China, Europe and International Security

This book examines the roles played by China and Europe in the domain of international security in the twenty-first century.

Bringing together Chinese and European expertise on the Sino–European Security relationship, this book positions Europe – both the EU and the major national actors – and China in a global security context. It offers not merely an elaboration of the theme of bilateral security relations, but also introduces a wider view on Europe and China as global security actors. The chapters cover four main themes: the perceptions of and actual relations between Europe and China as security actors; relations of China and Europe with third parties such as the US, Russia, and Iran; Europe and China as actors in multilateral security approaches; Europe and China as (potential) security actors in each other's technological domain or region.

Given the increasingly prominent roles that both China and Europe play in international security as permanent members of the UN Security Council (in the European case, through the informal and partial representation via the UK and France), through their extensive global economic interests, and their important relations with the USA, this book provides a timely examination of the current state and future developments in the Sino–European relationship.

This book will be of much interest to students of international security, Chinese politics, EU studies and IR in general.

Frans-Paul van der Putten is a research fellow at the Clingendael Institute in The Hague, Netherlands. He is the editor-in-chief of *Itinerario: Journal on the History of European Expansion and Global Interaction*.

Chu Shulong is Professor of Political Science and International Relations at the School of Public Policy and Management and Deputy Director of the Institute of International Strategic and Development Studies at Tsinghua University in Beijing, China.

Asian security studies
Series Editors:
Sumit Ganguly, *Indiana University, Bloomington* and
Andrew Scobell, *US Army War College*

Few regions of the world are fraught with as many security questions as Asia. Within this region it is possible to study great power rivalries, irredentist conflicts, nuclear and ballistic missile proliferation, secessionist movements, ethnoreligious conflicts and inter-state wars. This book series publishes the best possible scholarship on the security issues affecting the region, and includes detailed empirical studies, theoretically oriented case studies and policy-relevant analyses as well as more general works.

China, Europe and International Security

Interests, roles and prospects

Edited by
Frans-Paul van der Putten
and Chu Shulong

Routledge
Taylor & Francis Group

LONDON AND NEW YORK

First published 2011
by Routledge
2 Park Square, Milton Park, Abingdon, Oxon, OX14 4RN

Simultaneously published in the USA and Canada
by Routledge
711 Third Avenue, New York, NY 10017

*Routledge is an imprint of the Taylor & Francis Group,
an informa business*

First issued in paperback 2012

Typeset in Sabon by Glyph International Ltd.

British Library Cataloguing in Publication Data
A catalogue record for this book is available from the British Library

Library of Congress Cataloging-in-Publication Data
China, Europe, and international security : interests, roles, and
prospects / edited by Frans-Paul van der Putten and Chu Shulong.
    p. cm.
1. Security, International. 2. Europe–Relations–China.
3. China–Relations–Europe. 4. Europe–Foreign relations–21st century.
5. China–Foreign relations–21st century. I. Putten, Frans-Paul van der.
II. Shulong, Chu.
JZ6005.C45 2010
355'.033051–dc22   2010007851

ISBN13: 978-0-415-58580-4 (hbk)
ISBN13: 978-0-203-84460-1 (ebk)
ISBN13: 978-0-415-53253-2 (pbk)

Contents

List of illustrations

Figure

Tables

About the authors

Dr Nicola Casarini is Marie Curie Research Fellow at the Robert Schuman Centre for Advanced Studies (RSCAS) of the European University Institute (EUI). He was previously Jean Monnet Fellow in the RSCAS. He obtained his PhD in international relations from the London School of Economics (LSE) in October 2006 and was a visiting fellow at the European Union Institute for Security Studies (EUISS) in Paris in Autumn 2005. His work has so far concentrated on EU–China and EU–Asia relations, European foreign policy, Asian security affairs, and transatlantic relations. He is the author of *Remaking Global Order: The Evolution of Europe–China Relations and its Implications for East Asia and the United States* (Oxford: Oxford University Press, 2009), *The Road towards Convergence: European Foreign Policy in an Evolving International System*, co-edited with Costanza Musu (Houndmills: Palgrave, 2007), *The Evolution of the EU–China Relationship: From Constructive Engagement to Strategic Partnership* (Paris: EUISS, Occasional Paper No. 64, October 2006), and a number of scholarly articles and book chapters.

Chen Songchuan, MA, is a PhD candidate at the Institute of International Strategic and Development Studies at Tsinghua University, Beijing. Chen Songchuan has an MA in Law (International Relations) from Beijing Normal University. From 2003 to 2007 Chen worked as a lecturer in the College of Humanities and Law at the North China University of Technology, in Beijing. Recent publications include 'Pacifism and the 21st Century', *Journal of Contemporary Asia-Pacific Studies*, 4, 2008, and 'Harmony Strategy Thinking: The New Strategic Logic to Solve the Globalization Challenge', *Journal of Socialist Theory Guide*, 3, March 2008.

Dr Chu Shulong is Professor of political science and international relations at the School of Public Policy and Management and deputy director of the Institute of International Strategic and Development Studies at Tsinghua University in Beijing, China. He was previously director for the North American Studies Division of the China Institute of Contemporary International Relations. He is also a Professor at China's Ministry of

Foreign Affairs' Party School and an adviser to China's Central Television (CCTV) international reporting. Dr. Chu's major areas of research are international security, US foreign strategy and China policy, Sino–US relations, and China's foreign and security strategies. His most recent publications include *The Sino–US Relations in the Post-Cold War Era, Basic Theories of International Relations,* and *China's Foreign Strategy and Policy.*

Dr Feng Feng is a post-doctoral research fellow at the Institute of International Strategic and Development Studies at Tsinghua University, Beijing. Dr Feng has a PhD in International Politics from the Institute for International Strategy Studies at the Party School of the Central Committee of the CPC, and an MA from the School of International Studies at Peking University. Recent publications include 'Too Early for China to Talk about Exceeding US and Japan,' *World Newspaper,* 7 December 2004, 'The Rise of Brazil and Its Impact on the World Order', *Journal of Latin American Studies* 27(4) 2005 and 'Sino–EU Relations and China's Democratization', *Qilu Journal,* 2, 2008.

Susanne Kamerling, MSc, is a training and research fellow at the Security and Conflict Programme and Clingendael Asia Studies at the Netherlands Institute of International Relations 'Clingendael'. She has a background in political sciences and social geography. Her research interest is the role of China and India in regional and international security, and she also focuses on maritime security, piracy, and international maritime cooperation. She is editor of the Dutch magazine *China Nu,* and secretary of the Netherlands Society for International Affairs.

Willem van Kemenade, MA, started his career as a freelance journalist in 1968 with initial assignments in Africa and the Indian subcontinent. He studied History and Chinese in Amsterdam and Leiden. From 1977 to 1997 he was based in Hong Kong, Taipei and Beijing as the China/East Asia Correspondent for NRC Handelsblad. His first book *China, Hong Kong, Taiwan Inc.: The Dynamics of a New Empire* (New York, 1997), was also published in Dutch, German, Chinese and Turkish. Since the mid-1980s, he has been lecturing at business schools in Holland, Belgium and China and in recent years also at various programmes of Clingendael. Van Kemenade's special focus in recent years has been China's relations with all the major powers, in particular with the US, Japan, the European Union, India and most recently Iran. Recent publications include: 'China's Post-Olympic Rise and its Place in the Global Concert of Nations', in Jaap de Zwaan, Edwin Bakker and Sico van der Meer (eds) *Challenges in a Changing World: Clingendael Views on Global and Regional Issues* (The Hague, 2008); 'Détente between China and India: The Delicate Balance of Geopolitics in Asia', Clingendael Diplomacy Paper 16, 2008; 'Between Beijing and Paris: From abnormally good to pragmatic normalcy', *China Brief*, July 2007; 'China and Japan, Partners or Permanent Rivals', Clingendael Diplomacy Paper, 2006.

Janka Oertel, MA, received her Master of Arts in political science and sinology at the University of Kiel in 2007. She was a Carlo-Schmid-Fellow in 2004/5 at United Nations Headquarters in New York. Currently, Janka Oertel is a visiting fellow at the Stiftung Wissenschaft und Politik (German Institute for International and Security Affairs) in Berlin, and is working on her PhD thesis entitled 'China and the United Nations' as a scholarship holder of the German National Academic Foundation. Her main fields of research include the foreign and security policy of the People's Republic of China, United Nations reform and United Nations peacekeeping.

Dr Frans-Paul van der Putten is a research fellow with Clingendael Asia Studies and the Security and Conflict Programme of the Clingendael Institute in The Hague, Netherlands. His main area of interest is the relevance of China's rise for international security, in particular regarding China's relations with Europe and the United States. He studied history at Leiden University and previously worked as a researcher at Nyenrode Business School. He is the chief editor of *Itinerario: Journal on the History of European Expansion and Global Interaction,* published by Cambridge University Press.

Dr May-Britt U. Stumbaum is a senior research fellow and the head of the EU–China project in the China and Global Security Programme at the Stockholm International Peace Research Institute (SIPRI). Her research focuses on EU–China security relations and differing EU/US approaches towards China's rise. Her current work on transfers of dual use high technology to China and the differing regimes the EU and the US apply is based on studies facilitated by the Fritz Thyssen Foundation. Recent publications include the monograph on *The European Union and China: Decision-making in EU foreign and security policy towards the People's Republic of China.*

Dr Gudrun Wacker works at the Research Unit Asia, Stiftung Wissenschaft und Politik (German Institute for International and Security Affairs), in Berlin. Previously she held positions at the Bundesinstitut für Ostwissenschaftliche und Internationale Studien (Federal Institute for Russian, East European and International Studies), Cologne (September 1992 to December 2000), and the department of Sinology of the University of Tübingen (November 1983 to August 1992). She studied sinology and linguistics at the Free University Berlin, Shih-fan Ta-hsüeh in Taipei and the University of Tübingen (MA 1981), and obtained her PhD from the University of Tübingen 1991 (topic: Advertising in the People's Republic of China). Her main fields of research are Chinese foreign and security policy; EU–China relations, Sino–Russian and Sino–Central

Asian relations; China and the Asia-Pacific region; Chinese domestic development and minority policy (with special consideration of Xinjiang), telecommunications and the Internet in China. She did research at Harvard University and the Hoover Institution for War, Revolution and Peace from October 1982 to April 1983.

Dr Wang Bo is post-doctoral research fellow at the Energy Technology Innovation Policy Research Group, Belfer Center for Science and International Affairs, Harvard Kennedy School, Cambridge MA, United States. Previously Wang Bo was lecturer of International Relations and Deputy Director at the Department of International Politics, School of Humanities and Social Sciences, University of International Business and Economics, Beijing, China. He has a PhD from the China Foreign Affairs University (2006) where he wrote a thesis on US Oil Policy. Recent publications include 'China's Environmental Diplomacy', *American Journal of Chinese Studies*, April 2008, and *US Oil Policy* (Beijing: World Affairs Press, 2008).

Dr Xuan Xingzhang is currently an honorary researcher at the Center for Strategic and International Studies of the Chinese Central Party School (CCPS). His research interests are global development and international relations theory. Xuan Xingzhang graduated from the CCPS. He has published various articles in the *Journal of World Economics and Politics, Foreign Affairs Review* and *Contemporary International Relations*. His monographs include *The Blue Blood Company* (2004, 2006) and *Establishing Advantages* (2009).

Dr Yang Xiaoping is a research professor at the Institute of Asia-Pacific Studies, at the Chinese Academy of Social Sciences (CASS). Her research focuses on China's foreign policy, Sino–US relations and global governance. She graduated from the Chinese Central Party School. She has published in various Chinese-language journals that are included in the Chinese Social Sciences Citation Index (CSSCI). She is also the translator from English into Chinese of Ruth Benedict's *The Chrysanthemum and the Sword: Patterns of Japanese Culture*.

Dr Zhang Yanbing is assistant professor at the School of Public Policy and Management of Tsinghua University. Previously he was Programme Director of the Master in International Development programme at the same institution. In 2006 Zhang Yanbing obtained a PhD from Sheffield University with a thesis on 'Liberal and Social Visions in Post-Deng China: Neo-Authoritarianism and Its Critics'. His research areas are political theory, political economy, and international political economy.

Introduction

*Frans-Paul van der Putten
and Chu Shulong*

Together with the United States, Europe and China are the most influential actors in international security. Since the Cold War, relations between the US and Europe have constituted the most important bilateral relationship in international security. As a result of China's growing importance in recent years, Washington's relations with Beijing are now rivalling and possibly exceeding the importance of those with Europe. In this great power triangle, US–Europe and US–China relations are well-studied topics. However, how China and Europe relate to and affect one another in international security is still a new and little developed field of study. This book aims to contribute to a greater understanding of the roles that Europe and China play in international security.

Approach and definitions

This volume brings together the expertise and perspectives of fourteen authors, seven from China and seven from Europe. Jointly, the eleven main chapters address the questions and issues raised in the final section of this introductory chapter.

Thematically, the focus of this book is on international security. Any type of security issue that is relevant for international relations is included in the analysis. Depending on the issue at stake and the author's perspective, each chapter addresses either traditional security topics (involving inter-state relations), non-traditional security topics (involving such topics as development, human rights, fragile states, peacekeeping and piracy), or a mixture.

The two main actors in this book are China and Europe. While the former is a state and represented as such by its government, the latter is both a group of states and an international organisation. The member states of the European Union (EU) are represented in Europe's external affairs both directly and through the EU. In some ways, the EU is a distinct actor that operates alongside its member states, while in other ways it represents its members. Put differently, countries that are EU member states may act as such but they can also act on their own behalf, or – especially in the security sphere - as members of NATO. Twenty-one European countries are members of both the EU and NATO. This group includes the three lead-ing European countries: the UK, Germany and France.[1] Although in dealing with the European side, many of the chapters in this book are focused largely on the EU, wherever relevant the scope involves also interests and activities by EU member states – individually or as a group – that fall outside the collective EU framework. The overall theme of this book relates to China–Europe relations, rather than China–EU relations.

Issues in security studies on Europe and China

There is abundant literature on Europe's contemporary role in international security.[2] Three basic elements emerge from this:

1   Europe has allowed the United States to take the main responsibility for its security.
2   Europe's own approach to international security emphasises norms setting and multilateral institution building rather than employing hard power and a realist perspective.
3   Europe directs its security policies towards countries and regions that are geographically close – Eastern Europe, the Middle East and Africa – and largely keeps a distance from security issues in other parts of the world (Afghanistan being one of the few exceptions).

There is consensus on the historical dimension: Europe was at the centre of global security affairs until the mid-twentieth century and, after the end of the Cold War, the European Union emerged as a major security actor alongside the US. However, there seems to be significant confusion as to where the EU is headed. Some regard Europe as an emerging global security actor,[3] while others have called Europe a declining power.[4] To some extent this discrepancy can be explained by noting that the former group tends to focus on the growing institutional capacity of the EU, while the latter looks more at the long-term change – from the early twentieth century onwards – in the position of European countries relative to the rest of the world. Still, there is no consensus on what Europe's future as a security actor is likely to be, and so this is a theme for further research and debate.

On China's security role there are likewise a number of frequently recur-ring observations:

1   China is preoccupied with its domestic stability and favours stable foreign relations.[5]
2   Although China's military power is developing rapidly, it remains limited in terms of geographic reach and technological capabilities.[6] The country's main military asset is its long-range nuclear strike force.
3   In the long term China is widely seen as potentially rivalling the United States as the main power in international security affairs.[7]

In the case of China, the main controversy does not relate to China's potential as a great power. Although authors generally accept that the future pace of China's economic growth is the key variable, most also seem to consider it likely that growth will be sufficiently substantial to support the country's role as one of the leading powers of the twenty-first century. The greater uncertainty seems to relate to how China will use its power.[8] While Chinese authors tend to emphasise that China will not use violent means to achieve great power status,[9] the views of non-Chinese authors are more open-ended.[10]

While much has been and continues to be published on Europe's and China's respective role in international security, how these roles relate to each other is still a relatively new area of research. Two main categories of relevant publications can be identified.[11] In the first place, there are publications dealing primarily with the bilateral security relationship between China and Europe. The dominant contextual theme in this body of literature is the unbalanced nature of Sino–European relations. The economic dimension is well-developed, but the security dimension is very limited. The main issue in bilateral security relations that is discussed in literature is the EU arms embargo against China.[12] Two closely related topics are the Taiwan issue[13] and technological cooperation.[14]

In the second place, a number of authors have considered how the Chinese and European roles fit into the broader picture of global security relations. Three important topics that these authors have focused on are the influence of the US on Sino–European relations,[15] Chinese and European attitudes towards multilateralism in global governance,[16] and their roles in conflict management.[17]

Key questions

This volume aims to pick up the above-mentioned themes and develop them further, by addressing three main questions:

1 *How do Europe and China view each other's security roles?* One important issue in this context is whether China regards Europe as a leading security actor in the coming decades, and vice versa. It is particularly relevant to understand how each power assesses the other's influence in relation to that of the US, Russia and other security actors. Another issue is whether Europe and China regard one another as a potential security threat, especially in the long run.
2 *In which direction is the bilateral security relationship developing?* If it is true that this side of bilateral relations is underdeveloped, then it is important to understand what has been causing this. Two causes that are often put forward are the lack of a European security role in East Asia, and Europe's inability to develop security relations with China independently from the US. It is important to consider what the

consequences are of increasing military deployments by both actors in regions such as the Indian Ocean and Africa, and of the NATO presence in Afghanistan. Whereas until recently Europe and China conducted their military affairs in separate parts of the world, this is no longer the case. Likewise it is relevant to assess how the growing tendency of Washington and Beijing to address global affairs bilaterally might induce Europe to modify its strategic position towards China.

3 *How are China's and Europe's changing roles affecting international security?* Such changes may take place at various levels. To begin with, because of the centrality of the US role in global security affairs, any change in the trilateral relationship between China, Europe, and the United States is bound to have major repercussions. To a lesser extent, the same is true for the Europe–China–Russia relationship, since Russia is a permanent member of the UN Security Council. Furthermore, China and Europe exert major influences on the direction and pace of global security governance. To which extent these two actors manage to find common ground in this context will be of great significance for the global security architecture. A key topic is the balance between the principle of national sovereignty versus intervening on grounds related to human security. And closely related to this is the way in which Europe and China – as outside parties – contribute to crisis management in regions such as Africa, the Middle East and Asia. Joint crisis management can be both a basis for more strategic interaction between China and Europe, and a stabilising force in many parts of the world.

Each of the chapters in this book will address one or more of these issues. The concluding chapter of this volume will then return to the three main questions, and assess whether the available insights point the way to a more coherent perspective on China and Europe in international security.

Notes

1 Belgium, Bulgaria, Czech Republic, Denmark, Estonia, France, Germany, Greece, Hungary, Italy, Latvia, Lithuania, Luxembourg, Netherlands, Poland, Portugal, Romania, Slovakia, Slovenia, Spain, United Kingdom.
2 A good example is Álvaro de Vasconcelos (ed.), *The European Security Strategy 2003–2008: Building on common interests*, Paris: EU–ISS report 5, February 2009.
3 E.g., Marcin Zaborowski, 'Security Issues: EU perspective', in Stanley Crossick and Etienne Reuter (eds), *China–EU: A common future*, Singapore: World Scientific, 2007, p. 41.
4 E.g., Frans-Paul van der Putten, 'Time for Europe to Take a Long, Hard Look at Its Global Decline', *Europe's World*, Summer 2009, pp. 19–23.
5 Bates Gill, *Rising Star: China's new security diplomacy*, Washington DC: Brookings Institution Press, 2007, p. 10; Chu Shulong, 'The US, China and the International Order', *Contemporary International Relations*, August 2009.

6 Michael D. Swaine, 'China's Regional Military Posture', in David Shambaugh (ed.), *Power Shift: China and Asia's new dynamics*, Berkely: University of California Press, 2005; Sophie-Charlotte Brune, Sacha Lange and Janka Oertel, *China's militärische Entwicklung: Modernisierung und Internationalisierung der Streitkräfte*, Berlin: Stiftung Wissenschaft und Politik, October 2009.

7 Martin Jacques, *When China Rules the World: The rise of the Middle Kingdom and the end of the Western world*, London: Penguin Books, 2009; Fareed Zakaria, *The Post-American World*, New York: W.W. Norton & Company, 2008, pp. 127–8.

8 Related to this is the question of how peaceful China's rise will be: Andrew Scobell, 'China's Rise: How peaceful?', in Sumit Ganguly, Andrew Scobell and Joseph Chinyong Liow, *The Routledge Handbook of Asian Security Studies*, London: Routledge, 2009.

9 Zheng Bijian, 'China's "Peaceful Rise" to Great Power Status', *Foreign Affairs*, September–October 2005; Zhu Feng, 'China's Rise Will Be Peaceful: How unipolarity matters', in Robert S. Ross and Zhu Feng (eds), *China's Ascent: Power, security, and the future of international politics*, Ithaca: Cornell University Press, 2008.

10 Roy Kamphausen, David Lai and Andrew Scobell, *Beyond the Strait: PLA missions other than Taiwan*, Carlisle, PA: Strategic Studies Institute, US Army War College, 2009, 21–2; Susan L. Shirk, *China: Fragile superpower*. Oxford: Oxford University Press, 2007.

11 Possibly the most comprehensive overview – one that combines the two categories – is Bates Gill, 'European Union–China Cooperation on Security Issues', in David Shambaugh and Gudrun Wacker (eds), *American and European Relations with China: Advancing common agendas*, Berlin: Stiftung Wissenschaft und Politik, June 2008.

12 May-Britt U. Stumbaum, *The European Union and China: Decision-making in EU foreign and security policy towards the People's Republic of China*, Baden-Baden: Nomos, 2009; Nicola Casarini, 'The Evolution of the EU–China Relationship: From constructive engagement to strategic partnership', Paris: EU–ISS occasional paper 64, October 2006; Stanley Crossick, 'The Arms Embargo: EU perspective', in Stanley Crossick and Etienne Reuter (eds), *China–EU: A common future*. Singapore: World Scientific, 2007; Guo Xiaobin, 'The Arms Embargo: China perspective', in Crossick and Reuter (eds), *China–EU*.

13 Jean-Pierre Cabestan, 'The Taiwan Issue in Europe–China Relations: An irritant more than leverage', in David Shambaugh, Eberhard Sandschneider and Zhou Hong (eds), *China–Europe Relations: Perceptions, policies and prospects*. London: Routledge, 2008; Men Jing, 'Taiwan', in Crossick and Reuter (eds), *China–EU*.

14 Casarini, *EU–China Relationship*; May-Britt U. Stumbaum, 'Risky Business? The EU, China and dual-use technology'. Paris: EU–ISS occasional paper 80, October 2009.

15 Bates Gill, 'The United States and the China–Europe Relationship', in Shambaugh et al. (eds), *China–Europe Relations*; Ruan Rongze, 'China–EU–US Relations: Shaping a constructive future', in Shambaugh et al. (eds), *China–Europe Relations*; Andrew Small, 'The US Factor', in Crossick and Reuter (eds), *China–EU*; Marcin Zaborowski, *US China Policy: Implications for the EU*. Paris: EU–ISS analysis paper, October 2005; Bates Gill and Gudrun Wacker (eds), *China's Rise: Diverging US–EU perceptions and approaches*, Berlin: Stiftung Wissenschaft und Politik, August 2005.

16 Volker Stanzel, 'The EU and China in the Global System', in Shambaugh et al. (eds), *China–Europe Relations*; Liselotte Odgaard and Sven Biscop, 'The EU and China: Partners in Effective Multilateralism?', in David Kerr and Liu Fei (eds),

The International Politics of EU–China Relations, Oxford: Oxford University Press, 2007; Alyson J.K. Bailes and Anna Wetter, 'EU–China Security Relations: The "softer" side', in Kerr and Liu (eds), *International Politics of EU–China Relations*; Zaborowski, 'Security Issues', pp. 43–4; Xing Hua, 'Security Issues: China perspective', in Crossick and Reuter (eds), *China–EU*; Gustaaf Geraerts, Chen Zhimin and Gjovalin Macaj, 'The Reform of the UN', in Crossick and Reuter (eds), *China–EU*.

17 Emma van der Meulen and Frans-Paul van der Putten, 'Great Powers and International Conflict Management: European and Chinese involvement in the Darfur and Iran crises'. The Hague: Clingendael security paper, January 2009.

1 Europe's views on China's role in international security*

May-Britt U. Stumbaum

Introduction

While the European Union is emerging as a global actor, it is struggling to adapt its perspective to an ever-stronger People's Republic of China (PRC) and to develop a security perspective on China that is shared among EU member states. Given the EU's extensive interests in the East Asian region and China's growing global role, it is high time for the European Union to define its policy towards the rising Asian power. This chapter aims to analyse the view Europe has on China's role in international security and how the EU can pursue a security relationship to further its own interests.

For decades, the Sino–European relationship was characterised as a 'secondary relationship', a derivate of the Cold War that was shaped by the 'tyranny of distance' and the 'primacy of trade'.[1] In short, trade was predominant and China just too far away to matter to Europe in security aspects. Trade was and still is the backbone of the relationship; despite some more independent moves by, for example, the then French President Charles de Gaulle or British policies regarding Hong Kong, the relationship overall was overshadowed by and subordinated to the bipolarity of the Cold War's US–Soviet confrontation. Catalysed by the acrimonious debate about the lifting of the arms embargo in 2004/2005,[2] Europe's perception of China is changing, driven by two concurrent developments: the EU is setting out as a global actor and the PRC is resuming its place among great powers. Nowadays, the EU is searching for its own defence identity while trying to adapt its policies to an ever more powerful China. Wherever the EU is active today, whether in peacekeeping missions in Africa, counter-piracy missions in the Gulf of Aden or in proliferation efforts, climate change initiatives or fighting the current financial crisis, it meets Chinese troops, initiatives and interests. As one of the five permanent members of the UN Security Council, China is an active member and the 16th largest troop supplier to UN peacekeeping missions. Regarding new security threats such as environmental degradation and pandemics, China has been the main emitter of CO_2 since 2007 and therefore key to any climate change policies. SARS and the Avian Flu both originated from China. In the 2008/9 financial crisis, China holds extensive currency reserves and is one of the only economies still growing while Western economies are shrinking. In sum, China is an inextricable part of the solution of global challenges – and sometimes part of the cause as well. In recent papers, the European Union has acknowledged China's significance in coping with global security issues, yet the EU finds itself hurrying to adapt to the rapidly growing power of an ever more confident China. This chapter lays out the EU's perception of China, areas of common interests, and tools and fora for a collaborative approach with China. It sheds some light on the remaining stumbling blocks in the way of a meaningful security partnership with the People's Republic of China and concludes with an outlook on the EU's security perspective on China.

Changing attitudes within the EU–Chinese relationship

After a blossoming relationship, leading to the declaration of the 'EU–China strategic partnership' in 2003, the romance has worn off what was once dubbed the Sino–European 'love affair'[3] and its 'very serious engagement'.[4] With the EU having no major deployments in East Asia, and no existing strategic interests that could run against its development, the relationship had been developing rapidly; unlike the United States, the European Union has neither sizable troop deployments in East Asia nor a comparable system of security alliances.[5] However, ongoing trade frictions, uneasiness about China's policies in Africa and elsewhere, and heated arguments over human rights during the 2008 Olympic torch relay have created a strain on the relationship. In December 2008, the Chinese side cancelled the annual EU–China summit at very short notice, reportedly as a sign of protest against French President Sarkozy, then President of the EU, who had agreed to meet the Dalai Lama as a private person.[6] On the European side, recent years have seen public attitudes towards China's rise crumbling in major European countries such as France, Great Britain and Germany, with the percentage of people being favourable towards China dropping between 2005 and 2008 from 65 per cent to 47 per cent in Britain, from 58 per cent to 28 per cent in France and from 46 per cent to 29 per cent in Germany.[7]

Nevertheless, both sides express their determination to 'make the marriage work'.[8] To cite Javier Solana, 'the EU perceives China both as an important economic player and also as a catalyst of stability and conflict resolution'.[9] It is 'among the few strategic partners of the EU in the world'.[10] China's burgeoning influence in East Asia and global affairs alike has been acknowledged by European decision-makers. The PRC has acquired an increasingly high profile in politics concerning Sudan and Zimbabwe as well as Iran or the North Korea six-party-talks. As one of the five permanent members (P5) in the UN Security Council, China's contribution to troop-intensive international missions is constantly growing.[11] The PRC has become a force to be reckoned with in all international affairs concerning the European Union, from climate change to the economic downturn; in the current financial crisis, most hopes are set on China's enormous accumulated financial reserves deriving from the trade surpluses that the PRC runs with major partners.[12] The European Council stated in 2007 that

> the policy choices of China, now emerging as a global player, are of strategic importance to the EU ... The EU has a big interest in encouraging China to take on its global responsibilities, notably in the political, economic, commercial and monetary fields as well as to play a constructive role in the promotion of effective multilateralism and the resolution of international and regional issues.[13]

Along with the United States, the EU aims to encourage China to become a formally called 'responsible stakeholder'[14] of the Western-shaped international system and

> wants to work alongside China in addressing key international problems, since the two sides are both strong economically, and are both looking to make constructive and meaningful contributions to the stability of our regions and of the wider international community.'[15]

It is somewhat telling that the European Union is using broad, vague terms to describe 'its aspirations for the EU–China security relationship; the PRC, on the other hand, draws a much more detailed picture in its 2003 China Policy Paper on the European Union, the first of its kind, including: jointly combating terrorism and proliferation; contributing to the solution of the issue of anti-personnel landmines and explosive remnants of war. The paper proposes to maintain high-level military-to-military exchanges, and to develop and improve a strategic security consultation mechanism. In particular, it recommends the exchange of more missions of military experts, and to expand exchanges in respect of military officers' training and defence studies.[16] Indeed, there are several areas where both entities seem to have similar concerns and potential for cooperation, although they might differ in the connotation of the same terminology.[17]

Areas of cooperation in security aspects

The EU considers a broad array of issues as part of the EU–China agenda, while the promotion of 'effective multilateralism' lies at the heart of European policies. At the EU–China summit in November 2007, both sides spoke of the importance of 'effective multilateralism', their 'strong support for a fair, just and rules-based multilateral international system with the UN playing a central role' and their joint commitment to combat global and regional security challenges. Challenges included terrorism, realising peace, stability and 'effective denuclearisation' of the Korean peninsula. They also commented on the emerging regional architecture in Asia, the Israel–Palestine conflict and Kosovo.[18]

Responding to the changed security environment, China and the European Union, together with individual member states such as France, Germany and the United Kingdom, have embarked on expanding their security concept in similar ways: terms for this new security concept range from 'new security concept'[19] to 'comprehensive security'[20] and 'extended security concept' (*erweiterter Sicherheitsbegriff*).[21] All emphasize the changing nature of risks and threats in the twenty-first century, underlining the pre-eminence of international terrorism, the influence of non-governmental actors and the asymmetrical nature of new confrontations. They also include challenges that go far beyond purely military concerns, including demographic shifts, pandemics and the securing of natural resources. They agree that the challenges of today are global in nature and require concerted responses by the international community. In other words, they necessitate extensive international cooperation.

The recently confirmed European Security Strategy (ESS) of 2003 names five key challenges: terrorism, proliferation of weapons of mass destruction, regional conflicts, state failure and organised crime. It adds as 'global challenges' poverty, pandemics, environmental degradation and catastrophes, and securing resources.[22]

The latter seem to be very promising areas for cooperation between the EU and China, offering ample opportunities to develop ways of jointly addressing these challenges. As stated in the Joint Communiqué of the 11th EU–China summit in May 2009, the 'global economic and financial crisis, climate change and energy security'[23] feature most prominently on the EU–China agenda. On 'soft security' issues such as environmental protection and climate change, the EU can offer extensive expertise. Moreover, as the difference in the political systems – democracies in Europe and a one-party-system in China – matter less in these new areas. And these challenges can be addressed supranationally in the EU, as, for example, EU environmental sector programmes under the aegis of the European Commission. As drastically illustrated by the debate about lifting the EU's arms embargo on China, the EU is facing difficulties defining common ground in the CFSP when it comes to China.[24]

But the EU also strives for cooperation according to the key challenges identified in the ESS, such as proliferation and terrorism. The 2007–13 China Country Strategy Paper states that

> in the field of co-operation on foreign and security policy, particular attention will be given to combating WMD proliferation, WMD agents, materials and know-how, and conflict prevention. The challenge is to facilitate the booming legitimate exchanges of people, goods and services, while limiting abuse. Co-operation in the area of justice, freedom

and security, will focus on combating terrorism, fighting organised crime including money-laundering, corruption, trafficking of human beings, crime prevention, small arms and light weapons, illicit drugs and drugs precursors. Illegal migration is both a humanitarian concern and a politically sensitive issue on which the EU and China have engaged in regular consultations to reinforce administrative co-operation and the facilitation of people-to-people exchanges, for example through the Tourism Agreement (or Authorised Destination Status agreement – ADS).[25]

A key challenge within this set of threats and a major potential for Sino–European cooperation is the stabilisation of failing states, particularly in Europe's neighbouring and resource-rich continent, Africa. Besides diplomatic initiatives, the EU approaches this challenge through extensive development aid programmes as well as by the deployment of peacekeeping troops. China also has vested interests and wields significant influence in the region. It has set up favourable relationships with critical states such as Zimbabwe and Sudan, extensively enlarged its engagement in African countries and continues to supply an increasing number of troops to UN-mandated peacekeeping missions. In September 2009, China was the 14th biggest troop supplier to UN Peacekeeping missions, with 2,155 troops comprising engineers, logistic and medical troops.[26] On the other hand, the EU has been increasingly involved in peacekeeping missions since its first European Security and Defence Policy (ESDP) operation in March 2003 in the Republic of Macedonia, 'EUFOR Concordia'. Three of them are still continuing in Africa: two in the Democratic Republic of Congo, and one in Guinea Bissau.[27] Since 13 December 2008, the EU also operates Operation Atalanta in the Gulf of Aden.

With both entities having vested interests in securing resources from African states, cooperation between the EU and China will be crucial to avoid unintended consequences of clashes of interests.

Tools and fora for EU security cooperation with China

With the EU itself being an international institution and focusing on 'effective multilateralism', the EU favours regional integration and cooperation in international institutions. The EU offers three different levels for cooperation with China:

1   the international level at international institutions;
2   the European level with dialogues and programmes between the EU and China; and
3   the national level with bilateral initiatives between China and individual member states of the EU.

At the United Nations, Sino–European cooperation takes place between individual member states with China within the United Nations. France and the United Kingdom are both permanent members of the UN Security Council; furthermore, as all EU member states are members of the UN, the member state holding the EU Presidency also represents European interests at the UN. On the regional level, the EU is, together with China, active at the Association of Southeast Asian Nations (ASEAN) Regional Forum (ARF) and the Asia–Europe Meeting (ASEM). The bilateral cooperation on the European level is underpinned by the annual EU–China summit and gatherings ranging from regular working groups to annual meetings of heads of states, complemented – though not coordinated – with high-level visits by member states' delegations. As David Shambaugh points out, the 'intensity of interaction between European and Chinese officials is thus considerable. The architecture is overlapping and often confusing, but the totality of exchanges is impressive'.[28]

The actual work takes place in working groups at the Council of the European Union and 27 sectoral dialogues of the European Commission. The content of these groups are aligned with the division of competences between the different EU pillars, as they are formally known:[29] the supranational 1st pillar with the Commission's central role and the intergovernmental 2nd and 3rd pillars. At the Council, the EU conducts dialogues with China on human rights, illegal migration and human trafficking, non-proliferation, arms exports and Asian affairs. Council working groups such as the Africa Working Party (COAFR), the Working Party on Global Disarmament and Arms Control (CODUN) and the Working Party on Non-Proliferation (CONOP) meet regularly with their Chinese colleagues to discuss common challenges.

Furthermore, the EU engages in direct military exchanges with China in common peacekeeping operations and through bilateral programs of its member states. The EU has officially encouraged greater Chinese peacekeeping activity and several European countries, such as the United Kingdom, France, Sweden and Norway, have provided peacekeeping training assistance and engaged the People's Liberation Army (PLA) on peacekeeping matters; for example on the run up to the UN peacekeeping missions in Liberia and the Democratic Republic of Congo (DRC), the United Kingdom was involved in training PLA officials prior to their deployments. Countries such as France, Germany and the United Kingdom, but also smaller states such as the Netherlands, have exchanged military officers with China for training at their respective defence colleges.[30] The recent set-up of the EU's naval operation Atalanta offered for the first time the possibility of interacting with Chinese naval forces on a European level, after several member states' navies had already paid port visits in previous years; in 2004, China held separate joint naval exercises off the Chinese coast with France and the United Kingdom in March and June respectively.[31]

Stumbling blocks in EU security cooperation with China

In developing a security perspective on China, the EU faces several internal and external challenges and the differences in political systems of the two entities. While the EU is evolving as a global actor itself, it has to adapt its security perspective of a country that used to be perceived as 'weak and far away' and not on the 'immediate mind map' of European politicians[32]; a country that has also been rapidly climbing up the ranking of powerful countries and has become a crucial factor in solving today's global challenges. As further explained below, the EU has so far been struggling due to a lack of sufficient personnel at the European level, a knowledge deficit about China's intentions and military build-up and due to its internal division of competences and external pressure.

Internally, the EU's security and defence policy is still nascent. Security and defence policy is still a national domain and located in the CFSP where the role of the Commission is strictly limited. Most security affairs are dealt with on the national level, such as common manoeuvres with the PLA, the exchange of officers and intelligence gathering – with little coordination among EU member states. Military staff at the European level (EUMS) are limited and carefully guarded in their competences by the member states, as is the civilian personnel at the Council. While about 100 people are concerned with China at the European Commission, there are only a few at the Council. The EU's Situation Centre is aiming to build up its experts on China, but it is facing difficulties recruiting them from within the EU pool of officials.[33] Countries such as the UK, France, Sweden and others are gathering intelligence on China and sharing them bilaterally, but intelligence sharing at the European level still poses major difficulties. Alerted by the arms embargo debate and China's rapidly growing and non-transparent defence expenditures, the Commission called for an improvement of the EU's 'analytical capacity on China's military development'.[34] However, the deficit of human resources, information and competences on the European level has remained. With whom should Chinese officers collaborate if not with individual member states? And who could make sure that no unintentional information is given to Chinese officers if the coordination of EU member states functions, if at all, only bilaterally between individual member states? So far, the PLA has sent only non-combat troops to peacekeeping operations where Europeans would have a chance to learn on the ground about the Chinese capabilities and perspectives. The Operation Atalanta offers a good opportunity to gather intelligence on the Chinese navy within a European operation.

Stumbling blocks between both parts consist of a different definition of today's challenges, competing interests and the differing political systems. By using almost identical terminology, the EU and China seem to share a lot of security concerns and agree that global challenges can only be addressed by collaboration. However, both sides differ in their connotation of this terminology[35] as well as in their (often competing) interests. Using the example of 'effective multilateralism' that both entities promote, the EU's definition of multilateralism differs from China's, which equates multilateralism with multipolarity.[36] And China's emphasis on the principle of non-interference in its policies towards African despots is contrary to the EU's newly developing strategic culture that 'fosters early, rapid, and when necessary, robust intervention'.[37] On the African continent, China's model of 'effective governance' that offers loans with no strings attached undermines the EU's model of 'good governance' where compliance is sought through conditional loans.[38] On energy security questions, China perceives itself as a 'late-comer' that has to deal with those regions that have not been tapped by others, such as critical and failing states in Africa, Latin America and the Middle East. Having limited faith in the international market, China favours acquiring high-priced exclusive access to resources, whereas Europeans and Americans fear that their steady supply based on the international market will be jeopardised. In short, despite largely congruent security outlooks, both sides differ in the details and compete in their interests.

Overcoming differences in connotation and competition in interests are hampered by the lack of trust between both sides that stems from a difference in the political and social systems. China's 'new security concept' as laid out by the Chinese government underlines that in this

> world of diversity ... security cooperation is not just something for countries with similar or identical views and modes of development, it also includes cooperation between countries whose views and modes of development differ.[39]

Speaking on the 'comprehensive strategic partnership' between the EU and China in May 2004, Chinese Prime Minister Wen Jiabao stressed that the partnership 'transcends the differences in ideology and social system and is not subjected to the impacts of individual events that occur from time to time'.[40] Despite this rhetoric, with security issues being so close to a nation's core, it is clear that differences do matter. The continuing EU' arms embargo on China – in spite of the strategic partnership and the Joint Declaration on Non-Proliferation – illustrates the European unease about Chinese military issues. The non-familiarity and the lack of understanding of the Chinese political system, the opacity of the PLA and the military build-up, the deficit of historical exchanges due to the distance and increasing frictions between both sides on trade and human rights issues have not been helpful in promoting trust in the 'strategic partnership'.

Finally, there are external influences on the EU that are trying to shape a security perspective on China. The acrimonious debate about the arms embargo in 2004 and 2005 did not only reveal how the EU could be split from the outside,[41] but also made it very clear to European decision-makers that any trade of military-relevant goods with China, particularly with the lack of a security perspective, are a matter of concern for the EU's, and its member states', most important ally, the United States of America. Unlike the US, the EU does not patrol the East Asian waters to keep the Sea Lines of Communication (SLOC) open, even though 90 per cent of the EU's external-trade is sea-borne with the Straits of Malacca as one of the maritime choke points. At the peak of the embargo debate, former US Secretary of State Condoleezza Rice underlined US irritation with the EU's policy impact on East Asia by pointing out that 'it is the US, not Europe that has defended the Pacific'.[42] The EU responded to the crisis and US concerns with the establishment of the 'Guidelines on the EU's Foreign and Security Policy'. As not all EU member states' share the US' perspective on China, the external pressure exercised by the United States has definitely catalysed, but also aggravated the development of a common European security perspective on China.

Outlook

The financial crisis has further accelerated China's rise back to its place among the great powers and put additional pressure on the EU to develop a comprehensive approach when dealing with China. For decades, China was a country 'just too far away and too weak' to matter to the Europeans in security aspects. This has changed. Today, European decision-makers and analysts acknowledge that China represents an inevitable factor in addressing global challenges. The EU will need to engage with the growing power in all policy fields if it wants to tie China into the Western-shaped international system while retaining and extending its own influence.

Collaboration between the EU and China is happening on all three levels, internationally, bilaterally at the European level and bilaterally at the national level of EU member states. Collaboration encompasses the regular meetings of EU working groups on such issues as non-proliferation, Africa or arms control, political and economic dialogues and frequent meetings with Commission officials in 27 sectoral dialogues that often have an indirect security reference. With both entities increasing participation in international peacekeeping missions, there are also growing opportunities for military-to-military exchange on the ground. The EU and its member states are collaborating with China nowadays in the training of its peacekeepers, the exchange of military officers between national defence academies, joint military manoeuvres, science and technology cooperation including dual-use technologies such as space and energy, and in environment and resource security aspects.

However, collaboration is hampered by internal and external factors that influence the EU's shaping of a security identity for the EU–China strategic partnership. Obstacles include the division of competences with the EU structure and the lack of counterparts for Chinese military personnel at the European level as well as the lack of expertise on a Chinese military and political system that appears somewhat opaque and non-familiar. While in-depth expertise on China is still missing in Europe on a greater scale, Chinese officials have gathered very good information on how to work with the EU and its member states and have trained countless experts to work in the administration and academic institutions. Interaction between the EU, EU member states and the China are manifold, but rarely coordinated. A decreasingly favourable view of China among European member states' publics puts additional strain on the room to manoeuvre for European decision-makers. The US's concerned and sometimes suspicious view of EU–Chinese interaction further aggravates the conditions in which European and national officials and politicians are trying to shape a European security perspective on China. Until now, there has been no debate on a European level on possible scenarios for a European reaction should the United States and China start a local war over Taiwan.

The EU is facing an international system in flux: From the Straits of Malacca to the Gulf of Aden, to the financial crisis and Afghanistan/Pakistan, it seems that China and the United States – the emerging great power and the declining hyperpower – are currently figuring out their relationship with each other, thereby influencing the future shape of the international system. Bound to each other by interdependent trade relations and treasury bonds, both countries appear like two bears that are cautiously dancing around and eying each other while they find out their respective future spheres of influence and power level. If the EU wants to be an influential part of this future order, it needs to adapt a realistic approach in its policy towards China and define its interests, its available tools and the policy moves it needs to pursue its interests. The EU needs to determine what its 'Unique Selling Point' is to avoid a new bipolarity, or 'G2' as dubbed by Zbigniew Brzeziński.[43] In short – in order to actively pursue the EU's interests, the EU needs to choose wisely its instruments in order to influence the music to which those two powers dance. For this, it has to adapt its security policy towards the People's Republic of China.

The EU today is struggling to define a common security perception of China in times when the EU and China are emerging actors. A broad array of possible areas for cooperation faces a broad range of obstacles to realise these potentials. However, European interests as laid out in the European Security Strategy require the EU to address them in cooperation with other major powers; China is, after the United States of America, the prime partner with which the EU has to work to address global challenges. In order to turn the EU–Chinese relationship into a genuine 'strategic partnership', European decision-makers have to define a timely common security perspective on China.

Notes

* The research on which this chapter is based was made possible by the support of the Fritz Thyssen Foundation.

1 Michael B. Yahuda, 'The Sino–European Encounter: Historical influences on contemporary relations', in David Shambaugh, Eberhard Sandschneider and Hong Zhou (eds), *China–Europe Relations: Perceptions, Politics and Prospects*, New York: Routledge, 2008, p. 21.
2 For a good overview of why the EU should take a more active approach towards East Asia, see Frans-Paul van der Putten, 'The EU Arms Embargo against China: Should Europe play a role in East Asian security?', Social and Cultural Research, Occasional Paper 7, Hong Kong Shue Yan University, January 2009; May-Britt Stumbaum, 'The Invisible Ban: EU maintains weapons embargo on China', *Jane's Intelligence Review: Chinawatch*, December 2008, pp. 52–3; John Fox and Francois Godement, 'EU–China Relations: A power audit', European Council of Foreign Relations, London 2009.
3 David Murphy and Shada Islam, 'China's Love Affair with Europe', *Far Eastern Economic Review*, 12 February 2004, pp. 26–9.
4 'If it is not a marriage, it is at least a very serious engagement': Romano Prodi, 'Relations between the EU and China: More than just business', speech at the EU–China Business Forum, Brussels, 6 May 2004.
5 Roberto Menotti, 'European–Chinese Relations in the Post-Bipolar International System: The political dimension', Centro Studidi Politica Internazionale (CeSPI), Occasional Papers, Rome, September 1995; David Shambaugh, 'China and Europe: The emerging axis', *Current History*, September 2004; Lanxin Xiang, 'An EU Common Strategy for China?', *The International Spectator* 36(3), 2001, pp. 89–99.
6 'Brussels Stunned as Beijing Cancels EU–China Summit', *Euractiv.com*, 27 November 2008, available at: http://www.euractiv.com/en/foreign-affairs/brussels-stunned-beijing-cancels-eu-china-summit/article-177550.
7 China's activism in the crisis year of 2008, however, seems to have had a positive impact on public opinion and the attitude has become more favourable again, although support did not reach previous high levels. 'Opinion of China', PEW Global Attitudes Project, available at: http://pewglobal.org/database/?indicator =24 (11 September 2009).
8 David Shambaugh, Eberhard Sandschneider and Zhou Hong, 'From Honeymoon to Marriage: Prospects for the China–Europe relationship', in Shambaugh et al., *China–Europe Relations*. Comments by the Chinese Foreign Minister Yong Jiechi, 'Work Together to Build a Common Future', speech at the Royal Institute of International Affairs, London, 5 December 2007, available at: http://www. fmprc.gov.cn/eng/wjdt/zyjh/t387186.htm.
9 'Javier Solana meets Wen Jiabao', Council of the European Union, S022/09, Brussels, 30 January 2009.
10 'EU Seeks Solid, Comprehensive Development of Strategic Partnership with China, Says Solana', interview, *People's Daily online*, 24 November 2007, available at: http://english.people.cn/90001/90776/90883/6308790.html.
11 For an overview, see Bates Gill and Chin-hao Huang, 'China's Expanding Peacekeeping Role: Its significance and the policy implications', SIPRI Policy Brief, February 2009.
12 In 2008, the EU's trade deficit with the PRC alone grew by 19 million euros an hour, reaching 169.6 billion euros by the end of the year. Since China's accession to the World Trade Organisation (WTO) in 2002, EU–China trade has almost quadrupled, making the PRC the EU's second largest trade partner after the United States: 'Global Europe: EU–China trade in facts and figures', European Commission, Directorate General for Trade, May 2009, available at: http:// trade.ec.europa.eu/doclib/docs/2009/january/tradoc_142202.pdf.
13 'Guidelines on the EU's Foreign and Security Policy in East Asia', Council of the European Union, PRESS, Brussels, December 2007, p. 3. See also Marcin

Zaborowski (ed.), 'Facing China's Rise: Guidelines for an EU strategy', European Union Institute for Security Studies (EUISS), Chaillot Paper 94, Paris, December 2006.

14 Deputy Secretary Robert Zoellick statement on conclusion of the Second US–China Senior Dialogue, Washington DC, 8 December 2005, available at: http://www.america.gov/st/washfile-english/2005/December/20051208165226ajesrom0.4026758.html.

15 Javier Solana, 'EU and China: Strategic Partners with Global Objectives', interview, *People's Daily*, 17 March 2004; May-Britt Stumbaum, 'Common Threats – Common Action? Opportunities and Limits of EU–China Security Cooperation', *The International Spectator*, September 2007, 42(3), pp. 351–70.

16 Ministry of Foreign Affairs, 'China's Policy Paper on the European Union', Beijing, October 2003, available at: http://www.mfa.gov.cn/eng/wjb/zzjg/xos/dqzzywt/t27708.htm (13 September 2009).

17 On this aspect, see Stumbaum, 'Common Threats – Common Action?', pp. 351–70.

18 'Joint Statement of the 10th China–EU Summit', Presidency of the European Union, Beijing, 28 November 2007, available at: http://www.eu2007.pt/ue/ven/noticias_documentos/20071202china.htm (14 September 2009).

19 'China's Position Paper on the New Security Concept (CPP)', Ministry of Foreign Affairs, Beijing, 31 July 2002, available at: http://www.mfa.gov.cn/eng/wjb/zzjg/gjs/gjzzyhy/2612/2614/t15319.htm (14 September 2009).

20 Used for the first time by Japanese Prime Minister Masayoshi Ohira in the 1970s, see Raymond Feddema, Akio Igarashi and Kurt Radtke (eds), *Comprehensive Security in Asia: Views from Asia and the West on a Changing Security Environment,* Leiden: Brill, 2000.

21 Used by German Foreign Minister Frank-Walter Steinmeier in his inaugural speech in Berlin on 23 November 2005.

22 'A Secure Europe in a Better World: European security strategy', Council of the European Union, Brussels, 16 December 2003, available at: http://www.consilium.europa.eu/uedocs/cmsUpload/78367.pdf; Álvaro de Vasconcelos (ed.) 'The European Security strategy, 2003–2008: Building on common interests', ISS report 5, February 2009.

23 11th EU–China Summit, joint press communiqué, Council of the European Union, 10234/09, Prague, 20 May 2009.

24 For an analysis of decision-making in the EU on China policies, see May-Britt U. Stumbaum, *The European Union and China: Decision-Making in European Union Foreign and Security Policy towards the People's Republic of China,* DGAP Schriften zur Internationalen Politik, Baden Baden: Nomos, 2009.

25 'China Strategy Paper 2007–2013', European Commission, Brussels, 2007, p. 4, available at: ec.europa.eu/external_relations/china/csp/07_13_en.pdf (14 September 2009).

26 'Ranking of Military and Police Contributions to UN Operations', UN report, 31 August 2009, available at: www.un.org/Depts/dpko/dpko/contributors/2009/aug09_2.pdf (14 September 2009).

27 For an updated overview of ongoing and concluded ESDP missions, see http://www.consilium.europa.eu/showPage.aspx?id=268&lang=EN.

28 Shambaugh, 'China and Europe: The emerging axis', p. 247.

29 The Treaty of Lisbon has abolished the pillar structure. The impact of the new structure, however, still needs to be seen.

30 Bates Gill and Melissa Murphy, 'China–Europe Relations: Implications and policy responses for the United States', CSIS, Washington DC, May 2008, p. 18; interview with Dutch civil servant.

31 'China, France to Hold Joint Naval Exercises', *Xinhuanet*, 12 March 2004, available at: http://news.xinhuanet.com/english/2004-03/12/content_1363257. htm (14 September 2009).

32 William E. Griffith, 'China and Europe: Weak and Far Away', in Richard Solomon (ed.), *The China Factor*, Englewood Cliffs, NJ: Prentice Hall, 1981.

33 Interview with Council of the European Union official, 20 June 2009.

34 'EU–China: Closer partners, growing responsibilities', European Commission, COM(2006) 632 final, Brussels, 24 October 2006, available at: http://eur-lex. europa.eu/smartapi/cgi/sga_doc?smartapi!celexplus!prod!DocNumber&lg=en& type_doc=COMfinal&an_doc=2006&nu_doc=631.

35 For the different connotation of the same terminology, see Stumbaum, 'Common Threats – Common Action?'

36 See Kay Möller, 'Europe's Policy: Neither multipolar nor multilateral' in Gudrun Wacker (ed.), 'China's Rise: The return of geopolitics?', Stiftung Wissenschaft und Politik, research paper RP01, Berlin, 2006, p. 71; Zuqian Zhang, 'Sino–French Relations Need a Lot of Nursing', *The Straits Times*, 6 October 2004; 'France's Voice in the World', *The Economist*, 11 November 2003.

37 'A Secure Europe in a Better World', p.11. However, Chinese foreign policy is in transition. The Chinese leadership has reacted increasingly consciously of its international image and has been testing a more engaging policy, e.g. vis-à-vis Sudan, North Korea and Iran; see S. Kleine-Ahlbrand, 'China Jumps In', *International Herald Tribune*, 1 February 2007.

38 See Bernt Berger and Uwe Wissenbach, 'EU–China–Africa Trilateral Development Cooperation: Common challenges and new directions', German Development Institute, Discussion Paper 21p, Bonn, 2007.

39 'China's Policy Paper on the European Union', p. 2.

40 'Vigorously Promoting Comprehensive Strategic Partnership between China and the European Union', speech by Wen Jiabao at the China–EU Investment and Trade Forum, Brussels, 6 May 2004, available at: http://www.fmprc.gov.cn/ce/ cebe/eng/zt/t101949.htm (15 September 2009).

41 See Stumbaum, *The European Union and China*, 2009, chapter 6.

42 Roland Watson, Richard Beeston and David Charter, 'US Chill Gives Europe Cold Feet on China Arms Sales', *The Times*, 22 March 2005, available at: http:// www.timesonline.co.uk/tol/news/world/europe/article434141.ece.

43 Elizabeth Economy and Adam Segal, 'The G2 Mirage: Why the United States and China are not ready to upgrade ties', *Foreign Affairs*, 5(86), May/June 2009; Henry C. K. Liu, 'Brzezinski's G-2 Grand Strategy', *Asia Times Online*, 22 April 2009, available at: http://www.atimes.com/atimes/china_business/kd22cb03. html (3 September 2009).

2 China's views on Europe's role in international security

Zhang Yanbing

This chapter aims to provide an up-to-date assessment of China's views on Europe's role in international security. A striking phenomenon in Chinese contemporary international and strategic studies is that a number of studies on Europe have appeared in recent years, partly due to the increasingly important Sino–European relations and partly the growing role of Europe in the international system. European studies in the Chinese context can be roughly put into three categories:

- studies on the political, economic and social situations of the single European nation-states, mainly the major powers such as France, Germany, Britain, Italy and Spain, and their relations with China;
- research about European integration and Sino–European relations;
- studies on Europe's role at the global level, and China and Europe's relations with other great powers, for example US–China–Europe and Russia–China–Europe.

This kind of categorization implies that China essentially faces Europe at three distinct levels: individual states, Europe as a political entity and Europe as a global power. Compared with publications of the first two categories, studies of the third category are certainly less numerous. But it is exactly this category of studies this chapter tries to review, with the purpose of discussing Europe's international role from a Chinese perspective. Some studies within the second category, when discussing Sino–Europe relations, also imply China's understandings of Europe's international role, so they should not be ignored. More importantly, Chinese government' official statements on Europe's international role, although there are only a few, should be highlighted. The official statements influence intellectual inquiries, and vice versa. Essentially, 'China's' views on Europe's international role is derived from views expressed by the Chinese government and China's international and strategic studies community.

This chapter consists of three parts. Part one provides China's general views on international security and argues that, when dealing with international affairs, China's primary concern is still its own national security and development. Part two analyses Europe's role in international security from the Chinese perspective. The basic three points here are that Europe is a peaceful power, Europe is a great soft power and Europe is a growing power. Part three is a brief conclusion and offers some policy implications of the above findings for both China and Europe.

China's views on international security in general

China's current views on international security are still largely influenced by the strategic thinking of Deng Xiaoping, China's past paramount leader and the architect of China's opening up and reform policy. 'China's National Defence in 2008', the white paper published in January 2009, expresses how China understands international security. It says that although 'the world is undergoing tremendous changes and adjustments', 'peace and development remain the principal themes of the times, and the pursuit of peace, development and cooperation has become an irresistible trend of the times'.[1] It was Deng who provided this kind of understanding of the world order for China and designed China's development road under this understanding after he came back to power in 1978.

Like his predecessor Mao Zedong, Deng was primarily a nationalist. The starting point of their consideration about the relationship between China and the world was how to secure China's national security and foster China's development. But Deng's visions were different from those of his predecessor in two ways: the basic judgement of the international security situation; and how to balance national security and national development. These two points are tightly linked with each other.

During Mao's period, China's perception of the world order was that the world was in a period of war and revolution. Thus, the primary concern of the New China was how to survive during the Cold War, particularly with the threat from the US in the early years of its establishment. In the 1950s, China originally allied with the Soviet Union, but, once Mao found that the Soviet Union might also threaten China's national security, the Sino–Soviet split opened up. In the 1960s, China tried to oppose US and Soviet Union hegemony, and experienced a highly difficult security situation. The military clash between China and the Soviet Union on Zhenbao Island in 1969 more or less proved that the greater threat came from the Soviet Union, and forced China to say farewell completely to its former ally. In order to deal with the threat from the Soviet Union to its national security, China turned to the US and the West generally. At the beginning of the 1970s, the US needed China's help because of its struggle with the Soviet Union globally in general and its failure in Vietnam in particular. This paved the way for Nixon's visit to China in 1972. Meanwhile, in 1971, China's seat in the United Nations and membership of the UN Security Council were handed to the People's Republic. China's security situation changed dramatically because of these two great events, opening up a new era.[2]

Deng essentially inherited a more favourable international security situation than Mao had ever enjoyed. Following Nixon's visit to China, China established formal diplomatic relations with the US, Japan, Germany, and many other nations, and entered many international organizations as well. Sino–Soviet relations also improved during the 1980s. This made China certainly feel much safer than before. Meanwhile, looking back, the current wave of economic globalization had its origins in the early 1970s, and the global political and economic situation as a whole had certainly changed since then. The changing world situation guided Deng to believe that 'peace and development are the principal themes of the times'.[3] History has proved that he was right.

The difference between Deng and Mao on how to balance national security and national development directly came from the different international situations they faced. In Mao's view, and perhaps also in reality, China's national security was fundamentally threatened and national development therefore had to serve national security. The strategy of copying the Soviet heavy industry-oriented developmental model in the 1950s was the result of this model's apparent strength. After all, the Soviet Union had defeated Nazi Germany in the Second World War. For a nation like China, which wanted to survive and had to quickly build up a national defence industry, this model was certainly attractive. But when Mao found the Soviet model had its own problems in the late 1950s, he began to search China's own development road. The Great Leap Forward was Mao's attempt in this direction, and the Third Front Construction was the inevitable outcome of China facing up to the threat from both the US and the Soviet Union in 1960s.

Deng cared about China's national security, mainly national sovereignty and unification, as much as Mao, but, with the changed international situation, he argued that national development meant national security. In his own words, 'development is the only hard truth'. When he became China's top leader in the late 1970s, the key concern of Chinese government became how to foster China's economic development. Opening up to the outside world and to domestic economic reform are tools for development. Although the starting point might be that 'peace and development are the principal themes of the times' and China followed this overall trend passively, once it decided that economic development should be the nation's primary concern, it also assumed an active role in creating a beneficial international environment for its development. Gradually, 'peace, development and cooperation' have become the guiding principle when China thinks and deals with foreign affairs.[4]

The Tiananmen Event in 1989 and the subsequent collapse of the socialist bloc have not changed the vision of China's leaders on the world situation and China's development path. In fact, the fall of the Soviet Union, from a realist perspective, meant that the threat from the North to China finally disappeared, although the relationship between China and the West, and particularly the US, has since become more complicated. During that turbulent period, Deng drafted his famous 28-characters guide to China's foreign policy in the post-Cold War period:

1 *lengjing guancha*, observe and analyse developments calmly;
2 *chenzhuo yingfu*, deal with changes patiently and confidently;
3 *wenzhu zhenjiao*, secure our own position;
4 *taoguang yanghui*, conceal our capabilities and avoid the limelight;
5 *shanyu shouzhuo*, keep a low profile;
6 *juebu dangtou*, never become a leader; and
7 *yousuo zuowei*, strive for achievements on global affairs.[5]

Deng's strategic thinking has been largely inherited by his two successors, Jiang Zemin and Hu Jintao, both of whom were selected by Deng. This kind of leadership succession has not only guaranteed China's political stability but also the continuation of opening up, reform and development policies.

China is still on the road designed by Deng. Therefore, China's views on international security at the moment can be summarized as:

1 China is primarily concerned with its national security, and because the Taiwan issue and the Tibet issue relate to China's sovereignty and national unity, China does not concede on these issues;
2 When China's national security is not under fundamental threat, China focuses mainly on its national economic development;
3 Try to construct a peaceful international environment for economic development, by building good relationships with neighbouring countries as well as other great powers;
4 The Asia-Pacific Region is the main focus when security issues are concerned;
5 China avoids confrontations with other major powers and does not hope to be too involved in global affairs;
6 Support multilateralism and multipolarization in dealing with global issues.

China's views on Europe's role in international security

With China's views on international security in general having been clarified, we can now turn to China's views on Europe's role in international security. Generally speaking, this includes three interlocked aspects:

1 As far as the traditional security issue is concerned, Europe is a peaceful power and wages peace at the global level.
2 Europe is the great soft power in the world. It leads the world ideologically.
3 Europe's power is growing, and whether it will become more powerful depends largely on the future of its political integration, since its major

member states are also global players and sometimes have different views on international security issues.

Europe as a peaceful power

China's leaders since Deng Xiaoping have generally taken a positive view on Europe's role in international security and believed Europe is an importance force to wage peace globally. A recent study in China summarizes Deng's understanding of Europe's role in international security as following:

1   During the Cold War period, China felt sympathetic towards Europe's difficult position between the two rival superpowers and worried that war might break out in Europe;
2   China believed Europe was an important force in waging peace because it had suffered so much in the two World Wars and the Cold War;
3   China supported European integration and believed that, when European countries stayed together, Europe could become more powerful;
4   China hoped that Europe would have its own independent external policies rather than simply following the US.[6]

Deng's successors have generally inherited this kind of understanding of Europe's role in the world. For example, when he attended the first Asia–Europe Meeting in 1996, China's former primer Li Peng said that

> colonialism and the two World Wars had caused great tragedies to Asian and European people, these kinds of tragedies should not appear again and Asian and European people cherish peace.[7]

When China's former President Jiang Zemin visited Germany in 2002, he said that

> in order to achieve mankind's peace and development in the twenty-first century, Europe has the capacity to play more important role and it should do that ... China will always support Europe to keep peace and promote development in the world.[8]

When China's current President Hu Jintao visited London in 2005, he said that 'both China and Europe have the responsibility to keep world peace and promote mutual development'.[9] China's policy paper on the European Union, published for the first time in 2003, clearly states that China's first EU policy objective is to 'promote a sound and steady development of Sino–EU political relations, and to work with the EU to contribute to world peace and stability'.[10]

There are two main reasons why China views Europe/the EU as a peaceful power or a power for peace. The foremost reason is Europe does not threaten China's own national security. As discussed in the first part, China, like other nations, looks to its own security before paying attention to international security more generally. It is unimaginable that China would regard a nation that threatens its national security as a peaceful power. As China's EU Paper indicates,

> there is no fundamental conflict of interest between China and the EU and neither side poses a threat to the other ... the common ground between China and the EU far outweighs their disagreements.[11]

From a geopolitical perspective, compared with other major powers, the EU certainly deserves such a positive evaluation from China on its national security issues. When Deng Xiaoping met Mikhail Gorbachev in 1989, he had illustrated China's concern on its national security from a historical perspective. He stated that, since the Opium War, the countries that had taken the greatest advantage of China and that hurt China most deeply were Japan and tsarist Russia, and, at certain times and concerning certain questions, the Soviet Union. After the establishment of the People's Republic, the main threats to China's national security had come mainly from the US and the Soviet Union.[12] In 1962, there was also a war between China and India. Certainly, these are now history, but, as Karl Marx once said, 'the tradition of all dead generations weighs like a nightmare on the brains of the living'.[13] In the foreseeable future, there may be conflicts between China and the US, Russia, Japan or India, for various reasons – such as the Taiwan issue or territorial disputes. But it is nearly impossible for China and Europe to be faced with serious security difficulties between them.

Secondly, China takes a positive view on the world security situation as a whole. In China's vision, during the post-Cold War period the world was going to become multipolar, and a multipolar world is good for peace and development. When the Cold War ended with the disintegration of the Soviet Union in 1991, the US emerged as the world's sole superpower. China believes that 'it is gradually becoming a consensus shared by the international community that world affairs should not be monopolized by a superpower.'[14] China advocates global multipolarity:

> Multipolarity constitutes an important base for achieving a durable peace in the world. It is conducive to building a new just and reasonable eco-political order, setting up a relatively stable international political framework and promoting exchanges and cooperation.[15]

The Political Reports delivered by the General Secretaries to the Chinese Communist Party's National Congresses can be treated as the guiding principles of the China's global and national development strategy. From the 14th Congress in 1992, these political reports[16] have always described the world becoming multipolar. The current global economic crisis has given rise to the G-2 concept, that is, the idea of the world being governed by the US and China. Many countries hope that China will play a more important global role, but China itself is quite indifferent. For example, when he attended the 11th EU–China summit, China's premier Wen Jiabao told European leaders that the G-2 notion was wrong, and that a multipolar world and multilateralism were the main trend.[17]

Further, from the Chinese perspective, both China and Europe are poles and can work together to build up a peaceful multipolar world. In the recent years, the EU has been increasingly regarded by the Chinese people as 'a pole of the world'.[18] In many Chinese's opinions, Europe is an active advocate of world multipolarity and has adopted a policy of multilateralism in dealing with international relations.[19] The 'EU and China, both endorsing the idea of peaceful development, are becoming important players to maintain world peace and forces to lever against hegemonic politics.'[20] China knows that the US and the EU are different in terms of the interests, goals and methods of their global strategies:

- the US sees as its priority in its post-Cold War global strategy the prevention and containment of any power which might challenge US interests or threaten US superpower;
- whereas the EU respects diversity and believes that problems in global security are caused by multiple factors and that multilateral cooperation and international frameworks such as the UN will work increasingly effectively.[21]

    The EU embraces the idea that for the resolution of international crisis, armed force should be used as a last resort after all possible peaceful resolutions are exhausted, and that the use of armed force must be based on the UN Charter and other international laws.[22]

In China's international and strategic studies circle, discussions focus on the multipolar world and Europe's important role within it. Within the *Strategic and Security Review* published annually by the China Institutes of Contemporary International Relations (CICIR), the EU was described as 'Seeking Big Roles' in the multipolar world in 2002–2003',[23] as going 'from regional power to global power' in 2004–2005',[24] and as aiming to 'increase its international influences during the crisis' in 2008–2009.[25] A recent work by the Chinese Academy of Social Sciences also argues that European integration will balance the US as the only superpower in the world and will contribute to a multipolar world.[26]

Europe as a great soft power

If Europe is a power for waging peace, where does Europe's power come from? In China's view, Europe is primarily a great soft power. The concept of soft power was proposed by Joseph S. Nye in 1990.[27] According to Nye, there are three major ways to affect others to get the required outcomes: one is to threaten coercion (sticks); the second is to pay (carrots); the third is to attract them or co-opt them, so that they want what you want. Soft power is the ability to obtain what the required outcomes through co-option and attraction rather than the stick and carrot methods.[28]

Since the concept was defined, Chinese scholars have focused their research on this concept and have written many articles on it.[29] Many of China's international and strategic studies community describe Europe as a great soft power in the world. Qin Yaqing, the deputy president of China's Foreign Affairs University, argues that

> in the post-war period, Europe's international influence mainly exhibited as a soft power ... European integration as a development road is certainly attractive ... its soft power mainly includes peaceful ideas, institutional design and polices.[30]

Qin's colleague Zhu Liqun argues that, 'as the biggest soft power in the world, the EU plays an irreplaceable role in constructing the world order positively ... on the international level, the EU mainly plays the role as a civilian power and transformative power.'[31] Wu Yikang, the director of Chinese Society for EU Studies, argues that 'the soft power of the EU is obvious and no one else in the world can compare with it.'[32]

Several reasons contribute to China's understanding of Europe as a great soft power and they need to be discussed in detail one by one. Firstly, the Chinese generally have respect for European civilization and Europe's achievement in modern history. Chen Lemin, the former director of European Studies centre of the Chinese Academy of Social Sciences, stated that

> when world politics is concerned, Europe was certainly 'marginalized' in the 20th century compared with the previous several centuries ... but the real treasure of Europe lies in its history that lasts from ancient Greece and ancient Rome to the Medieval period and to the present, and in its cultural achievements like Philosophy, Literature, Aesthetics, History, Law and so on.[33]

A recent survey of international and strategy studies in the People's Republic has summarized European Studies in China in this way. It says

> the EU member states are far away from China and, from a geopolitical perspective, they have become not that important. But these countries had been deeply involved in China's modern history. Britain, France and Germany used to be the world's great powers. Although during the post-war period, they have been in decline, they are still very important both regionally and globally. Because of the historical reasons and the

realistic concerns, the Chinese government and the intellectual circle have always cared about European and Sino–European relations studies ... since the establishment of the People's Republic, European and Sino–Europe relations studies have been the key agenda of China's international studies.[34]

These two statements more or less represent China's views toward Europe. Although in the hard power aspect European countries are in relative decline, its civilization and achievements are still very attractive, which points to the soft power of Europe.

Secondly, European integration demonstrates a new way of dealing with international security peacefully. There are massive studies in contemporary China about European integration. But most of them are mainly about European integration itself and there are only a few which discuss the soft power exhibits in European integration. The most important work on this topic to have appeared in China in recent years perhaps is *Ideas, Institutions, and Policies: A Study of the European Union's Soft Power*, edited by Qin Yaqing.[35] In this book, Qin and his colleagues argue that 'soft power mainly comes from three resources, culture or ideas, institutions and policies'.[36] They also discuss how each of these three aspects of soft power has manifested itself in European integration. Their main argument is that

> the fundamental change in post-war Europe is the change of ideas and the formation of a new international relations culture with peace as its core. The core of Europe's soft power is the idea of peace constructed by the Europeans in the last several decades. The other two important ideas are cooperation and community. Cooperation is the way for peace, and cooperation leads to integration.[37]

During the process of integration, collective identity was constructed and the idea of a security community began to have its foundation. In their understanding, the soft power of the EU's institutions comes from their guarantees of the idea of peace and from constructing this idea in an institutional way. The soft power of policies largely depends on whether these policies are legitimate, reciprocal and effective.[38]

But when Qin and his colleagues' discussion turns to how Europe's soft power works on the international scale, their reasoning becomes quite cautious. They argue that the ideas of peace, democracy, cooperation, development and environmental protection are certainly universal values. But Europe's way of institutionalizing these ideas is not universal. The EU model is based on Europe's unique history and culture.[39] Qin and his colleagues' arguments are certainly controversial, but at least they have clarified that Europe's soft power lies mainly in its ideas and that these ideas are powerful forces.

The ideas that back up European integration are only a small part of the powerful ideas produced by the Europeans. More importantly, it has to be conceded that all influential modern ideologies are essentially produced by Europeans; for example, classical liberalism, socialism, Marxism, Keynesianism, nationalism and fascism in the pre-war period, and neo-liberalism, feminism, environmentalism and neo-conservatism in recent decades. To some extent, it may be argued that mankind is living in an ideological context that was created by Europeans. Keynes once argued that

> practical men, who believe themselves to be quite exempt from any intellectual influences, are usually the slaves of some defunct economist ... I am sure that the power of vested interest is vastly exaggerated compared with the gradual encroachment of ideas.[40]

If Keynes was right, European integration might have paved a way for perpetual peace of the world in the future.

Thirdly, as far as the impact of powerful European ideas on international security is concerned, beyond the exemplary role of European integration in the traditional security field, the most important European contribution in recent decades has been the legitimization of environmentalism in the non-traditional security field. For instance, one Chinese scholar comments that

> climate change has become an increasingly important political element as well as social concern in the EU. The EU has taken the opportunity of Germany being the president country of the G-8 to bring the issue to international attention.[41]

There is no space here to illustrate the process of the worldwide rise of environmentalism. But environmentalism is a product of post-modern Europe and the Europeans have always been the pioneers in promoting this idea and trying to institutionalize it globally. The most recent major attempt by the Europeans in this field is *The Stern Report* and the next will be the Climate Change Conference in Copenhagen. In political science, power is often understood as agenda setting and initiation. From this perspective, Europe is certainly a global power and still guides the direction of mankind.

China's view of Europe as a great soft power is partly from the international role Europe plays and partly its hard power, and is still in a process of development. In the Cold War era, the then European Community (EC) refrained from developing institutionalized cooperation in the area of security and defence among the member states. Since the Cold War, due to difficulties existing in European political integration, the EU is generally deemed as a civilian power rather than a military alliance. The main components of the European model dealing with international relations and international conflicts are 'institutionalization' and 'multilateral in-situation building'.[42] It is by the efforts of the EU and its member states taking an active part in institution building on different levels that European values, norms and rules have been exported. In recent years, some European scholars have defined the concept of 'EU normative power'. More specifically, normative power means that global politics and the global economy are run by norms and notions, a concept that has been studied in Chinese academic circles. For instance, Cui has examined the conceptual evolution of EU normative power and discusses the EU's advantages and limitations as a global normative power.[43]

The European model is arousing increasingly greater attention in the international arena, but it has certain shortcomings. There are systemic problems in European security strategy, such as vaguely defined European defence policy, unclear defence priorities, proper instruments of execution and a struggle for internal unity.[44] To implement a unified security policy remains a huge challenge for the EU. If the EU wants to possess a decisive leadership role in the world, it must act as one; and decisions, particularly ones concerning diplomacy and defence, should be made at the EU level. But it is impossible in the current EU infrastructure because member states are responsible for their own territorial defence. Moreover, unlike the US, the EU does not have a security presence or defence commitments in many areas of the world. This situation has both advantages and drawbacks. On the one hand, as a non-threatening power with no claim to hegemony in such regions, the EU is more trusted and less feared than the US. On the other, with the renaissance of realpolitik thinking in the region, the EU faces the simple challenge of being taken seriously.[45]

Europe as a growing power

How to overcome these shortcomings is related to the third general view of China toward Europe, that Europe's power is growing. Whether it will become more powerful depends on the future of its political integration. Chinese thinking on Europe as a growing power implies four interlinked aspects. First, the achievement of European integration is certainly impressive. But the achievement still lies mainly in the economic field. It means that, secondly, European political integration still faces many difficulties and, thirdly, whether Europe will become an independent military force and has its unified defence and security policies is still an open question. Fourthly, China believes that European integration will be more successful in the future. We'll take these points one by one.

Europe integration has achieved a very high level of supranational cooperation that goes much further than in any other region in the world. There is no doubt that the European integration has a profound impact on Europe, as it has developed into an EU of 27 member states from the original 6 member states. The EU's integration has been thought by the Chinese to be a powerful driver for stability and peace in Europe. Most Chinese observers agree that Europe has achieved a historic transformation by its integration, which signifies that Europe has finally found a peaceful developmental path after a long history of frequent warfare. According to one Chinese scholar,

> the European integration and the EU have made great progress in breaking through the traditional transnational cooperation and have contributed to the peaceful transformation of the regional order and the construction of European security community.[46]

In recent years, the EU's own development has steadily augmented its relevant role and influence in the world. China has a very positive view of the EU integration's implications for the rest of the world. China's current president, Hu Jintao, once stated that

> the European Union is the world's largest regional group that enjoys the highest level of integration. It has achieved progress in both interior construction and enlargement in recent years and thus taken a more important place on the world stage.[47]

One scholar wrote that 'the European integration has undoubtedly led the EU to be in the limelight of the world stage'.[48] Also, 'Europeans have presented the world with a new model of international social institutions, as a sharp contrast to the concept of the US.'[49] The factors that have been driving European integration further in recent years are also debated:

> The industrialization and market economies upheld in western European countries provide preconditions for economic integration; however, to avoid wars among each other after the Second World War was the main motivation of forming an economic union among western European countries. The economic globalization, energy crisis and high technology development promoted European economic integration to go further.[50]

It is generally accepted in China that economic integration is the cornerstone of the EU's 50 years of integration. Its economic and trade cooperation has expanded continuously and the euro is now 10 years old. Today, the EU is the biggest economy in the world. According to a survey and a preliminary analysis conducted by the Research Group of the Institute of European Studies of the Chinese Academy of Social Sciences (CASS) in 2008, as far as the EU's position and role in current international politics are concerned, 46.0 per cent of respondents considered them very important, and 39.1 per cent quite important, a total of 85.1 per cent. This indicates that most Chinese people recognize that the EU plays a significant role in international politics. It is worth noticing that in this survey the consensus rate of the Chinese public as to the EU's position in the international political system is even higher than its position in the international economic system: 46.0 per cent for very important, with 35.1 per cent for quite important.[51]

However, China has not been hugely positive about the level reached so far in the EU's integration or world multipolarity. Many Chinese scholars have noticed the difficulties that Europe has gone through in the process of integration, in particular in the political field. For instance, in 2005, France and the Netherlands voted 'No' against the European constitution, which was deemed a big setback for further European integration.[52] The Irish 'No' vote in June 2008 put on hold key EU institutional reforms as well. Some believe that such difficulties reveal the deep-rooted clash of interests between individual member states and the EU as a whole.[53] The difficulties in political integration make implementing a unified security policy of the EU a very big challenge. Although political relations have made significant forward strides in Europe,[54] Europe has been underperforming in international security. A recent study argues that 'considering its economic power, the power and position the EU enjoys in world politics is too low'.[55]

Since the end of the Cold War, the EU has certainly adopted several treaty revisions and resolutions, as it agreed to develop a Common Foreign and Security Policy (CFSP) in order to build an autonomous military capacity. But European security and defence policy followed several different paths during the 1990s, developing simultaneously within the Western European Union, NATO and the European Union itself. Within them, a NATO-based European security and defence identity is still regarded as the core element by a number of Chinese authors.[56] This is based on the fact that Europe still relies heavily on the US to protect its security. For instance, it was clear that Europe could not deal by itself with the Kosovo crisis in 1999 and it had to rely on the US and NATO to solve the crisis.[57] Moreover, it did not sufficiently take into account the UN or other international organizations.[58] The weakness of the EU's CSDP became much clearer when the Iraq War broke out in 2003. Essentially, when dealing with this international security issue, Europe was split into two groups, a New Europe and an Old Europe, borrowing Rumsfeld's conceptions. 'The CSDP is the core of European political integration, but it has always worked on a low level.'[59]

Finally, as far as the future of European integration is concerned, most Chinese literature holds a relatively positive view. For instance, Zhen Qirong believes that the CFSP will continue to develop and the current difficult situation of European political integration may only be caused by the fact that it is still a recent development, since the CFSP has only been developing for 15 years and the EU itself is only 50 years old. The EU will tackle the difficulties it faces and put its integration forward, and will contribute to Europe's stability and world peace through its integration.[60] In Chen Zhimin's opinion, the EU is in the process of militarization and is actually 'a superpower in the making', though he does admit that the military power of the EU is limited and believes it is impossible for the EU to turn into a superpower like the US. He also believes that its militarization does not mean the demise of the EU as a civilian power. Rather, to some extent, militarization fills up the capacity gap which the EU had to face during the Cold War, and may enable the EU to carry out its missions as a civilian power more effectively.[61]

Conclusions and policy implications

This chapter has outlined the three main aspects of China's views on Europe's role in international security, based on a discussion of China's vision of international security in general. From the Chinese perspective, due to the rapid development of economic integration and launching of common foreign economic policy and European political cooperation, Europe has been able to play an important role in the world as a peaceful power, a great soft power and a growing power when international security is concerned. These findings have several important policy implications:

- First, Europe should cherish the positive views China holds about it. China's fundamental interest is its national security. As far as the Taiwan issue and the Tibetan issue are concerned, Europe should respect China's sovereignty and its determination to protect its national unity. Europe should try to avoid becoming involved in such sensitive issues as the internationalization of the Tibetan issue or the selling of weapons to Taiwan, which would certainly annoy China. A sound Sino–European relationship is the foundation for both sides to cooperate in the field of international security. To threaten China's national security will not only harm Sino–Europe relations but also international security.
- Secondly, Europe should keep to its role as a peaceful power, play a more important role as a great soft power and make European integration more successful in order to contribute to international security. China supports European integration and hopes Europe will become stronger. However, the future of European integration will be mainly determined by the efforts of the Europeans themselves. It largely depends on whether the Europeans can solve their internal difficulties and deal with their relations with the US and Russia artfully. European integration has achieved a lot, but in order to build a United States of Europe, there is still a long way to go. What China can do is to improve Sino–Europe economic cooperation in order to foster European economic recovery. A unified and well-developed European economy is the foundation of European political integration.
- Finally, China and Europe share many common interests without direct conflicts of interests. The intensification of long-term and comprehensive cooperation in all fields, such as the environment, climate change, the risk of a new pandemic, energy supplies, natural resources and so

on is in the fundamental interests of both sides and will contribute to world peace and development. Some ideas proposed by Europe, such as peace, sustainable development, multilateralism and environmental protection, have universal values. But Europe cannot achieve these in the international system all by itself. China should support these ideas by practising them itself and working with Europe on the global scale. Europe's power is growing and China is becoming stronger.

Both sides cherish peace and development. Good cooperation between them will contribute to global peace and development.

Notes

1 'China's National Defense in 2008', available at: http://www.gov.cn/english/official/2009-01/20/content_1210227_3.htm (14 June 2009).
2 Niu Jun (ed.), *China's Diplomacy in the Post Cold War Years*, Beijing: Peking University Press, 2009, pp. 17–26.
3 Deng Xiaoping, 'Heping he Fazhan Shi Dangdai Shijie de Liangda Wenti' ('Peace and development are the principal themes of the times'), 1985, available at: http://web.peopledaily.com.cn/deng/ (14 June 2009).
4 Zheng Qirong (ed.), *Gaigekaifang Yilai de Zhongguo Waijiao, 1978–2008* ('Chinese diplomacy since the reform and opening up, 1978–2008'), Beijing: Shijie Zhishi Press, 2008, pp. 6–16.
5 Ibid., pp. 16–27.
6 For a good summary of Deng Xiaoping's view of Europe's role in international security, see: Ding Yansong, 'Deng Xiaoping's Viewpoint of European Safety and the Pushing of Sino–EU Relations', *Journal of Daqing Normal University* 29(1), 2009.
7 Li Peng's speech at the first Asia–Europe Meeting, available at: http://news.xinhuanet.com/world/2008-08/29/content_9735292.htm (14 June 2009).
8 Jiang Zeming's speech at the German Association for Foreign Policy, available at: http://www.people.com.cn/GB/shizheng/20020410/706739.html (15 June 2009).
9 Hu Jintao's speech available at:http://politics.people.com.cn/GB/1024/3845867.html (15 June 2009).
10 Available at: http://www.fmprc.gov.cn/ce/cehu/chn/ztbd/zcwj/t64156.htm (15 June 2009).
11 Ibid.
12 Deng Xiaoping, 'Let Us Put the Past Behind Us and Open a New Era', 1989, available at: http://english.peopledaily.com.cn/dengxp/vol3/text/c1970.html, (15 June 2009).
13 Karl Marx, 'The Eighteenth Brumaire of Louis Bonaparte', 1852, available at: http://www.marxists.org/archive/marx/works/1852/18th-brumaire/ch01.htm (15 June 2009).
14 'Multipolarity Plays Key Role in World Peace: Chinese Vice President', *People's Daily*, 6 November 2001, available at: http://english.peopledaily.com.cn/english/200111/05/eng20011105_83945.html (14 June 2009).
15 'Major Points of Hu Jintao's Speech at FIRI in Paris', *People's Daily*, 6 November 2001, available at: http://english.peopledaily.com.cn/200111/06/eng20011106_83972.html (14 June 2009).
16 These reports can be found at: http://cpc.people.com.cn/GB/64162/64168/64568/index.html (15 June 2009).

17 Wen Jiabao criticized the G2 concept: http://news.sina.com.cn/w/2009-05-22/000915663617s.shtml (18 June 2009).
18 Research Group of the Institute of European Studies, 'A Survey and Preliminary Analysis of the Chinese Perception of the EU and China–Europe Relations', Beijing: Chinese Academy of Social Sciences, Working Paper Series on European Studies 2(1), 2008.
19 Lin Ling, 'Oumeng Waijiao zhong de Duobianzhuyi Linian' ('Multilateralism in EU's Diplomacy'), *Guoji Ziliao Xinxi* (*'International Materials and Information'*), 2, 2009.
20 Zhou Hong and Shen Yannan (eds), *Ouzhou Fazhan Baogao, 2004–2005: Da Oumeng, Xin Ouzhou* ('Annual Development Report of Europe, 2004–2005: Great European Union, New Europe'), Beijing: Social Science Academic Press, 2005.
21 Ibid., p. 13.
22 Zhou Hong and Shen Yannan, eds, *Ouzhou Fazhan Baogao, 2006–2007: Ouzhou de Guoji Weiji Guanli,* ['Annual Development Report of Europe, 2006–2007: Europe Union's International Crisis Management'], Beijing: Social Science Academic Press, 2007, p. 7.
23 China Institute of Contemporary International Relations, *Strategic and Security Review,* Beijing: Shishi Press, 2003, pp. 49–52.
24 Ibid., pp. 181–200.
25 Ibid., pp. 315–36.
26 Zhou Hong (ed.), *European Union as a Power,* Beijing: Social Sciences Academic Press, 2008.
27 Joseph S. Nye, Jr, 'Soft Power', *Foreign Policy,* Fall 1990.
28 Joseph S. Nye, Jr, *Bound to Lead: The Changing Nature of American Power,* New York: Basic Books Inc. Publishers, 1990, p. 34.
29 Qin Yaqing (ed.), *Ideas, Institutions and Policies: A Study of European Union's Soft Power,* Beijing: World Knowledge Press, 2008, pp. 3, 41.
30 Ibid., p. 19.
31 Zhu Liqun ed., *Guoji Tixi he Zhongou Guanxi* ['International System and Sino–European Relations'], Beijing: World Knowledge Press, 2008, p. 4.
32 Wu Yikang (ed.), *Ouzhou Yitihua de Zouxiang he Zhong-Ou Guanxi* ('Orientation of the European Integration and China–EU Relations'), Beijing: Shishi Press, 2008, p. 186.
33 Chen Lemin, *20 Shiji de Ouzhou* ('Europe in the 20th Century'), Beijing: Sanlian Press, 2007, p. 4.
34 Wang Jun and Dan Xingwu, *Zhongguo Guoji Yanjiu Sishi Nian* ('China's International Relations Studies in the Past 40 Years'), Beijing: Central Compilation and Translation Press, 2008, pp. 178–9.
35 Qin Yaqing (ed.), *Ideas, Institutions and Policies'.*
36 Ibid., p. 6.
37 Ibid., p. 9.
38 Ibid., pp. 16–19.
39 Ibid., p. 19.
40 John Maynard Keynes, *The General Theory of Employment, Interest, and Money,* Amherst, NY: Prometheus Books, 1997 [1936], p. 383.
41 Zhou Hong and Shen Yannan (eds), *Ouzhou Fazhan Baogao, 2007–2008: Ouzhou Lianmeng 50 Nian* ('Annual Development Report of Europe, 2007–2008: Europe Union of 50 Years'), Beijing: Social Science Academic Press, 2008.
42 Zhang Jun, 'EU's Behavior in ASEM as a Civilian Power', *Chinese Journal of European Studies,* 24(1), February 2006.
43 Cui Hongwei, 'Guifanxing Qiangquan' Oumeng yu Zhongou Guanxi de Hexie Fazhan' ('The Harmonious Development of the Relationship between Normative Power EU and China'), *Social Science* 11, 2007.

44 Sven Biscop, Andrew Small, Stan Sloan and Feng Zhongping, 'European Security Strategy and its Impact on the United States and China', 2009, available at: http://carnegieendowment.org/events/?fa=eventDetail&id=1282&prog=zgp,zru &proj=zted (14 June 2009).
45 Marcin Zaborowski, 'Developing a European Security Perspective on China', Paris: EU Institute for Security Studies, 3 March 2006, available at: http://www.iss.europa.eu/uploads/media/rep06-06.pdf (14 June 2009).
46 Zhu Guichang, 'European Integration and the Construction of European Security Community', Paper presented to the International Conference on European integration and the Transformation of European Political and Social Order 19–21 October 2007, Weihai, China.
47 'Major Points of Hu Jintao's Speech at FIRI in Paris', *People's Daily*, 6 November 2001, available at: http://english.peopledaily.com.cn/200111/06/eng20011106_83972.html (14 June 2009).
48 Zhou Hong and Shen Yannan (eds), *Ouzhou Fazhan Baogao, 2007–2008*, p. 6.
49 Zhou Hong and Shen Yannan (eds), *Ouzhou Fazhan Baogao, 2004–2005*.
50 Zhou Hong and Shen Yannan (eds), *Ouzhou Fazhan Baogao, 2007–2008*, p. 7.
51 Research Group of the Institute of European Studies, Chinese Academy of Social Sciences, 2008, 'A Survey and Preliminary Analysis of the Chinese Perception of the EU and China–Europe Relations', Working Paper Series on European Studies 2(1), 2008.
52 Zhou Hong and Shen Yannan (eds), *Ouzhou Fazhan Baogao, 2005–2006: Ouzhou Xianfa de Mingyun* ('Annual Development Report of Europe, 2005–2006: The Fate of the European Constitution'), Beijing: Social Science Academic Press, 2006, p. 9.
53 Zheng Qirong (ed.), *EU CFSP in a Globalizing Era*, Beijing: Shijie Zhishi Press, 2008, p. 36.
54 Xiong Guangkai, *International Situation and Security Strategy*, Beijing: Tsinghua University Press, 2006, pp. 333–4.
55 Zheng Qirong (ed.), *EU CFSP in a Globalizing Era*, p. 351.
56 Ibid., pp. 354–65.
57 Ibid., p. 359.
58 Zhou Hong and Shen Yannan, eds, *Ouzhou Fazhan Baogao, 2006–2007: Ouzhou de Guoji Weiji Guanli*, ['Annual Development Report of Europe, 2006–2007: Europe Union's International Crisis Management'], Beijing: Social Science Academic Press, 2007, p. 6.
59 Ibid., p. 355.
60 Zheng Qirong (ed.), *EU CFSP in a Globalizing Era*, p. 365.
61 Chen Zhimin, 'The Militarizing of the European Union: From Civilian Power to Military Power?', *European Studies* 5, 2004, pp. 79–92.

3 Bilateral security relations between China and Europe

Wang Bo

Introduction

China and the EU are both key players in international relations. They are the largest economies in developing and developed countries respectively. China and EU member states Britain and France are three of the five United Nations Security Council permanent members. Both sides recognize each other as important players in international arena. Both regard each other as key political and economical partners.[1] The China–EU strategic partnership proclaimed by both sides in 2003 is a manifesto of the importance of the relationship each side attached to. In the 'strategic partnership', the China–EU security relationship is an integrated part of the partnership. However, the security relationship shows a rather complex scenario. On the one hand, the conventional security relationship in the domains such as arms sale and military personnel exchange is playing a very insignificant role among the overall relationship; on the other, the unconventional security relationship in the domains of energy and climate change is playing a much more ostentatious role. Also, due to the fact that the EU represents a large number of member states, the China–EU relationship is constrained by the fact that there are different voices inside the EU.

Security relations in this study are categorized into two groups:

- conventional security relations, which include arms sales and arms control, military personnel exchange, cooperation on regional and world conflicts (including antiterrorism cooperation);
- unconventional security relations, which mainly cover energy and climate change and other environmental security issues.

China–EU conventional security relations

In comparison with the political and economic relations between China and EU, the relations in the field of conventional security are both relatively insignificant and complex.

a) *The arms embargo issue*

In the bilateral security relationship, the EU's arms embargo against China is both serving as an indicator of the relationship and as the barrier to the security relations in other fields such as military personnel exchange and training, etc. The European Union imposed the arms embargo against China in the wake of the Tiananmen Square incident in Beijing on 4 June 1989. The purpose was to put pressure on the Chinese government to end 'repressive actions against those who legitimately claim their democratic rights'.[2] But with the fast development of political and economical relations, the two sides claimed one another as a 'strategic partner' in 2003. The embargo turned to be an ostentatiously inharmonious issue with this high profile partnership. Chinese government strongly urged the EU side to lift the embargo. Lifting of the embargo became one of the key objectives in China's EU Policy Paper.[3] The Chinese leadership considers the embargo an insult to the strategic partnership relation, and argues that it is a product of Cold War mentality. Chinese government claims that the lifting of the embargo will not result in China's large-scale arms importation from EU.[4] The EU member States leaders such as France and Germany had in the beginning proposed the lifting in order to fit the overall environment of the EU–China strategic partnership. However, due to external factors such as US pressure, and internal factors such as disagreement among EU members and the linking of the embargo with other issues such as human rights and the Taiwan issue, the embargo is still there and makes the lifting a prolonged dilemma for both sides.[5] This issue typically reflects the constraints that China–EU security relations face.

External factors beyond China–EU relations

The most important external factor is US. As the hegemonic power in the Western alliance, the US has a profound influence on the EU in security issues. In EU security strategy, maintaining the transatlantic strategic alliance with US through NATO is the cornerstone of EU security. In 2003, when EU leaders were seriously considering the lifting of the embargo, the US were strongly opposed to the EU's move. George W. Bush stated openly, 'there is a deep concern in our country that transfer of weapons would be a transfer of technology to China, which would change the balance of relations between China and Taiwan, and that is of concern'.[6]

Among the formal and informal alliance network in the Asia Pacific region, China is the key actor that both the US and other regional actors are trying to hedge. The Taiwan Strait has been the most volatile spot in the region. Therefore, the US would not let other actors, such as the EU, undermine its position. The EU's move to lift the embargo would mean that America's allies would assist its rival.[7]

Another external factor is Japan. Japan also openly opposes the EU's lifting of the embargo.[8] The outspoken reason is that lifting the embargo would cause instability between the Chinese mainland and Taiwan which in turn would affect Japan's and regional security. But the implicit reason is much more than that. Due to both historical legacy and geopolitical factors, Japan and China are regional rivals in security. Without a stable and reliable regional security mechanism that can build real confidence between them, Japan could hardly leave China to develop its military power without check.

Obviously, in the EU's overall security strategy, Asia–Pacific security is far less important than it is in the security agenda of the US and Japan.[9] Therefore, when the lifting of the embargo was challenged by the EU's two most important allies, it had to weigh its decision very cautiously.[10]

EU internal factors: hard to reach consensus among member states

In principle, all the members support the common EU foreign policy and security policy, but in practice, due to different interests and policy priorities in their China policies, reaching a consensus among the 27 member states has proved to be a hard, or even impossible, task.[11] In the recently published 'A Power Audit of EU–China Relations' by John Fox and Francois Godement, the authors place the 27 EU member states into four groups according to the features of their relationship with China: Assertive Industrialists, Ideological Free Traders, Accommodating Mercantilists and European Followers.[12] Though the categorization is based mainly on the economic and political relations, as both the EU as a whole and most EU member states link China's human rights and the Taiwan and Tibet issues to their security relations with China, this categorization largely reflects China–EU security relations. Meanwhile, China also has also taken advantage of trade issues at times when political tensions resulted from the above-mentioned issues. Therefore, this chapter utilizes the categorization by Fox and Godement to look at the policies of different EU members in regard to the lifting of arms embargo against China.

According to Fox and Godement's analysis, though not strictly coinciding with the real scenario, the Assertive Industrialists and Ideological Free Traders tend to be critical towards closer security ties with China due to political reasons. The Accommodating Mercantilists are more likely to compromise over political difference in exchange of business interests. Therefore, these countries do not pose a serious hindrance over the development of security relations; they tend instead to improve the security relations for better commercial relations. The European Followers tend to be small countries and do not have their own independent position on relations with China but rely on the EU's collective positions.

Assertive Industrialists include the Czech Republic, Germany and Poland. This group is willing to stand up vigorously to China on both political and economic issues, and is ready to pressure China with specific demands for a given sector, to support anti-dumping measures, or to threaten other trade actions. They contribute towards European divisions because some, including Germany, have doubts about an integrated EU approach and still prefer to compete with other member states for Beijing's ear. The Czech Republic and Poland have a strong anti-communist movement domestically, and they do not have strong interest in the Chinese domestic market. They are, therefore, the "EU members most 'hostile' towards China.

Germany's policy toward China is more complex due to its strong business stake in China. There is a strong split domestically as to its policy towards China. This split is demonstrated through the partisanship in its parliament and change of government. When German Chancellor Gerhard Schröder proposed to lift the arms embargo he met strong domestic resistance. On 28 October 2003, the German Parliament, including the vast majority of Chancellor Gerhard Schröder's own Social Democrats and virtually all of Foreign Minister Joschka Fischer's Green party, passed a resolution opposing Schröder's attempts to lift the embargo. On 11 March 2004, leaders of the four German political parties representing Germany in the European Parliament sent an open letter to Schröder urging him to abandon his support for arms sales to China.[13] When Merkel became chancellor, German criticism towards China on Tibetan and Human rights issues increased and incentives to lift of the embargo faded away.

The Ideological Free Traders are Denmark, the Netherlands, Sweden and the UK. While they are ready to criticize China on political issues, they consistently oppose restricting their trade relations with China. This group, therefore, neither promote the lifting of the embargo nor provide the main voices against it.

The Accommodating Mercantilists are Bulgaria, Cyprus, Finland, Greece, Hungary, Italy, Malta, Portugal, Romania, Slovakia, Slovenia and Spain. They share the assumption that good political relations with China will lead to commercial benefits. They see anti-dumping measures as a useful tool and oppose awarding China the market economy status. They compensate their readiness to resort to protectionist measures by shunning confrontation with China on political questions. This group, therefore, has the most incentives to lift the arms embargo for a better political relationship so as to benefit commercial relations.

France is a special case. During Chirac's presidency, France could well have been put in the latter group. However, since Sarkozy's presidency, France has begun to follow a more critical policy towards China on political issues, which fits more closely in the category of Ideological Free-Traders. Currently it would be more difficult for the French government to advocate the lifting of arms embargo than in Chirac's time.

The European Followers are mainly Austria, Belgium, Estonia, Ireland, Latvia, Luxembourg and Lithuania. This is the most European-spirited group that follows, rather than leads, EU policy towards China. Many do not consider a relationship with China to be central to their foreign policy. Their strategy adds to EU weakness by feeding the perception that China is not a key European priority – even as they rely on EU support to protect them from pressure on issues like Taiwan or Tibet.[14] This group has a smaller economic stake in China and mostly does not have high-level political dialogues. Yet due to their small size, they have more sympathy with the Tibetan independence movement. This sentiment would naturally lead to their suspicion of the lifting of the arms embargo though they are not the leading opponents.

The divisions among EU members on the issue of lifting the arms embargo largely coincide with Fox and Godement's analysis. China generally has better and more stable security relations with 'accommodating mercantilists' and 'European followers' groups as these countries are not likely to challenge China on security issues by linking human rights or Taiwan. Chinese military visits with these countries are more regular.[15] But with other countries the security relations are more complex since they are more likely to be affected by human rights, Taiwan and Tibetan issues. Whenever these issues become volatile or governments in these countries change, the security relations succumbed to these political controversies.

France (Jacques Chirac) and Germany (Gerhard Schröder) first officially proposed the lifting in December 2003. The proposal was supported by Italy and Spain. By May 2004, the UK, Finland and Netherlands had joined the supportive camp. But Germany, Sweden and Denmark's parliaments opposed the lifting.[16] Not only did the member states parliaments vote against lifting the embargo, but the EU parliament too voted against the lifting. In its resolution against the lifting passed on 19 November 2003 the vote was 572:72.[17] Later on, the new German Chancellor Merkel and new French President Sarkozy raised their voices in criticizing China's human rights and the Tibetan issue. With two of the leading EU states' contingency with China, their motivation to lift the embargo was greatly weakened.

The EU leaders' intention to lift the embargo also encountered strong resistance in public opinion. Since December 2003, European newspapers have run at least 70 different commentaries about the China arms embargo – the vast majority strongly against lifting it. The influential German newspaper *Frankfurter Allegemeine* called the decision 'dangerous'. The *Berliner Zeitung* was dumbfounded at the EU's eagerness to sell weapons to Beijing and despaired, 'China, China, China … We are watching, flabbergasted, the unanimous motions of the Peoples' Congress in Beijing' that call for unleashing war against Taiwan. Austria's influential *Die Presse* asked, 'even if we disregard the US warnings, is it really wise to open the EU arms floodgates to China?'[18]

Factors relating to China

On the China side, though both the public opinion and government are in support of strong collaborating relations, there are other issues that affect the lifting of the embargo.[19] Lifting the embargo not only means increasing the arms trade with the EU, but also, or more importantly, shedding an infamous history legacy. As the Chinese Foreign Affairs Ministry officials stress, the only other countries with which the EU maintains an arms embargo are Zimbabwe, Sudan and Burma.[20] Therefore, the lifting of the embargo is more a political issue than a security one. But human rights, Tibetan and Taiwan issues all concern the core interests of either China' or the Chinese Communist Party'. Therefore, the Chinese government can hardly step back significantly in exchange for the lifting of the embargo, which is more a symbolic gain.

Though the EU has no direct security stake in East Asia security, a conflict across Taiwan Strait would inevitably affect EU indirectly.[21] The Anti-Secession Law passed by the Chinese Peoples' Congress on 14 March 2005 was proof that for the Chinese authorities national territorial integrity is a far greater priority than the EU's possible lifting of the embargo. However, the Taiwan issue was reduced to a minor factor when Ma Yingjiu was elected as Taiwan's president in 2008. As Ma sticks to the 'One China' principle, the Taiwanese pro-independence movement has lost momentum. The trend of reconciliation across the Taiwan Strait makes the Taiwan issue no longer a chief barrier in EU's decision to lift the embargo.

But for the human rights and Tibetan issues it is a different story. While Chinese political reform has been largely stagnant since 1989, Chinese booming economy and education has increased citizen's' awareness of their civil rights. As corruption and inequality among social groups are getting aggravated, this will lead inevitably to larger and more frequent civil protest movements. The internet in a sense plays the role of civil rights educator and organizer and catalyst of civil protests. While the government tries to hold on to its vested power and interests, Chinese social transformation is doomed to be accompanied by more and more human rights issues. This will add tension to the China–EU relationship.

The Tibetan issue is not simply linked with national autonomy but also one innately linked to China's democratization, without which it is hard for the Chinese leaders to grant the autonomy demanded by the Dalai Lama group. But the overseas Tibetans' anxiety for their future fate grows as the Dalai Lama is approaching old age. They would very likely try to attract more attention from the international community in the future. Therefore, a more visible Tibetan issue would be a negative factor for the EU to lift the embargo. China intentionally postponed the EU summit scheduled in December 2008, when France was in the chair, as a punishment for the French president meeting the Dalai Lama in spite of China's strong protests.[22] This diplomatic war made China–EU relations drop to the low tide of the strategic partnership.

Lifting the embargo would not lead to a dramatic increase of China's import of arms equipment and technologies from the EU. As the above mentioned factors, the US and Japan would not allow EU's arms sales to undermine their security interests in the Asia–Pacific region. The EU is itself planning to raise the threshold of arms transfer by upgrading its Code of Conduct for arms export. [23]

Therefore, even if the embargo against China is lifted, China could still not import the high tech arms that it really needs. Currently China's main arms equipment and technology provider Russia can provide most of the arms it needs. In turn, the Russian defence industry gets the money it needs to sustain its arms development. In the period 1990–2007 Russia sold China $25 billion worth of weapons.[24] Though this sole arms import source has left China with many vulnerabilities from bargaining with Russia, the generally friendly Sino–Russian relations since the end of Cold War makes the source a reliable one.

Though lifting the arms embargo is a key issue in China–EU security relationship, it is not a top priority for either side in their respective overall agendas. Due to their own internal constraints, neither side would compromise significantly in exchange for the lifting of the embargo. The division of power in the EU and in EU individual member states makes a consensus on lifting the embargo even harder to reach.

b) Prevention of proliferation of weapons of massive destruction (WMD) and missiles in China–EU security relations

Preventing the proliferation of WMD and missiles has been another key issue in China–EU security relations and plays a major role in both sides' security strategies. The two parties have maintained well-coordinated working relations. As stated in China's Defence White Paper, 'China firmly opposes the proliferation of weapons of mass destruction (WMD) and their means of delivery and actively takes part in international non-proliferation efforts.'[25] As early as December 2003, the Chinese government issued the White Paper on China's Non-Proliferation Policy and Measures (2003).[26]

Though China remained outside of the international non-proliferation regime in the first few decades after the People's Republic was founded, it has been consistently taking positive steps to merge into the international community since its open door policy in the late 1970s. China has joined all international treaties and international organizations in the field of non-proliferation: the Treaty on the Non-proliferation of Nuclear Weapons (NPT), the Biological Weapons Convention (BWC) and the Chemical Weapons Convention (CWC). As a rising power, China is playing an increasingly important role in international non-proliferation efforts. The most notable one is its initiating and hosting of the Six-Party Talks on denuclearization of the Korean Peninsula.

The EU's Security Strategy defines that 'Proliferation of Weapons of Mass Destruction is potentially the greatest threat to our security.'[27] EU countries experienced the terror of the nuclear arms race between the US and the Soviet Union during the Cold War era. In the post Cold War era, the EU has been facing new security challenges such as regional conflicts and terrorism. The proliferation of WMD would aggravate these new threats. It has therefore been consistently pushing its non-proliferation activities.

The consensus and willingness to cooperate on non-proliferation issues are expressed explicitly in the 2004 Joint Declaration of China and EU on Non-proliferation and Arms Control.[28]

Coordination in nuclear crises in North Korea and Iran

Two highlights in China–EU cooperation on non-proliferation issues are coordination on the North Korea and Iran nuclear crises and EU engagement in China's export control personnel. North Korea's nuclear programme has clearly threatened regional stability as well as China's security interests. The recent North Korean nuclear test near the Chinese border demonstrated the immediate threat to China and the whole region. Though the North Korean nuclear crisis has no immediate impact on the EU, it affects the EU's interests by setting a bad example, particularly for Iran's nuclear programme, which the EU is working hard to stop. The EU has no direct involvement in the Six-Party Talks but indirectly the UK, France and Germany have been playing a relevant role in the UN Security Council. In this context, the EU has expressed its compliments on the great efforts made by China.[29]

The situation in the Iran nuclear crisis is different from that in North Korea. As the Middle East is the most important source of oil and gas imports for both China and the EU, the peaceful resolution of the crises would benefit both parties. Due to the hostile US–Iran relations, the EU has been playing a pivotal role in persuading Iran to give up its nuclear programme. However, this has proved to be very difficult to achieve. The China–EU dialogue on the Iran nuclear issue takes place at summits, at ministerial as well as working levels. The EU side conducts talks with China mainly through the bilateral channels of the UK, France and Germany.

Though both China and the EU share common interests in the peaceful resolution of the crisis, China holds different principles and approaches from that of EU. On the one hand non-interference in domestic affairs has been one of the pillars of China's foreign policy, and is hard to alter in the Iran case. On the other hand, China acknowledges Iran's right to develop nuclear power for civil use, which is different from EU and US' suspicion of Iran's real intention of developing nuclear power.[30] The differences do not only result from the different perceptions on non-proliferation but also from different positions and interests. China itself has been and still is the victim of an arms embargo; therefore, it is in sympathy with Iran's situation. Also, China has a huge stake in the oil and gas resources in Iran. Therefore, Chinese approach to Iran is more appeasing than the more coercive EU position. However, different approaches allow China more leeway to serve as a reconciler between the EU and Iran, which helps to ease the tension and might eventually lead the peaceful settlement of the issue. The EU mainly has leverage on Iran through the EU-3 (UK, France and Germany).[31] The recent developments of the 'Iranian and North Korean nuclear issues' have proved that prevention of WMD is an important mutual interest for China and the EU.

EU's engagement on China's export control personnel

Though the EU is not as ostentatious in the non-proliferation of WMD as the US, it carries out practical engaging programmes in raising the awareness and capacity of Chinese stakeholders such as bureaucrats, researchers and enterprises in the field of non-proliferation. Through EU-Outreach Projects, the EU and China have organized three seminars for over 200 Chinese researchers, customs officials and industry managers. These awareness-raising and capacity-building programmes have proved to be very success-ful as a bottom-up approach in coordination with the top-down approach of summit meetings and joint declarations.[32]

Military visits and personnel exchanges

Military personnel visits and exchanges are also important elements in and indicators of bilateral security relations. A true strategic partnership in a security sense would mean high-level and intimate personnel exchanges. These exchanges would normally include military leaders' visits, sending military attachés, ship visits, joint military seminars, joint military exercises and training of military officers, etc.[33] These exchanges can help build confidence in each other's security objectives and achieve interactive effects in making new security strategies.

In China's EU Policy Paper, military personnel exchanges and training are the two core objectives of China's EU policy in the security field. It states,'

> China and the EU will maintain high-level military-to-military exchanges, develop and improve, step by step, a strategic security consultation mechanism, exchange more missions of military experts, and expand exchanges in respect of military officers' training and defense studies.'[34]

These security objectives are largely tied into China's political agenda, which is aimed at enriching the EU–China strategic partnership. [35] In the actual practice of China–EU military personnel exchanges, the major elements are the sending of military attaches, military leaders' visits, fleet visits and joint military seminars.[36]

MILITARY VISITS

In 2007, there were 84 naval ship visits and visits of high-level military delegations from China to foreign countries and 84 foreign visits to China. Of these, 22 were military visits from China to the EU and 14 from the EU to China. In 2008, there were 84 and 73 respectively, of which 10 were Chinese military visits to the EU and 13 from the EU to China (see Table 3.1).[37] These exchanges of visits occurred mainly between China and EU core members such as Germany, France, UK and the Netherlands. This reflects the fact that the big actors are the most important in maintaining and improving China–EU security relations. Apart from these visits, there have also been small-scale military officer seminars between the major EU member states and China. China took part in six seminars with France and two with Germany. These seminars lasted less than two weeks each and provided medium- and high-level officers with platforms to exchange ideas on the key issues in their bilateral and regional security issues, such as Taiwan, WMD, etc.

TRAINING OF CHINESE MILITARY OFFICERS

Constrained by the arms embargo, EU members are not allowed to train Chinese military officers. Though France, the UK and Germany have quietly recruited a small number of Chinese military officers, due to the small scale their effects on engaging Chinese future security strategy is very limited. Even such low profile and small scale training incurred criticism by conservatives in EU.[38] Forbidding the training of Chinese military officers is in conflict with EU' policy of engagement with China. One of the most important contributions to the great achievements of China's modernization is learning from the West. However, due to both internal factors and external factors, the military sector remains one of the most isolated sectors in China in the sense of opening up to the West. This will inevitably prolong the transformation of the Chinese military outlook to the world and its domestic function.

As is well known, the Chinese army is not politically neutral but loyal to the Chinese Communist Party.[39] This feature makes the army's function not only to safeguard national security but also to safeguard the Party's ruling position. That is, the army plays a crucial role in China's political life. In any critical political aspect, the Chinese army's role should not be underestimated. The 1989 incident is the most illustrative case in point. As the most isolated sector, it has the most obsolete mentality both internationally and domestically. As the EU's strategic goal is to engage China to make it a responsible international partner and the Chinese military are experiencing a historical period of modernization, the latter two mentioned forms of military personnel exchange could have a significant impact on shaping

Table 3.1 Chinese military visits, 2007–2008

	Chinese military visits	Chinese military visits to EU	Foreign military visits to China	EU Military visits to China
2007	84	22	84	14
2008	84	10	73	13

Source: *White Paper on China's Defense in 2008.*

Chinese military personnel's concept of both international security as well as the military role in domestic political life.

The training of Chinese military officers would help the army play a more constructive role in China's political transition and would be in agreement with EU's strategic objectives toward China. As the EU and China do not have fundamental conflicting security interests, it would be both realistic and significant for EU to engage China in security by providing training assistance to Chinese military officers. The current low profile and small-scale training of a handful Chinese military officers can hardly play a significant role in shaping the Chinese military transformation.

JOINT MILITARY EXERCISES

In contrast to China's regular joint military exercises with Russia and other Shanghai Cooperation Organization members and other Asia-Pacific neighbours, there have been no China–EU joint military exercises so far in spite of being at the most advanced level of security significance. Apart from the above stated reasons, such as military embargo constraints and EU internal disunity, another factor is that, though both China and the EU claim to be global powers, their core interests relate to regional issues. Both are in essence regional powers whose prioritized interests are regional not global like the US. Their respective priorities are East Asia and Europe and bordering regions. Neither side has keen interest in the other's region.[40]

China–EU unconventional security relations: energy and climate security

Though the China–EU conventional security relationship is significantly constrained by external powers and internal barriers from both sides, in unconventional security fields such as energy and climate security the two sides share more complementary interests and fewer constraints. These fields have therefore seen substantial cooperation. In the domain of energy and climate security, the two sides regard each other as core partners, with complementing interests greatly outweighing the conflicting ones.[41]

a) *Common threats in energy and climate security*

Energy security

Energy security concerns are on the top of the agenda in the global highest levels of leaders. Both the EU and China are among the largest global energy consumers and greenhouse gas emitters. China and the EU together account for around 30 per cent of global energy consumption and 30 per cent of global emissions. And this share will grow. According to the International Energy Agency's forecast, global energy consumption will see an increase of

55 per cent by 2030. The EU will see a 0.4 per cent annual increase and China 3.2 per cent.[42]

The US National Petroleum Council Report issued in July 2007, concluded:

> It is a hard truth that the global supply of oil and natural gas from the conventional sources relied upon historically is unlikely to meet projected 50 per cent to 60 per cent growth in demand over the next 25 years.[43]

The volatile oil supply and price are common threats to the prosperity of China and the EU, both high-volume oil importers.[44] Their common interests provide a foundation for deepening collaborative efforts on energy and climate security over the next quarter-century. China's overall energy consumption has seen a dramatic increase alongside its continually fast growing economy since the reforms and open-door policy of the late 1970s. In 1978, it consumed 400 million tons of oil equivalent (mtoe). By 2006, the figure turned into near 1600 mtoe.[45] According to the International Energy Agency, China's energy consumption will reach 3,819 mtoe by 2030 doubling its 1,741 mtoe in 2005.[46]

From 2002 to 2004, some Chinese provinces suffered shortages of coal, oil and electricity, highlighting the fact that China's supply of energy is unable to provide stable support for its economic growth.[47] Heavy reliance on fossil fuel, particularly coal, has caused serious environmental problems. Fossil fuels provide 80 per cent of China's energy mixture, with coal responsible for 70 per cent of China's energy supply and 80 per cent of electricity. According to a joint report by Work Bank and China State Environmental Protection Agency, health costs of air and water pollution in China amount to about 4.3 per cent of its GDP. By adding the non-health impacts of pollution, which are estimated to be about 1.5 per cent of GDP, the total cost of air and water pollution in China is about 5.8 per cent of GDP each year.[48]

Fast growing oil consumption and import is another challenge for China's energy security. China is the world's second largest consumer of oil after the US. It is also the third largest oil importer. Before 1993, China was a net oil exporter. By 2008, 40 per cent of its oil was imported. As most foreign oil resources are located in politically volatile regions, securing a stable and affordable oil supply imposes a very challenging task for China.

The EU presently consumes the same amount of energy as China. But it is more dependent on foreign energy than China. According to the European Commission's Green Paper on security of energy supply, if no action is taken the EU's energy dependency will climb from 50 per cent in 2000 to 70 per cent in 2030:

- Some 45 per cent of EU oil imports originate from the Middle East; by 2030, 90 per cent of EU oil consumption will have to be covered by imports;

- 40 per cent of EU gas imports originate from Russia (30 per cent Algeria, 25 per cent Norway); By 2030, over 60 per cent of EU gas imports are expected to come from Russia with overall external dependency expected to reach 80 per cent.
- By 2030, 66 per cent of EU coal needs is expected to be covered by imports.[49]

Both China and EU are therefore facing the challenge of securing affordable and stable supply of energy. In 2005, China set the goal of a 20 per cent energy cut by 2010, the last year of its 11th Five-year Plan period.[50] This would mean a decrease from 1.22 to 0.98 ton of coal equivalent per unit of GDP. And it is hoped that there will be an additional 20 per cent increase in energy efficiency by 2020.[51] Similarly, in 2006, the EU adopted a target to increase its energy efficiency by 20 per cent by 2020. With the expected increase in economic activity over the period, this could lead to an overall 13 per cent reduction in energy consumption.[52]

Climate security

Apart from energy security, another security issue both China and EU have to face is the threat of climate change. Solid scientific findings have proved that, due to human activities, the globe is getting warmer at an aggravated pace which will threat the welfare of the whole human community. The ground temperature in Europe and China has increased by approximately 0.8°C in the past hundred years.[53] This trend is being aggravated as increasing amounts of CO_2 and other greenhouse gases are emitted and gather in the atmosphere.

Business-as-usual scenarios project extreme temperature rises of 4–7°C by the end of the century. The Stern Review estimated the avoidable costs of inaction would be between 5 per cent and 20 per cent of GDP per year.[54] A responsible risk management strategy for policy-makers would be to keep to the low probability range of 2°C rise, as climate sensitivities appear higher than previously estimated. Then, global CO_2 emissions will have to peak in the next two decades and reduce by over 50 per cent by 2050. For developed countries, such as the member states of the EU, this implies moving to an essentially zero-carbon economy by around mid-century, with major developing countries such as China following well before the end of the century.[55]

b) China–EU cooperation on energy and climate security

Cooperation on energy and climate security in China–EU relations is not only high on profile but also solid in substance. There have been various levels dialogues and joint programmes with practical cooperation between China and the EU. The two sides established a policy dialogue on energy in

1994 that convenes high-level European and Chinese representatives from industry and administration. Cooperation in this field has subsequently been intensifying, especially with regard to clean energy. On a roughly annual basis, a bilateral energy conference is organized dealing with particular energy sources and technologies from a technical and practical perspective. Since 1999, when a delegation of the European Parliament, the European Commission and high-ranking industry representatives called on China to make an assessment of the cooperation between the EU and China in energy-related areas, clean technologies have gained prominence as a focal point of the energy partnership.

In 2004, China and the European Commission jointly unveiled the five-year Energy Environment Programme (EEP), which encourages the formulation of improved energy policies via assistance to central administrations and local authorities, and stimulates the development of new technologies by providing funds for feasibility studies.[56] During the following years, this was extended to various specific areas such as biomass resources, rural power supply and offshore wind power. Between 2004 and 2006, not less than 22 workshops and conferences were organized in the framework of the EEP.

In 2005, China and the EU signed two action plans, one with the objective of promoting clean coal technologies, and the other on industrial cooperation on energy efficiency and renewable energies.[57] The same year, China and the EU signed a memorandum of understanding (MoU) to develop a new strategic dialogue on energy and transport as well as a joint declaration on climate change. According to the joint declaration, a formal partnership was established aiming to cooperate on advanced technology on clean coal and other energy conservation and efficiency technologies.[58] Energy and climate change has since become the key topic of the summit. In 2006, Commissioner Andris Piebalgs signed another MoU with the Chinese government on near-zero emissions power generation technology.[59] A growing number of joint projects have come into existence, entailing all different energy sectors. Between 2001 and 2006, the EU has spent approximately $65 million supporting clean energy in China.[60]

In addition to the EU programmes, individual EU member states, mainly France, Germany, Italy and the UK, provide funding through grants and soft loans for energy- and climate-related projects.[61] Germany manages joint projects in all clean energy sectors. Between 2001 and 2006, German federal and state governments contributed at least $40 million to the promotion of new clean technologies.

The UK runs seven small-scale programmes with China. In 2007, Finland offered $3 million of technical assistance to 'support Nordic energy utilisation solutions' and Finnish energy technology exports such as gas boilers, heat distribution systems and electricity. The country also set up a working group to investigate opportunities for boosting environmental and energy technology trade with China. Between 2001 and 2006, the Netherlands spent up to $35 million to clean energy projects in China.[62]

A most notable achievement of China–EU cooperation in climate change mitigation is in clean development mechanism (CDM), one of the three flexible mechanisms under the Kyoto Protocol. China has approved 1,846 CDM projects, and 450 have been registered as of 16 January 2009 (meaning they are ready to proceed).[63] These CDM projects will enable China to issue about 0.16 billion tons CO_2 equivalent credits annually by the end of the Kyoto Protocol's first commitment period in 2012, which means that 56.8 per cent of total annual global emissions reductions under the CDM are taking place in China.[64] The great success of CDM projects in China should inspire policy makers from both sides that market mechanism facilitated by government policy are dynamic engines in realizing both energy and climate security.

c) Drivers behind cooperation in energy and climate security

The EU–China joint efforts to promote clean energy will bring a win–win situation.[65] What drives Europe to funnel substantial means and time into the energy partnership with China? As both China and EU are key energy consumers, assisting China to develop clean energy and diversify its energy structure will mitigate competition in the global energy market and therefore benefit the EU's energy security.

The development of clean energy will not only reduce greenhouse gas emissions and limit environmental damage but also bring immense commercial opportunities. Such fields as wind, solar energy, clean coal technologies, natural gas and bio-fuel are proving to have healthy effects. In these fields, the EU has the comparative advantage of advanced technology, while China has both a huge market and cheap labour in manufacturing. China has been a leading export market for European clean energy technologies. For instance, between 2001 and 2006 exports of wind turbines to China amounted to $201 million. In the same period, $230 million worth of hydropower turbines were sold. Photovoltaic systems represented a total export volume of $196 million.[66] China has already produced 80 per cent of the world's energy-saving lamps – many of which are based on technology created in the EU.[67]

Taking wind and solar energy as examples, many European companies successfully bid for a part of China's expanding wind energy market. The Spanish wind turbine fabricant Gamesa, Danish Vestas and German Nordex are in the top five suppliers of wind power installations to China. In 2006, over 50 per cent of the high-capacity wind turbines installed in China were imported from Denmark.[68]

China's localization strategy in the energy generation equipment manufacturing stimulates the transfer of the production to China. China will create eight to ten other manufacturing enterprises by 2015, producing wind power equipment components with an annual production capacity worth $2.66 billion.[69] The Chinese comparative advantage in labour price helped the reduction of the cost of equipment (by 50 per cent) which would help greatly overcome the cost hurdle for large-scale instalment of wind turbines.[70] Meanwhile, the export of Chinese produced wind turbines to the EU market can also reduce the EU's cost in installing such turbines. In 2005, the EU–China trade flows in solar systems reversed as Chinese firms started to export high-end products to Germany.[71]

Rationale behind the cooperation in climate security

Because of the US Bush Administration's sceptical policy on international climate change cooperation, the EU in recent years has been playing the leadership role in ratifying the Kyoto Protocol and continuing the post-Kyoto Protocol negotiations. As the new largest greenhouse gas emitter, China's choices matter. As China will see a fast-growing period of energy capacity building, China's immediate decisions about its infrastructure needs and patterns of consumption will have a decisive impact on global efforts to stabilize greenhouse gas emissions and the feasible rate of reduction to sustainable levels. China emissions accounted for 19 per cent of global CO_2 emissions in 2005 and is expected to rise to about 27 per cent by 2030. In preliminary estimates for 2006, China topped the list of CO_2-emitting countries, surpassing the US by an estimated 8 per cent. However, China's per capita carbon emissions level is over three times less than the EU average and six times less than the US average.[72]

China's strategic aspiration towards an innovation-based economy with science-based development is in line with the vision for a low-carbon transition. A focus on developing and deploying advanced climate technologies is also consistent with China's aspiration to move up the global value chain,[73] making China the number one EU target. China's active participation in the international climate change negotiations is in the interests of the EU international climate security strategy. Currently, the EU is seeking to persuade China to meet and continue to set higher domestic targets for energy efficiency standards and share of renewable energy, and to make use of economic tools such as pricing and trade/investment incentives. The EU also expects China to prioritize the development of clean coal technologies, including carbon capture and storage. Finally, the EU expects China to agree a global emissions stabilization goal and to commit to specific targets on greenhouse emissions in post-2012 climate negotiations, or, at least, to set some sectoral reduction targets.

The Chinese side, though it ratified the Kyoto Protocol early in 2003, has not committed to any binding reduction target withholding the principle of 'common but differentiated' responsibilities between developed and developing countries. Instead, the Chinese government put the ambitious voluntary reduction targets by setting the goal of lowering 20 per cent of energy intensity by 2010 from the 2005 base. The rationale behind this voluntary reduction approach is in the following sections.

CHINA IS EXPECTING A SUBSTANTIAL GROWTH IN ENERGY CONSUMPTION
IN THE NEXT 20 YEARS

Though the technology advancement is likely to change the 'business as usual' scenarios, Chinese policy makers are apprehensive in making binding commitments that will leave little space for the nation's grand dream of rejuvenation.[74]

CHINA INVESTS MUCH HOPE IN GAINING FINANCIAL AND TECHNOLOGY
ASSISTANCE TO AID ITS SUSTAINABLE DEVELOPMENT AS WELL AS GREENHOUSE
GAS EMISSION REDUCTION

As China's energy intensity is 40 per cent above the EU average, to upgrade Chinese energy generation and consumption sectors requires massive investment of capital and advanced technology.[75] For a nation with 60 per cent of its population with no health and retirement insurance and badly underinvested in education, it is hard for it to have sufficient money to realize such a transfer from a high carbon intensity economy to low carbon one without substantial international assistance. Therefore, China is very active in participating in carbon trading and joint research and demonstration clean energy projects. These projects bring China substantial money in assisting the research and development and capacity building in energy and climate.

For instance, the Energy and Environment Programme for 2004–2008 is a €42.9 million joint funded scheme that addresses a number of energy security and climate protection projects, including clean coal technology. Another one is the EU Framework Programme, in which China was involved in 28 projects with a total project cost of €66 million. Half of these projects related to carbon capture and storage technology.[76]

The EU weighs disproportionately as China's income source from the clean development mechanism. It is expected that the EU could be purchasing 77 per cent of carbon credits generated in China through CDM by 2012 to help meet its compliance with the Kyoto Protocol. It means, on the one hand, that EU countries benefit greatly from China's participation in the carbon trading system by lowering their carbon reduction cost. On the other hand, this means that the CER income will provide billions of additional capital in assisting China's low carbon development. The additional carbon income helps to overcome the cost hurdles when introducing higher cost foreign technology (equipment and training).[77]

China's primary goal is to ensure the EU's engagement on climate change supports rather than hinders its economic development. EU investment and technologies in energy are desirable for China's development. EU funds in supporting China's research and capacity-building are beneficial to China's climate change mitigation and adaptation efforts.[78] Participating in EU–China cooperation on climate change not only brings China money and technology in aiding its economic development but also improves China's image as a responsible state in international community. [79]

d) Challenges and solutions in the China–EU relations in energy and climate change security

The main theme of cooperation in China–EU energy and climate chorus is also challenged with some weak tones and discords.

China's quest for overseas oil and gas caused EU
concern for energy security as fellow consumers

Though the EU welcomes China's growth into an economic strong power, it is watching China's expansion of energy demand with growing unease. The following aspects of China's energy policy cause some concern in the EU:

> China invests in some energy-rich 'states of concern', for example in Iran, Sudan, Burma/Myanmar, Turkmenistan and Uzbekistan, whilst ignoring the nature of political leadership there. Refraining from interfering in other states' internal affairs is a longstanding cornerstone of China's foreign policy, but in this case, its posture directly undermines whatever leverage the EU could have in promoting reforms in these countries.

The EU is also concerned about China's overseas investments aimed at securing long-term and exclusive contracts.

> Almost all Chinese energy companies remain state-owned or state-controlled and their investment plans are heavily influenced by the government's calculations rather than expectations of profitability. In the view of the EU, these practices often run against the principles of the open market and free competition as well as contributing to the increase in energy prices.[80]

Also, China's emergence as a new destination for Russian natural gas diminishes the EU's leverage that stems from its position as a leading export market for Russian gas. EU is concerned that Russia might try to optimize its central position as a land bridge between east and west, by creating new gas pipelines to China.[81]

The EU's concerns are justifiable from their own perspective. However, it intentionally or unintentionally neglects the fact that China, as a new emerging oil consumer and importer, faces an unfavourable competition environment. The conventional oil resources have already been manipulated either by the powerful Western multinational oil companies or by the national oil companies of the oil producing countries. Access to oil resources still falls outside of the scope of institutions of the international energy cooperation regime, the International Energy Agency (IEA). Under such unfavourable situation, China has no other alternatives but to seek its own resources. The EU should therefore recognize China's legitimate right to seek oil and gas resources without violating international law. China has no obligation to sacrifice her own energy security for no reward.

A bilateral coordination mechanism should therefore be established. In order to coordinate the two sides in the world energy resources market, both a regular dialogue mechanism at ministerial level and a coordinating and communicating mechanism composed of both energy enterprises and researchers should be established to coordinate their stances and reach consensus in regard to behavioural norms exploring energy resources.

Also, China should become a full member of the IEA as, which would benefit both China and the EU's energy security. The IEA, as a coordination and cooperation mechanism among Western energy (particularly oil) consuming countries since the first oil crisis in 1970s has been playing a very important role in sharing energy information, carrying out joint energy research programmes and, most importantly, coordinating members' policy in time of oil disruption. Though China has been the second largest energy consumer, it is still outside of this mechanism. While the EU complains about the lack of transparency in China's energy reserves, etc., it has not yet decided to include China as a full participating member in this mechanism. To include China in such a mechanism would be a historical step to enhance China–EU cooperation on energy security.

Different priorities and approaches between China and EU in energy and climate security

As the EU prioritizes the climate change threat at the top of the bilateral relations, expecting China to make a formal commitment to reduction, China puts development ahead of climate change threat and insists on a voluntary reduction approach. While the EU expects China to open its market to EU low carbon equipment to achieve both the climate objective and financial gain, China hopes to obtain both financial assistance and technology transfer in formal training of know-how and production licences.

To fill the gap and realize win–win objectives, China and EU should reach a consensus on the approaches to realize a low carbon economy in the future as well as sustain China's economic development. As stated in the Bali Road Map in 2007, China supported the Bali action plan, which in 1(b)(ii) called for: 'Nationally appropriate mitigation actions by developing country parties in the context of sustainable development, supported and enabled by technology, financing and capacity-building, in a measurable, reportable and verifiable manner.'[82]

An EU–China road map in climate change mitigation and sustainable development should be drawn up. In realizing the blueprint of cooperation in 'a measurable, reportable and verifiable manner' would eventually lead to China's formal commitment to the GHG emission target. The approaches should be more practical, coordinated and ambitious.

A sectoral coordination mechanism should be established that covers important sectors such as power generation, renewable energy, manufacturing industries, building, etc. The mechanism should have both working team and ministerial level coordination meetings. The working teams for each sector should investigate and bring about plans for cooperation to help realize the research, development, demonstration and deployment of new low-carbon technologies. The team should also list the available technologies that can assist China to realize energy conservation and improve energy efficiency. This sectoral approach is similar to the Asia-Pacific Partnership on Clean Development and Climate (APP) initiated by the US. However, it should avoid the failure of APP by adding real substance to it rather than just rhetoric on paper and in meeting rooms.

A substantial funding from EU to aid the technology transfer to China and more favourable tax and tariff policies from both sides are essential to the success of this cooperation. This approach will demonstrate the seriousness of the EU's intention to engage China in climate mitigation and sustainable development and provide concrete assistance for China to lower its emissions. These steps will demonstrate an assured roadmap to a low-carbon economy for Chinese decision makers and eventually lead to China's binding reduction commitment in the framework of the UNFCCC.

The combined economic might of the EU, the world's largest single market, and China, the fastest-growing economy, can provide unprecedented opportunities to generate benefits of scale that will lower the costs of climate-friendly goods and services globally. By working together, China and the EU could become the de facto engine of global low-carbon transformation and eventually realize the security of energy and climate change in a win–win approach.

Conclusions

China–EU relations are generally most uneventful and friendly in comparison to China's relations with the US and Japan. Security relations are one of the pillars in their 'strategic partnership'. But conventional security relations are asymmetrically weak compared with economic and political relations or unconventional security relations. The weakness can be attributed to the interference from a third actor, mainly the US; the difficulty in reaching a consensus among EU member states (and inconsistency between different administrations within individual member states); and the heterogeneity of the two political systems that has resulted in the human rights issue, which has been a great hindrance for security relations. Unconventional security relations such as energy and climate security are more vocal and constructive than the conventional one in the bilateral relations.

In conventional security relations, since convergent interests far outweigh divergent ones and each party's strategic goals are more complementary than conflicting, a closer security engagement in forms of high level military dialogue, exchange of military personnel, joint military exercises and particularly lifting of the arms trade embargo would not only promote trust and understanding but also stimulate the bilateral cooperation in other issues, such as economic cooperation, and political dialogue, and eventually lead to a more positive role in shaping China's transition track. A punitive approach of linking the security issues with other issues are destructive in their relations and eventually would lead to a vicious circle. Delinking the security issues from other issues would bring constructive effect to the tension in other issues.

In unconventional security relations such as energy and climate change security, the EU should take a more comprehensive, practical and broad envisioned strategy to engage China in clean energy development and climate change mitigation. Formal bilateral and multilateral mechanisms are both key to the success for the engagement.

Notes

1 Gustaaf Geeraerts, 'In the Eyes of the Dragon: Chinese perceptions of the EU as a global actor', BICCS Asia Paper 1(4), 2 December 2007, available at: http://www. vub.ac.be/biccs/documents/6),%20In%20the%20Eyes%20of%20the%20Dragon, %20Chinese%20Perceptions%20of%20the%20EU,%20Asia%20Paper%20vol%5 B1%5D.%201%20(4),%20BICCS,%20Brussels..pdf.
2 European Council, 'Declaration on China', Madrid: 27 June 27 1989, annex I of EU, European Union Factsheet, European Union: Brussels, n.d. available at: http://ue.eu.int/uedocs/cmsUpload/FACTSHEET_ON_THE_EU_ AND_CHINA. pdf.
3 China's EU Policy Paper, October 2003, available at: http://www.fmprc.gov.cn/ eng/topics/ceupp/t27708.htm.
4 Chinese Foreign Ministry speaker Qin Gang at a press conference on 19 December 2006, available at: http://www.fmprc.gov.cn/chn/gxh/mtb/fyrbt/t284105.htm; see also: Chen Gang, 'China Foreign Ministry Speaker: EU's Arms Embargo against China is a product of Cold War', 18 November 2004, available at: http://news. xinhuanet.com/newscenter/2004-11/18/content_2233985.htm.
5 Richard A. Bitzinger 'A Prisoner's Dilemma: The EU's China Arms Embargo', *China Brief*, 4(13), available at: http://www.jamestown.org/single/?no_ cache=1&tx_ttnews%5Btt_news%5D=3828.
6 Press Conference, NATO, Brussels, February 22, available at: 2005.http://www. state.gov/p/eur/rls/rm/42523.htm. Detailed analysis of US concerns on the EU's lifting of the embargo against China can be found in Richard F. Grimmett and Theresa Papademetriou, 'European Union's Arms Control Regime and Arms Exports to China: Background and Legal Analysis', CRS Report for Congress, 1 March 2005.

7 US Department of Defence, 'Annual Report to Congress: The Military Power of the People's Republic of China 2005', Office of the Secretary of Defence, 19 July 2005, available at: http://www.defenselink.mil/news/Jul2005/d20050719china.pdf; US Department of Defense, 'Annual Report to Congress: The Military Power of the People's Republic of China, 2007', Office of the Secretary of Defense, available at: http://www.defenselink.mil/pubs/pdfs/070523-China-Military-Power-final.pdf; US Department of Defense, 'Annual Report to Congress: The Military Power of the People's Republic of China, 2009',Office of the Secretary of Defense, available at: http://www.defenselink.mil/pubs/pdfs/China_Military_Power_Report_2009.pdf.

8 'Japanese Foreign Minister Nobutaka Machimura made this clear in talks with his British counterpart Jack Straw who was in Tokyo on Thursday. Irish Prime Minister Bertie Ahern announced that the ban will probably be lifted by mid-2005. Mr Machimura said "It is extremely worrying as this issue concerns the peace and security environments not only in Japan but also in East Asia as a whole."': 'Japan Against Lifting Arms Sale Ban Against China', *Asia News*, 11 January 2005, available at: http://www.asianews.it/index.php?art=2395&l=en

9 Bernt Berger and Heather Gilmartin, 'The Quiet Europeans? Appraising Europe's Commitment to East Asian Security' in: H.J. Giessmann (ed.), *Security Handbook 2008*, Baden Baden: Nomos, 2008, pp. 211–39. See also European Council, 'A Secure Europe In A Better World: European Security Strategy', Brussels, 12 December 2003, available at: http://ue.eu.int/uedocs/cmsUpload/78367.pdf; Javier Solana, 'Report On The Implementation of the European Security Strategy: Providing Security in a Changing World', Brussels, 11 and 12 December 2008, available at: http://www.consilium.europa.eu/ueDocs/cms_Data/docs/pressdata/EN/reports/104630.pdf.

10 However, according to Zaborowski, the importance of transatlantic considerations in this decision seems exaggerated if not misjudged. After all, America's other close allies Israel and Australia are selling arms to China, which so far has not led to meaningful frictions in Washington's relations with these states: Marcin Zaborowski, 'Security Dimension of EU–China Relations: A European Perspective', *Analizy natolinskie* 1(24), 2008, p. 4, available at: http://www.natolin.edu.pl/pdf/analizy/Natolin_Analiza_1_2008.pdf.

11 John Fox and Francois Godement, 'A Power Audit of EU–China Relations', Policy Report, European Council on Foreign Relations, 20 April 2009, pp. 21–2, available at: http://ecfr.3cdn.net/532cd91d0b5c9699ad_ozm6b9bz4.pdf

12 Ibid., pp. 22–7.

13 John J. Tkacik, Jr, 'EU Leadership Finds Little Public Support for lifting China Arms Ban', *WebMemo* 690, 17 March 2005, available at: http://www.heritage.org/research/asiaandthepacific/wm693.cfm; 'European Parliament opposes Lifting Arms Embargo Against China' *Asia News,* 20 December 2003, available at: http://www.asianews.it/index.php?l=en&art=177&dos=24&size=A; 'EU: China Must Stop Selling Weapons to Countries under UN Embargo', *Asia News,* 24 April 2008, available at: http://www.asianews.it/index.php?l=en&art=12103.

14 Fox and Godement, 'Power Audit'.

15 'China's National Defense in 2008', Appendix I available at: http://www.gov.cn/english/official/2009-01/20/content_1210227.htm.

16 Nicola Casarini, 'The Evolution of the EU–China Relationship: From Constructive Engagement to Strategic Partnership', Paris: European Union Institute of Security Studies, October 2006.

17 'European Parliament Opposes Lifting Arms Embargo Against China', *Asia News*, 20 December 2003, available at: http://www.asianews.it/index.php?l=en&art=177&dos=24&size=A.

18 Tkacik, 'EU Leadership'.

19 'A Survey and Preliminary Analysis of Chinese Public Opinion on EU and Sino–EU Relations' *European Studies* 2, Institute of European Studies, Chinese Academy of Social Sciences, April 2008, pp. 1–52.
20 Casarini, 'Evolution', p. 31.
21 'Asia as a Strategic Challenge and Opportunity for Germany and Europe', Asia-Strategy of the CDU/CSU Parliamentary Group, Decision from 23 October 2007, p. 5.
22 Leigh Thomas, 'China warns EU on Meddling in Internal Matters', 20 May 2009, available at: http://news.yahoo.com/s/afp/20090520/wl_asia_afp/euchinasummit.
23 United Kingdom Strategic Export Controls, 'Annual Report 2005', available at: http://www.official-documents.gov.uk/document/cm68/6882/6882.pdf.
24 Stephen Blank, 'Recent Trends in Russo-Chinese Military Relations', *China Brief*, 9/2, available at: http://www.jamestown.org/programs/chinabrief/single/?tx_ttnews%5Btt_news%5D=34389&tx_ttnews%5BbackPid%5D=25&cHash=745 8900c65.
25 'China's National Defense in 2008', chapter XIV: 'Arms Control and Disarmament', available at: http://www.chinadaily.com.cn/china/2009-01/20/content_7413294_16.htm.
26 'China's Non-Proliferation Policy and Measures', 2003, available at: http://english.gov.cn/official/2005-07/28/content_17957.htm.
27 European Council, 'A Secure Europe'.
28 'Joint Declaration of the People's Republic of China and the European Union on Non-Proliferation and Arms Control', 9 December 2004, available at: http://www.fmprc.gov.cn/eng/wjdt/2649/t173749.htm.
29 Fox and Godement, 'Power Audit', pp. 41–2. See also: 'Security Is "Key Priority" in EU–China Talks: Solana', Xinhua News Agency, 16 March 2004, available at: http://www.china.org.cn/english/international/90416.htm.
30 European Council, 'EU Strategy against the Proliferation of Weapons of Mass Destruction', 2003, p. 2, available at: http://trade.ec.europa.eu/doclib/docs/2004/august/tradoc_118532.en03.pdf.
31 Fox and Godement, 'Power Audit', p. 40.
32 Federal Office of Economics and Export Control, 'EU Outreach Projects: Pilot Project 2005/06 Annual Report', available at: http://www.docstoc.com/docs/5743761/Annual-Report-Pilot-Project-EU-OUTREACH-PROJECTS-PILOT-PROJECT.
33 'China's Defense in 2008'.
34 'China's EU Policy Paper', October 2003, available at: http://www.fmprc.gov.cn/eng/topics/ceupp/t27708.htm.
35 Kristen Gunness, '"China's Military Diplomacy in an Era of Change"', National Defense University symposium on China's Global Activism: Implications for US Security Interests', Fort Lesley J. McNair: National Defense University, 20 June 2006, available at: http://www.ndu.edu/inss/symposia/pacific2006/Gunnesspaper.pdf.
36 'China's Defense in 2008'.
37 Ibid.
38 Michael Smith, 'MoD Breaches EU Rules by Training Chinese Officer', *The Times*, 7 September 2008, available at: http://www.timesonline.co.uk/tol/news/uk/article4681845.ece.
39 Li Cheng and Scott W. Harold, 'China's New Military Elite', *China Security* 3(4), Autumn 2007, pp. 62–89.
40 Though China and EU have a great stake in the stability of each other's region, they do not have the right incentive and/or leverage in playing a significant role. China is seeking a low profile image in the international community. Europe is

stable with the guarantee of NATO and EU integration; the EU has an incentive to play a larger role but is constrained by US predominance in the region. See also the analysis by Stefano Silvestri, 'Revising the European Security Strategy: Arguments for Discussion', May 2008, available at: http://www.iai.it/pdf/IAI_Silvestri_300508.pdf.

41 'Climate Change, Trade Top Agenda at EU–China Summit', 20 May 2009, available at: http://www.euractiv.com/en/foreign-affairs/climate-change-trade-top-agenda-eu-china-summit/article-182507.

42 IEA, 'Research and Development Database', 2007, available at: http://www.iea.org/Textbase/stats/rd.asp .

43 US National Petroleum Council, 'Facing the Hard Truths about Energy: A Comprehensive View to 2030 of Global Oil and Natural Gas', 2007, p. 17, available at: http://downloadcenter.connectlive.com/events/npc071807/pdf-downloads/NPC-Hard_Truths-Executive_Summary.pdf.

44 Jiang Zemin, 'Reflections on Energy Issues in China', *Journal of Shanghai Jiaotong University* 42(3), March, 2008, pp. 346–59; Jozias van Aartsen, 'Why Energy Must Be at the Core of EU Security Thinking', *Europe's World*, Spring 2008.

45 BP, 'Statistical Review of World Energy', 2007.

46 IEA, 'World Energy Outlook 2007: China and India Insights', 2007, available at http://www.iea.org/textbase/nppdf/free/2007/weo_2007.pdf.

47 Liu Zhiyang, San Feng and Long Xiaobai, 'Chinese Perspectives on Energy and Climate Security: A study commissioned by the Interdependencies on Energy and Climate Security Project', London: Chatham House, February 2008, p. 3.

48 World Bank and SEPA, 'Cost of Pollution in China: Economic Estimates of Physical Damages', February 2007, available at: http://siteresources.worldbank.org/INTEAPREGTOPENVIRONMENT/Resources/China_Cost_of_Pollution.pdf .

49 European Commission, 'Green Paper: Towards a European strategy for the security of energy supply', 2000, available at: http://eur-lex.europa.eu/LexUriServ/LexUriServ.do?uri=CELEX:52000DC0769:EN:HTML.

50 People's Congress of China, 'The Eleventh Five-Year Plan for National Economic and Social Development of the People's Republic of China', part 1, chapter 3, 16 March 2006, available at: http://news.xinhuanet.com/misc/2006-03/16/content_4309517.htm.

51 Antony Froggatt, 'The EU and China: New perspectives on energy efficiency', *China Dialogue*, 22 October 2007, available at: http://www.chinadialogue.net/article/show/single/en/1411-The-EU-China-new-perspectives-on-energy-efficiency.

52 Ibid.

53 IPCC, 'Climate Change 2007 Synthesis Report', p. 30, available at: http://www.ipcc.ch/pdf/assessment-report/ar4/syr/ar4_syr.pdf.

54 Nicholas Stern, 'Stern Review on the Economics of Climate Change', London: HM Treasury, 2006.

55 'Changing Climates: Interdependencies on energy and climate security for China and Europe', London: Chatham House, November 2007, p. vii.

56 Energy Environment Programme (EEP), available at: www.eep.org.cn/index.php.

57 Energy Commissioner Andris Piebalgs, 'Towards a Closer EU–China Co-Operation in the Field of Energy', Speech 06/105, China–EU Energy Conference, 20 February 2006, available at: http://europa.eu/rapid/pressReleasesAction.do?reference=SPEECH/06/105&format=HTML&aged=1&language=en&guiLanguage=en.

58 'EU and China Partnership on Climate Change', 2 September 2005, available at: http://ec.europa.eu/environment/climat/pdf/china/joint_declaration_ch_eu.pdf.

59 Jonathan Holslag, 'Clouds Ahead: China's Energy Policy in the Light of Climate Change, and Options for Cooperation with the EU', Brussels: BICCS, 2008, available at: www.vub.ac.be/biccs/.../Holslag%20(2007),%20Clouds%20Ahead.pdf.

60 See www.delchn.cec.eu.int/en/Co-operation/Project_Fiches.htm.
61 'Changing Climates'.
62 Eeva Ahola, 'Finnish Energy Technology Heads to China', Helsinki: Ministry of Trade and Industry of Finland, 9 March 2006.
63 This statistic was updated on 17 March 2009. See: http://cdm.ccchina.gov. cn/WebSite/CDM/UpFile/File2158.pdf. See also 'The National Coordination Committee on Climate Change: CDM in China' (in Chinese), available at: http:// cdm.ccchina.gov.cn/WebSite/CDM/UpFile/File1839.pdf.
64 UNFCCC Database: http://cdm.unfccc.int/Statistics/Registration/AmountOf ReductRegisteredProjPieChart.html (16 April 2009.
65 Holslag, 'Clouds Ahead'.
66 UN Commodity Trade Statistics Database (HS 2002, 85023), (HS 2002, 8410), (HS 2002, 854140).
67 'Changing Climates', p. 7.
68 Holslag, 'Clouds Ahead', p. 5; Joanna I. Lewis, 'Technology Acquisition and Innovation in the Developing World: The case of wind turbine development in China', Powerpoint presentation at the Harvard China Seminar Series, Harvard University, 5 March 2009.
69 Holslag, 'Clouds Ahead', p. 5.
70 Interviews with Chinese wind power engineers, January 2009.
71 Rolf Hug and Martin Schachinger, 'Chinese Solar Modules Penetrating the German Market', *The Solar Server*, 10 November 2006, available at: www. solarserver.de/solarmagazin/solarreport_0806_chinese_e.html.
72 'Changing Climates', p. vii.
73 Ibid., pp. vii–viii.
74 Personal communication with Chinese officials and researchers from December 2008 to January 2009.
75 World Energy Council, 'Energy Efficiency Policies around the World: Review and Evaluation', January 2008, available at: http://www.worldenergy.org/publications/ energy_efficiency_policies_around_the_world_review_and_evaluation/2_energy_ efficiency_trends/1181.asp.
76 The EU is China's largest supplier of clean coal expertise and systems. In 2006, the European Commission and the Chinese government inked a Memorandum of Understanding on clean coal technologies that aims at encouraging the development of technology for the capture and underground storage of carbon dioxide emitted from coal-fired power stations. The EU is also assisting China to build a new power station by 2015 to demonstrate technologies both for carbon capture and storage. Individual member states such as Germany, the United Kingdom and the Netherlands launched projects to promote their know-how and products on the Chinese market: Cédric Philibert and Jacek Podkanski, 'International Energy Technology Collaboration and Climate Change Mitigation, Case Study: Clean coal technologies', Paris: OECD/IEA, 2006. German companies conquered a market share as much as 50% in the treatment, desulfurization, etc., of coal emissions: Holslag, 'Clouds Ahead'.
77 Wang Bo, 'Can CDM Bring Technology Transfer to Developing Countries: An empirical study of CDM projects in China', Energy Technology Innovation Research Group working paper, Cambridge, MA: Harvard Kennedy School, June 2009.
78 Fox and Godement, 'Power Audit', pp. 42–3.
79 Wang Bo, 'Understanding China's Climate Change Policy: From both international and domestic perspectives', *American Journal of Chinese Studies*, 2, October 2009.
80 Zaborowski, 'Security Dimension of EU–China Relations'. See also: Holslag, 'Clouds Ahead'.

81 'Putin Tells Asia: Russia is here to Stay', *Moscow News*, 36, 13 September 2007.
82 UNFCCC, Decision 1/cp.13: Bali Action Plan, March 14, 2008, p. 3. Available at: http://unfccc.int/resource/docs/2007/cop13/eng/06a01.pdf#page=3. Also, personal interview and communication from official, Ministry of Foreign Affairs, Beijing, January 29, 2008.

4 The rise and fall of EU–China relations in space and defence technology

Nicola Casarini

Introduction

Relations between the People's Republic of China (PRC) and the European Union in the fields of space and defence technology have gone through various phases, following closely the overall state of political relations between the two sides. Collaboration in these key – and sensitive – sectors reached a peak in the period 2003–2005, at the time of the so-called 'honeymoon' in Sino–European relations. The establishment of a comprehensive strategic partnership between the two sides in 2003 was accompanied by two substantial moves: the signature the same day of the political agreement allowing China to participate in the joint development of Galileo (the EU-led global navigation satellite system, an alternative to the dominant American GPS) and the promise by some EU policy makers to their Chinese counterparts to initiate formal discussions on the lifting of the EU arms embargo imposed on China in the aftermath of the Tiananmen Square crackdown on students. With these initiatives, the two sides intended to establish a techno-political linkage based on cooperation in high S&T matters, including plans for exploiting business opportunities from the two sides' aerospace and defence sectors. However, the US intervened to try to limit – if not stop altogether – some of those initiatives perceived to be detrimental to Washington's role and responsibility in East Asia. In summer 2005, the EU and its member states decided to shelve the proposal to lift the arms embargo, ending in this way the prospects for increased EU–China collaboration in defence technology. Space and satellite navigation cooperation continued, however, until summer 2008, when the publication of the second phase of the procurement for the remaining 26 satellites of the Galileo system officially excluded Chinese contractors.

This chapter examines the main themes and reasons provided by European and Chinese policy makers for fostering, and then halting, their cooperation in space and defence technology. It argues that this form of cooperation has been the most significant attempt by the EU and China to counter US primacy in technologically advanced and defence-related industrial sectors in the post-Cold War period. The intervention of the US in the period

2004–2005 was the key factor in convincing EU policy makers to scale down their collaboration with Beijing in space and defence technology. US opposition to initiatives perceived to be detrimental for Washington's role and responsibility in East Asia largely contributed to the reorientation of the EU's foreign and security policy on the positions of its American ally. The shelving of the proposal to lift the arms embargo in summer 2005 and the halting of Sino–European cooperation in satellite navigation in summer 2008 put a seal on EU–China cooperation in these sensitive and strategic policy fields.

Sino–European relations in space and defence technology had become possible in the aftermath of the end of the Cold War and thanks to major changes in the international system. It was in this new geopolitical landscape that the EU and China could establish a political framework and foster cooperation in security-related policy fields that would have been unthinkable during the bipolar era.

New possibilities

The end of the Cold War and the demise of the Soviet Union presented both China and the EU with a new geopolitical landscape conducive to the promotion of their bilateral ties in fields of policy of security and strategic nature, something that would have been unthinkable during the period of East–West confrontation. Alongside – and thanks to – changes in the international environment, both the EU and China pressed forward with the adoption of policies and programmes geared toward the modernisation of their respective space and defence sectors, with the aim of upgrading their security and defence-related capabilities and gain – especially for the EU – a more autonomous security and political role in world affairs. This contributed to creating the conditions for upgrading Sino–European relations in security and strategic policy at the beginning of the twenty-first century.

On 30 October 2003, the EU and China established a comprehensive strategic partnership. This upgrading was based on the idea that relations between the two sides had gained momentum and acquired a new strategic significance. In September 2003, the European Commission had released its fourth policy paper on China: 'A Maturing Partnership: Shared Interests and Challenges in EU–China Relations'. The document called for a strategic partnership with Beijing, stating that:

> It is in the clear interest of the EU and China to work as strategic partners on the international scene … Through a further reinforcement of their cooperation, the EU and China will be better able to shore up their joint security and other interests in Asia and elsewhere.[1]

In October 2003 the Chinese Ministry of Foreign Affairs released its answer to the European Commission's document. In 'China's EU policy paper' it was pointed out that 'China is committed to a long-term, stable and full partnership'. The declaration of strategic partnership was accompanied by two substantial moves: the signature the same day of the political agreement allowing China to participate in the joint development of Galileo (the EU-led global navigation satellite system, alternative to the dominant American GPS) and the promise by some EU policy makers to their Chinese counterparts to initiate formal discussions on the lifting of the EU arms embargo imposed on China in the aftermath of the Tiananmen Square crackdown on students. The top level Sino–European summit held at the end of October 2003 thus provided the political framework within which to advance cooperation in space and defence technology. The strategic partnership provided an opportunity within which to advance plans for a techno-political linkage based on cooperation in high S&T matters and attempts at exploiting business opportunities from the two sides' aerospace and defence sectors.

In the eyes of Chinese and European policy makers (in particular the political leadership of some of the large continental EU member states and senior officials in the European Commission), EU–China collaboration in security and defence-related policy fields would give meaning and substance to the two sides' declarations about strategic partnership. At the same time, it attracted the attention, and the concern, of the US and its East Asian allies, preoccupied that this form of cooperation would contribute to boosting Beijing's defence modernisation and power projection in the region. What worried US policy makers more was the role that Europe might play in helping Beijing's technological upgrading, including its military implications. Technology would lie, indeed, at the heart of the Sino–European strategic partnership. Over the years, Europe had become China's most important source of scientific expertise and advanced technology. Fostering high S&T cooperation with the EU and its member states would fall within the Chinese leadership's overarching goal of economic development and promotion of the country's comprehensive national power. At the same time, EU policy makers would consider a techno-political linkage with China as instrumental for advancing the EU's role as a global centre in high S&T, foster Europe's global competitiveness in key technologically advanced industrial sectors (such as aerospace and defence), and promote greater autonomy from Washington in foreign and security affairs. The strategic partnership would thus provide an opportunity for some key EU member states (and high-ranking elements within the European Commission) together with Chinese leaders to challenge US primacy in key high-tech and security-related industrial sectors. The chosen time (October 2003) also indicated increasing disaffection, in particular by the European allies, with US unilateral attitudes in world affairs.

In autumn 2003, a definitive geopolitical constellation presented itself. During the first part of the year, French and German political leaderships were in the driving seat in criticising, and opposing, the US-led Iraq war and, more generally, the Bush administration's unilateral attitude in world affairs.

France and Germany were also at the forefront in supporting stronger links with China, a line of action strongly backed by the European Commission presided over by Romano Prodi. In this situation, characterised by different transatlantic conceptions about global order as well as diverging opinions between the US and the EU vis-à-vis China's rise and its global role, the establishment of strategic partnership with provision of closer EU–China links in space and defence technology could take place. It was as much about commercial interests, and concerns, about global competitiveness in key high-tech sectors, as it was about different conceptions of global order.

The decision to invite China and other space-faring nations to jointly develop the Galileo satellite system derives, for instance, from different conceptions on the use of space and China's rise. The EU uses international cooperation in the Galileo project to disseminate trust and the peaceful use of space technology. The US appears to concentrate on leveraging the space to provide America and its allies an asymmetric military advantage. While the EU is more concerned in creating useful (i.e. commercial) space applications, the US seems to look at space from a different angle: the protection of its global interests and primacy in world affairs. Fostering Sino–European space cooperation was meant, primarily, to boost commercial activities. But it would also be a reaction to concerns over US uses, and intentions, of its space primacy. The Bush administration had opposed the Galileo project since the beginning as it was interpreted as paving the way, over time, for increased EU technological and operational autonomy from Washington. As a counter measure, the US included as many EU members and companies as possible in the Joint Strike Fighter project which, according to some observers, would serve as a Trojan horse for preventing the creation of a large EU defence-industrial complex able to challenge the American dominant position in the defence sector. Chinese leaders, on the other hand, showed their support for Galileo from the beginning. The support lent by China (one of the world's most important space-faring nations) for the Galileo satellite system was welcomed by European political and corporate leaders and allowed Beijing to access much-coveted European advanced space technology and expertise.

US policy makers repeatedly voiced their concern, and opposition, to this form of international cooperation, arguing that projects such as Galileo, including access to advanced Western space technology, would put China in a better position to acquire the most advanced early-warning systems and recognition satellites, which could help them in countering Taiwanese arms systems imported from the US as well as target US space assets in the area. Furthermore, US scholars and policy makers suggested a link between EU–China cooperation in Galileo and the proposal to lift the EU arms embargo on China. China's participation in the Galileo satellite system and the proposal to lift the arms embargo are, indeed, interconnected. For instance, some of the technologies needed by China to be able to read Galileo's encrypted features need special export licensing and, given its military applications, the technologies under discussion would fall under the provisions of the arms embargo. Moreover, the technologies directly connected to the manufacture of weapons systems which utilise satellite positioning and targeting also fall under the arms embargo. In order to circumvent these legal obstacles, since the end of 2003 those EU member state governments that have strongly supported China's participation in the Galileo project (i.e. France and Germany, but also Italy and Spain) have proposed that the arms embargo be lifted. The rationale can be summarised as follows: if China is considered by the EU a strategic partner reliable enough to cooperate in Europe's main aerospace project, why maintain an arms embargo imposed during the Cold War which 'does not correspond anymore to the political realities of the contemporary world'? In sum, the arms embargo issue is directly linked to China's participation in the Galileo project. The two initiatives, though quite different in nature and scope, must be seen, however, as two sides of the same coin: the upgrading of relations between the EU and China through a techno-political linkage. To better understand the significance of these two initiatives, we will now turn to a close examination of each one of them.

Satellite cooperation

From autumn 2003 to summer 2008, the EU and China collaborated in the development of Galileo, Europe's flagship aerospace project, in the framework of a political agreement between the two sides signed in October 2003. Galileo is a Global Navigation Satellite System (GNSS) that will offer both civilian and military applications once it becomes operational in 2013.[2] Galileo is an alternative to the dominant US Global Positioning System (GPS), though the EU and the US reached an agreement on the interoperability of the two systems in June 2004.[3] Galileo is designed to encircle the globe with 30 satellites in medium earth orbit, comprising 27 operational satellites and 3 reserves, plus two control centres on the ground.[4] According to the European Commission, the estimated cost of the project will amount to 3.4 billion euros.[5] It will provide users, ranging from aircraft and shipping to cars and trekkers, with a navigational fix accurate to within just one metre.

The European Union and the European Space Agency (ESA), kicked off the Galileo project in March 2002. On 30 October 2003, an agreement was reached for China's cooperation and commitment to finance 200 million euros (out of an estimated total cost at that time of 2.2 to 2.4 billion euros) of Galileo's costs. On 27 October 2003, the Council authorised the Italian Presidency of the EU to sign the 'Cooperation Agreement on Galileo between the European Community and the PRC'. The signature took place, significantly, during the sixth EU–China summit held in Beijing on 30 October 2003. According to the official wording:

> The agreement provides for co-operative activities on satellite navigation in a wide range of sectors, notably science and technology, industrial

manufacturing, service and market development, as well as standardisation, frequency and certification.[6]

Chinese leaders attached a lot of emphasis to this kind of cooperation with the EU. In the 'China's EU Policy Paper' of October 2003, the Ministry of Foreign Affairs stated that:

> China will, on the premise of equality and mutual benefit and a balance between interests and obligations, participate in the Galileo Programme and enhance cooperation in international 'big science' projects.

In February 2003, a joint Sino–European satellite navigation cooperation centre had been opened in Beijing. The China–Europe Global Navigation Satellite System Technical Training and Cooperation Centre (CENC) was meant to serve as a focal point for all activities on the GNSS as well as promote industrial cooperation with special attention given to development of applications. The CENC is jointly run by the Chinese Ministry of Science and Technology, the Chinese Remote Sensing Centre, the European Commission and the European Space Agency. According to the EU–China agreement, the main focus of Chinese participation would be on developing applications, as well as research and development, manufacturing and technical aspects of the Galileo project.

China agreed to invest 200 million euros in Galileo. In the first phase (i.e. the manufacturing and launching of the first four satellites of the constellation) Beijing pledged to spend 70 million euros, of which 5 million euros was the entrance fee. The EU-designated Chinese industrial partner for the Galileo project was the National Remote Sensing Centre of China (NRSCC). In October 2004, the Galileo Joint Undertaking and the NRSCC signed a Technical Agreement for the first phase of the implementation, including manufacturing and launch, of the first four satellites and a substantial part of the ground infrastructure.[7] The Technical Agreement included details regarding the amount of money that the Chinese government would invest in Galileo, with the proviso that these sums would remain inside the country and serve to build the Chinese infrastructure, components and services for the Galileo project. Moreover, the Agreement contained clear indication that the rights of the technology developed while working on Galileo would remain the property of the NRSCC.

By July 2008 (when publication of the ESA's tender package for the second phase of Galileo excluded Chinese firms) around 35 million euros had been contracted to Chinese industries and research institutes for developing various applications of the Galileo system in China. A number of projects had been agreed between the two sides and implemented, including: Galileo Fishery Application (FAS); China Galileo Test Range (CGTR); Project of Location Based Services Standardization (LBS); Galileo Laser

Retro-Reflector (LRR); Search and Rescue Transponder (SART); Early Galileo Service in China (EGSIC); Forward Link Service End-End Validation (EEV); Medium-altitude Earth Orbit Local User Terminal (MEOLUT).[8]

The number of projects and the amount of money invested to this point made China the most important non-EU partner in Galileo. Chinese officials recognise that without the active involvement of European partners and European expertise/know-how, including technology travelling to China, the local sub-contractors (companies and research centres) would have been unable to complete the above projects.[9] Among EU member states, French, German and Italian aerospace companies were at the forefront of collaboration with Beijing. While cooperation with Europe's aerospace sector provides China with access to advanced technology and know-how, it also allows EU firms a better entry into the promising Chinese market for aerospace products. In recent years, European companies have sold telecommunication satellites and other space technologies to Beijing. Furthermore, some European commercial remote sensing companies (like their American counterparts) have been selling spatial imagery to China. According to analysts and official documents, some low-resolution micro-satellites have been sold by France to China.[10]

Sino–European collaboration in the aerospace sector has security- and defence-related implications and as such are directly linked to the Chinese arms embargo issue. As mentioned earlier, some of the technologies directly connected to the manufacture of weapons systems which utilise satellite positioning and targeting fall under the arms embargo. In such a context, the existence of an arms ban would be a hurdle for closer Sino–European aerospace cooperation. In order to circumvent the legal obstacles represented by the arms ban, EU member states that supported China's participation in the Galileo project would also propose that the arms embargo be lifted so that increased cooperation in space and defence industry and technologies could take place.

The proposal to lift the arms embargo

The EU embargo on arms sales dates back to June 1989, when EU member states imposed it on the People's Republic of China in response to the PLA's crackdown on students in Tiananmen Square.[11] Along with the EC, the United States, other Western countries and Japan also condemned the massacre and imposed similar restrictions. Fourteen years later (autumn 2003), in a different geopolitical environment and with the establishment of the EU–China strategic partnership, France and Germany officially proposed to initiate discussions on the lifting of the arms embargo with the aim of creating the conditions for promoting Sino–European cooperation in defence industry and technologies, as well as boosting exchanges and cooperation in military affairs. As the Chinese Ministry of Foreign Affairs stated in its policy paper on the EU:

> China and the EU will maintain high-level military-to-military exchanges, develop and improve, step by step, a strategic security consultation mechanism, exchange more missions of military experts, and expand exchanges in respect of military officers' training and defense studies ... The EU should lift its ban on arms sales to China at an early date so as to remove barriers to greater bilateral cooperation on defense industry and technologies.[12]

For Chinese policy makers the lifting of the embargo was a political act necessary for moving beyond Cold War thinking. It would also give meaning and content to the newly established strategic partnership as well as lay the ground for closer Sino–European cooperation and exchanges on security and military matters.[13] Consultations, military exchanges and joint manoeuvres with the People's Liberation Army (PLA) have already been undertaken by some EU member states. For instance, Germany has held several rounds of high-level consultations on security and defence matters with China, underpinned by visits of high-ranking military and civilian representatives. Germany is also training PLA officers. France and China have established a strategic dialogue and held annual consultations on defence and security issues since 1997, complemented by the training of Chinese military officers. Since 2003, the UK has had an annual strategic security dialogue with Beijing and has been training PLA officers. It was in this context of growing Sino–European relations in the security and military spheres that the proposal to lift the arms ban begun to be discussed.

The advocates of an end to the arms embargo based their case on a number of arguments. First of all, they claim, China has changed. Since the 1989 Tiananmen Square crackdown on students, Beijing has significantly reformed its system of government and its economy, and improved relations with neighbours. It should be rewarded for this. Former French President Jacques Chirac, in particular, was in the forefront, dubbing the arms embargo as 'outdated'. In January 2004, Chirac stated that 'the ban no longer corresponds to the political reality of the contemporary world and therefore makes no sense today'.[14] Former German Chancellor Gerhard Schröder, during a state visit to China in December 2003, also declared that the embargo should be lifted.[15] By the end of 2003, Silvio Berlusconi, Italy's Prime Minister, and Jose Maria Aznar, the Spanish Prime Minister, had joined the same position. The proposal to lift the embargo was officially tabled by France and Germany at the European Council in Brussels in December 2003.[16] In the following months, Italy, Spain, the United Kingdom, Finland and the Netherlands joined the camp of the supporters of the lifting.[17] Despite the critical stance of the Nordic countries, an EU-15 consensus on initiating discussions on the lifting was reached within the CFSP framework.

The official position of the Council in favour of lifting the embargo claimed that the EU Code of Conduct (CoC) on arms sales and normal national arms export policies and controls would still apply, thereby preventing abuses when it came to exporting arms to China. EU officials added that, by treating China as a respected interlocutor, they could encourage its peaceful integration into the international community. They even argued that European weapons would be too expensive and that China had frequently declared that it had no intention of buying weapons from Europe. As such, the end of the embargo would principally serve to show that the EU did not discriminate against Beijing but treated it on a par with nations such as Russia.[18] For Chinese leaders, the embargo represented the past. Wen Jiabao, the Chinese Premier, declared that the embargo 'is a product of the Cold War and is totally outdated'.[19] For Chinese leaders, as long as the arms embargo remains in place, it represents an affront to China's dignity and international standing.[20] Li Zhaoxing, former Chinese foreign minister (2003–2007), stated on various occasions that the maintenance of the embargo was a form of political discrimination against Beijing. During the debate on the proposal, Chinese officials repeatedly stressed that the only other countries with an EU arms embargo were Zimbabwe, Sudan and Myanmar, noting that North Korea had not been subject to a similar ban.[21]

This idea of discrimination fits the victimisation narrative which has emerged in China since the early 1990s. In this sense, the lifting of the arms embargo by such an important Western player would allow China to regain honour and prestige and partly eliminate the humiliating experience of the past and show recognition of China as a respected interlocutor in security and defence affairs. It would also allow Beijing to have normal military relations with the EU and its member states and, in the process, send a clear message to those Taiwanese policy makers in favour of independence. Finally, for Chinese officials the lifting of the embargo would mean that China's transformation had reached the point where it could receive equal treatment as a full member of the international society and not be marginalised and discriminated against as if it was a rogue state.[22] Chinese leaders also recognised in private discussions that the lifting of the arms ban would greatly contribute in pushing forward Sino–European relations and that for this European companies would be rewarded. EU policy makers (in particular those from the larger member states) indeed expected in return some favourable decisions on the purchase of European commercial aircraft (especially Airbus), automotives, civil engineering and transportation infrastructure.[23]

The European Parliament and some national parliaments intervened in the debate, however, to oppose the lifting. On 28 October 2003, the Bundestag, including the vast majority of Chancellor Gerhard Schröder's own Social Democrats and virtually all of Foreign Minister Joschka

Fischer's Greens, passed a resolution opposing Berlin's attempts to lift the embargo. On 19 November 2003, the European Parliament passed a similar resolution with 572 votes against 72. On 11 March 2004, leaders of the four German political parties representing Germany in the European Parliament sent an open letter to Chancellor Schröder urging him to abandon his support. In the 2005 Annual Report on the CFSP, the European Parliament, with 431 votes in favour and 85 against, urged the Council once again not to lift the arms embargo. In that Report, MEPs 'call[ed] on the Council not to lift the arms embargo until greater progress is made in the field of human rights and arms exports controls in China and on cross-Strait relations'.[24]

Human rights concerns were not the only argument used by those opposed to the lifting of the embargo. From a security point of view, the opponents argued that, once the embargo had been lifted, China would be able to acquire European weapons systems – especially advanced early warning capabilities as well as surface-to-air and air-to-air missile systems – that could affect the military balance across the Taiwan Strait in Beijing's favour. In this context, it is important to recall that French and British military exchanges and joint manoeuvres with the PLA took place in 2004, during the debate on the proposal to lift the arms embargo. Joint manoeuvres are an important component of cooperation in military and security matters. Yet, they are also about display of the latest military equipment and technology. France and China held joint military exercises in the South China Sea in March 2004 (just before the presidential elections in Taiwan), the first ever naval manoeuvres involving China and a Western country. In June 2004, the UK held joint maritime search-and-rescue exercises with the PLA.[25]

The US intervened to strongly criticise – and oppose – the proposal to lift the arms embargo. The US government even voiced threats of retaliation in EU–US industrial and defence cooperation should the lifting occur. Opposition within Europe and elsewhere, in particular the US, led EU member states in June 2005 to officially postpone the issue, finding the timing inappropriate. A number of factors played in favour of postponement:

- strong opposition from the US and its East Asian allies;
- increasing uneasiness in many national parliaments and within the European Parliament;
- China's failure to provide clear and specific evidence of improvement of its human rights record;
- the passing of China's Anti-Secession Law in March 2005;
- the formation of a new, and more pro-American, European Commission; and
- accession to the EU of 10 new – more Atlanticist – members.

The postponement put a halt to plans for increased cooperation between the EU and China in defence industry and technologies. It also marked the end of the 'honeymoon' period in EU–China relations. It was a victory for the advocates of American primacy in world affairs (both in the US and in Europe) as it demonstrated to Washington's East Asian allies (and the Europeans as well) that the US was still firmly in command of major political decisions within the Western camp. Following the postponement, there was also a gradual reorientation of the EU's foreign and security policy in China and East Asia towards the US positions.

Turning around

The reorientation the EU's foreign and security policy in China and East Asia towards the US positions was embodied in the 'Guidelines on the EU's Foreign and Security Policy in East Asia' adopted by the Council of the EU in December 2007.[26] Work on the document began in summer 2005, immediately after the official postponement of the proposal to lift the embargo, and it was adopted by the Council of the EU 18 months later. This document put a seal on those elements of the EU–China relationship perceived to be detrimental to the US role and responsibilities in East Asia. The 'Guidelines' recognise the unique role of the US for regional security and stability:

> The US's security commitments to Japan, the Republic of Korea and Taiwan and the associated presence of US forces in the region give the US a distinct perspective on the region's security challenges. It is important that the EU is sensitive to this. Given the great importance of transatlantic relations, the EU has a strong interest in partnership and cooperation with the US on the Foreign and Security policy challenges arising from East Asia.[27]

From this document, it seems that the EU and its member states had aligned themselves with the US position, removing those initiatives that could be perceived in Washington (and Tokyo) as impinging on the strategic interests of the American ally in the region. The document continues, asserting that:

> The EU should also, in consultation with all partners, deepen its understanding of the military balance affecting the cross-strait situation; of the technologies and capabilities which, if transferred to the region, could disturb that balance; of the related risks to stability including the risk of miscalculation; and factor that assessment into the way that Member States apply the Code of Conduct in relation to their exports to the region of strategic and military items.[28]

Overall, the document appears to put a seal on any EU autonomous initiative vis-à-vis China on security and strategic matters that could be perceived, by the American ally and its East Asian partners, as detrimental for the region's strategic balance. This policy readjustment was accompanied (and caused) by changes in the political leadership in some of the larger EU member states (Germany and France in particular), the formation of a new (and more pro-American) European Commission headed by Manuel Barroso, and accession to the EU of the more Atlanticist Central and Eastern European countries. These developments contributed to the re-evaluation of priorities in EU–China relations. Alongside changes at the top political level, 'negative' perceptions about China emerged in European public opinion.[29] While the publication of the 'Guidelines' in December 2007 shelved any serious discussion on the lifting of the Chinese arms embargo, Sino–European space and satellite navigation cooperation continued on the ground. This was bound to be readjusted, however, following the more general realignment of the EU's foreign and security policy in China and East Asia with the US position.

On 1 July 2008, the European Space Agency (ESA) and the European Commission published the procurement criteria for the second phase of Galileo, the manufacturing, services and launch of the remaining 26 satellites of the European satellite system.[30] In the document, the tender was limited to a select number of countries divided into two groups. The first group – the inner circle with priority access to the procurement scheme – includes all 27 member states of the EU (as the procurement is entirely financed out of the EU budget). In the second group – the outer circle – there are a number of countries which can participate to the tender if they are signatories of the pluri-lateral 'Agreement on Government Procurement' (GPA) adopted in the framework of the WTO.[31] China, until that moment the most important non-EU partner in Galileo, was kept out of the second phase of public procurement, since Beijing is not a party to the GPA. However, a narrow escape route was included, which could pave the way for a 'political readjustment' of Sino–European cooperation in Galileo:

> In exceptional circumstances related to the nature and the availability of specific goods or services ... ESA may authorize the use of subcontractors established outside the territory of one of the Member States of the European Union or of a state that is a party to one of the above mentioned agreements.[32]

Both EU and Chinese policy makers asserted on various occasions that the final content and the mechanism of their satellite navigation cooperation would remain open and go through eventual 'readjustments', following the trend of political relations between the two sides.[33] Yet, the publication of the ESA public procurement scheme for the second phase of the Galileo system was a slap in the face for China, which had always regarded space and satellite navigation cooperation with the EU as a model for Beijing's international cooperation in big S&T projects. What could explain the decision by the EU to exclude China from the second phase of procurement and put into question the future prospects of the largest ever joint high S&T project between the EU and China? First, the political reorientation of the EU's CFSP as discussed above. In addition, a number of technical issues – with strategic implications –helped to convince EU policy makers to halt collaboration with China on satellite navigation; for instance, Europeans were becoming increasingly concerned about technology transfers and Intellectual Property Rights (IPR) enforcement.

EU member states appear to be more and more wary of a lack of significant progress in China's legislation and actions in relation to IPR, and increasingly concerned that the Chinese might use European advanced space technology to develop their own satellite system and challenge Galileo itself. This is related to preoccupations on possible competition between Galileo and China's own Global Satellite Navigation System: the *Beidou* (or Compass). The latter is expected to be completed with 30 satellites before 2015, with 10 or more new satellites scheduled to be launched in the period 2009–2011. Beidou is China's own strategic project planned to perform very much like the American GPS and the Russian GLONASS and be operational well ahead of the EU's Galileo system. Like the American GPS, the Beidou is not open to the outside world (unlike Galileo) and is controlled by the military as it is intended to be used for national security reasons. The Chinese GNSS is driven by the same motives as the other (competing) satellite systems: sovereign control over critical infrastructure, security purposes, industrial policy and manufacturing, global competitiveness and markets. It is also a powerful symbol of China's great power status, something to which Chinese leaders (and the population as well) are very sensitive.

Plans for a Chinese GNSS were unveiled in September 2007, when the Chinese government announced its intention to convert its regional system, of various Compass geo-stationary orbit satellites, into a fully fledged global navigation satellite system. At the same time, Beijing would continue to work (as the most-important non-EU partner) on the Galileo project, consequently raising concerns in Europe. In 2000–2001, EU and Chinese diplomats joined forces at the International Telecommunication Union (ITU) in Geneva to obtain the frequencies for Galileo. However, while the Galileo project was slowed down in Europe due to problems encountered by the public–private partnership, the Chinese continued to work on research, manufacturing and service applications for Galileo in China as well as on their own system. Since 2006/7, there seems to have been an overlap between the two projects (Galileo and the Beidou), in particular between the Galileo Public Regulated Service (PRS) and some Beidou frequencies, in a situation where the Chinese system appears to be in a more advanced phase of development than Galileo, with at least 10–12 satellites in orbit by the end of 2009 against only 2 for Galileo.[34] While US and EU policy makers (and technicians) have met at various times to discuss the interoperability, and frequency compatibility, between their two systems following the transatlantic summit in Ireland in June 2004, EU and Chinese officials have not yet resolved their outstanding issues, including the question of signal compatibility between Galileo and the Beidou.

In autumn 2003 (at the time of the signature of the Galileo agreement), cooperation with China was intended as a means of challenging US primacy in the aerospace sector, and the EU expected to stay ahead of China in the development of space-based satellite navigation technology and capabilities. However, due to slow European progress, coupled with significant Chinese advances, things turned out differently. Moreover, the US intervened to oppose EU–China cooperation in strategic and security-related fields and EU policy makers were persuaded to scale back their level of involvement with China. China, expecting more from cooperation with the Europeans in terms of technical know-how, system management, technology transfer, and market and signal access, pressed on with the development of its own satellite system. The result was a Chinese GNSS (the Beidou), which is expected to be fully operational in the Asian region by 2010–11, and by 2015 it may well have a global reach; the possibility is that it could challenge not only the American GPS but Galileo too. The challenge is not simply commercial. Since the Beidou satellite system is marketed mainly for national security uses, it would provide the PLA with additional means of boosting its military space capabilities. In this vein, the challenge to Galileo was seen in the context of the Chinese ASAT test of January 2007[35] and Beijing's advances of its military space programme. The ASAT test was followed by further pressure on the EU by US, and Japanese, policy makers to limit space cooperation with China. It seems that the ASAT test played a key role in convincing the EU to reconsider the level of their cooperation due to concerns about China's development of advanced space weaponry.

Chinese strategists are aware of the critical damage that could be wrought on the US if an adversary was able to deny Washington use of its space assets during a conflict. For instance, the capability of putting US satellites out of use, together with other communications or command and control systems that are space-based (not to mention the GPS for precision-guided munitions and tracking, reconnaissance satellites, and radar), would be vital for any prospect of Chinese success in a conflict over Taiwan – one of the most likely arenas which could bring the US and China into direct confrontation. Proving the vulnerability of US satellites was the aim of China's ASAT in January 2007, when the PLA destroyed an old Chinese weather satellite using an anti-satellite weapon. For US senior military planners, the Chinese ASAT test was a 'strategically dislocating' event, as significant as the Russian launch of Sputnik in 1957.[36]

The ASAT test also made a substantial impression on Beijing's neighbours such as Japan and South Korea, which had already begun the development of their own military space systems. In 2006, both countries launched new military reconnaissance satellites. The PLA saw both these burgeoning programmes as potentially aimed at increasing Seoul's and Tokyo's respective military space capabilities in the region. In the aftermath of China's ASAT test, both Japan and South Korea expressed concerns that their limited programmes could be directly threatened by China's growing capabilities and accused Beijing of breaching international law, in particular the Outer Space Treaty.[37] The Europeans too were preoccupied by the ASAT test and aired threats of backlash in space cooperation if China were to make further kinetic energy tests that would cause further space debris and breach international law. The EU and its member states have always argued that their cooperation with China on Galileo and other space-based technologies is aimed at civilian uses of the technology. The prospect of European technology being used for developing China's military space assets was unwelcome in Europe. The ASAT test provided, therefore, a serious warning to Europeans against civilian space cooperation with China. European parliaments and public opinion, let alone the governments more ready to use the 'China threat' discourse, found themselves in a difficult position in allowing their domestic space industries to cooperate with a China that was pursuing a space weapons programme. There was also a gradual realignment with the US and its East Asian allies – in particular Japan –seeking a containment of China's military space advances.

Strategic considerations coinciding with genuine concerns regarding technology transfers and the enforcement of IPR in China, as well as a perceived challenge from the Beidou system, caused leading EU policy makers to put a halt to EU–China space and satellite navigation cooperation and provided the basis for a political readjustment of their collaboration. With the publication of the ESA document in July 2008 which excluded Chinese contractors from the second phase of procurement of Galileo, what remained of the techno-political linkage between the EU and China initiated in autumn 2003 – and which attracted so much attention from the US and its East Asian allies – began to fade away.

Conclusion

Sino–European relations in space and defence technology reached a peak in the period autumn 2003 to summer 2005. In the aftermath of the official postponement of the proposal to lift the EU arms embargo on China (June 2005), the EU and its member states gradually realigned their foreign and security policy on China and East Asia with the positions of the American ally. Following the Chinese ASAT test, US policy makers applied further pressure on their EU counterparts in order to limit space cooperation with China. This coincided with genuine concerns by EU policy makers of a satellite challenge to Galileo coming from China's Beidou satellite navigation system.

As this chapter has sought to demonstrate, Sino–European space and defence technology cooperation has been characterised by ups and downs, following the overall political relations between the two sides and US intervention. Yet it is probable that, given certain conditions (new leadership in Europe, both at EU level and in the main national capitals, a Chinese leadership more prone to delivering political concessions, and a more neutral approach to EU–China relations by the US administration) EU–China space and defence technology relations could resume – and rise – again.

Notes

1 European Commission, 'A Maturing Partnership: Shared Interests and Challenges in EU–China Relations', COM (2003) 533 final, Brussels, 10 September 2003.
2 For more details on the technical, military and political aspects of Galileo see: Gustav Lindström and Giovanni Gasparini, 'The Galileo Satellite System and Its Security Implications', European Union Institute for Security Studies (EUISS), Occasional Paper 44, April 2003; see also: European Community, Regulation (EC) n. 683/2008 of the European Parliament and of the Council of 9 July 2008 on the further implementation of the European satellite navigation programmes (EGNOS and Galileo), Brussels, 9 July 2008.
3 'Agreement on the promotion, provision and use of Galileo and GPS satellite-based navigation systems and related applications (between the European Community and its Member States, of the one part, and the United States of America of the other part)', Dublin, 28 June 2004. On 26 July 2007, the United States and the European Union announced their agreement to jointly adopt and provide an improved design for their respective Global Navigation Satellite System (GNSS) signals. These signals will be implemented on the Galileo Open Service and the GPS IIIA new civil signal.
4 European Commission, Communication from the Commission to the European Parliament and the Council: Progressing GALILEO: reprofiling the European GNSS Programmes, COM (2007) 534 final, Brussels, 19 September 2007.
5 Ibid., p. 3.
6 Cooperation Agreement on a Civil Global Navigation Satellite System (GNSS) – Galileo – between the European Community and its Member States and the People's Republic of China, Beijing, 30 October 2003, p. 2; for more details on the political and strategic implications of EU–China satellite cooperation see Nicola Casarini, 'The Evolution of the EU–China Relationship: From Constructive Engagement to Strategic Partnership', Paris, EUISS, Occasional Paper 64, October 2006, pp. 26–9.
7 Galileo Programme Technical Agreement between the National Remote Sensing Center of China and the China Galileo Satellite Navigation Corporation, Beijing, 9 October 2004.
8 For more details see: Nicola Casarini, *Remaking Global Order: The Evolution of Europe–China Relations and its Implications for East Asia and the United States*, Oxford: Oxford University Press, 2009, in particular Chapter 5.
9 Interviews, MOST and CENC, Beijing, August 2008.
10 Council of the European Union, 'Eight Annual Report on the EU Code of Conduct on Arms Exports', 2006/C 250/01, Brussels, 16 October 2006, pp. 265–6.
11 At that time European countries issued the following statement: 'The European Council strongly condemns the brutal repression taking place in China … it thinks it necessary to adopt the following measures … interruption by the

Member States of the Community of military cooperation and an embargo on trade in arms with China', European Council Declaration on China, Madrid, 26–27 June 1989.

12 Chinese Ministry of Foreign Affairs, 'China's EU Policy Paper', Beijing, October 2003, Title V.

13 At the time, the international press used terms such as 'love affair' and 'honeymoon' to describe the state of Sino–European relations. See, for instance, David Murphy and Shada Islam, 'China's Love Affair with Europe', *The Far Eastern Economic Review*, 12 February 2004, pp. 26–9.

14 'Chirac Renews Call for End to EU Arms Embargo on China', *Agence France-Presse*, 27 January 2004.

15 'Schröder Backs Sales to China of EU Weapons', *Wall Street Journal*, 2 December 2003.

16 'European Council Presidency Conclusions', Brussels, 12 December 2003. Point 72 (p. 19) states, 'The European Council invites the General Affairs and External Relations Council to re-examine the question of the embargo on the sale of arms to China'.

17 James Kirkup, 'Blair's Backing for China Trade Angers Activists', *The Scotsman*, 11 May 2004.

18 Interviews, Chinese Ministry of Foreign Affairs, Beijing, and European Commission delegation in China, September 2004 and May 2005.

19 Quoted from *CNN World News*, 2 May 2004.

20 See for instance Chris Patten, *Cousins and Strangers: America, Britain and Europe in a New Century*, New York: Times Books, 2006, pp. 260–61.

21 Interviews, Chinese Ministry of Foreign Affairs, Beijing, September 2004 and May 2005.

22 Ibid.

23 Kristin Archick, Richard F. Grimmett and Shirley Kan, 'European Union's Arms Embargo on China: Implications and options for US policy', Congressional Research Service, Library of Congress, Washington DC, August 2005, p. 20.

24 European Parliament, 'Report on the Common Foreign and Security Policy' (Brok's Report), 28 November 2005, discussed and adopted by the European Parliament on 2 February 2006. Quotation from point 34.

25 For more details see: May-Britt Stumbaum, 'Engaging China – Uniting Europe? European Union foreign policy towards China', in Nicola Casarini and Costanza Musu (eds), *European Foreign Policy in an Evolving International System: The road towards convergence*, Basingstoke: Palgrave, 2007, pp. 57–75.

26 Council of the EU, 'Guidelines on the EU's Foreign and Security Policy in East Asia', 2842nd Council meeting (16183/07), Brussels, 20 December 2007.

27 Ibid., p. 3, point 8.

28 Ibid., p. 8, point 24.

29 See German Marshall Fund, 'Perspectives on Trade and Poverty Reduction: A survey of public opinion', Washington DC, 2007, p. 18, available at: http://www.gmfus.org/economics/tpsurvey/2007TPSurvey-FINAL.pdf.

30 European Space Agency, 'Galileo Full Operational Capability (FOC) Procurement: Tender Information Package', (ESA-DTEN-NG-DOC-03087), Paris, 1 July 2008.

31 On the pluri-lateral Agreement on Government Procurement see http://www.wto.org/english/tratop_e/gproc_e/gp_gpa_e.htm.

32 Ibid., p. 15.

33 Interview, European Commission, Brussels, October 2008 and Chinese Ministry of Science and Technology (MOST), August 2008.

34 Interviews, European Commission delegation in China and Chinese Ministry of Science and Technology, Beijing, August 2008.

35 This was a Chinese anti-satellite (ASAT) test strike against an old Chinese weather satellite. See 'Chinese Test Anti-Satellite Weapon', *Aviation Week*, 17 January 2007, available at: http://www.aviationweek.com/aw/generic/story_channel.jsp?channel=space&id=news/CHI01177.xml.
36 Quoted in Caitlin Harrington, 'China ASAT test prompts US rethink', *Jane's Information Group*, 30 April 2007.
37 Interviews, Japan and South Korean Mission to the EU, Brussels, October 2008.

5 Hegemonic cycles and Sino–European cooperation in crisis management

Xuan Xingzhang and Yang Xiaoping

In his book *Power and Prosperity,*[1] Mancur Olsen identified encompassing interests as the basis for different groups to work together.[2] China and Europe, which are situated at the two edges of the Eurasian Continent, and both overshadowed by American power, share huge strategic interests but are troubled by weaknesses generated by changes in the global strategic space. How will these changes influence Sino–European strategic cooperation? And what opportunities exist for both parties in the current global system?

The triangular relationship between China, the United States and Europe

The 1970s witnessed a watershed in international relations. According to the Egyptian economist Samir Amin, since the early 1970s, compared with the post-war period in terms of rapid growth, the world economy has been in a relatively long period of recession.[3] Also, according to World-System Theory, around 1970 US hegemony began to decline and the global financial system started to enter a new stage of expansion. This corresponds to the so-called Phase B (or downward period) in the Kondratieff's economic wave theory: a 50-year production decline for high- and low-wage goods. After Phase B, the economy enters phase A (the ascendant period), in which production of both high- and low-wage goods increases dramatically.[4] In contrast to Phase A, in Phase B the world economy is marked by declining profits, increasing financial liquidity, lower wages, merging industries, fierce competition between core countries and a floating exchange rate.[5] Phase B is a period of hegemonic decline, multi-polarization and increasing national competition. This is the stage the global economy is currently in.

Since the 1970s, cracks have emerged within both the capitalism and socialism camps. The pyramid-shaped economic structure in each camp – with the US and the Soviet Union at the respective tops – eroded. The rapid economic developments in Western Europe and Japan enabled them to reduce their dependency on the United States and increase the competition between them. A similar development took place in the socialism camp.

This actually reflected the changes of the international power structure which resulted from the cyclical fluctuations in the world's political and economic system. Along with the cyclical fluctuations, decentralization and centralization occurred simultaneously.

As Gilpin pointed out,

> During the early phase of an interdependent world economy, polarization effects predominate over spread effects. Over time, however, due to the growth of efficiency in the periphery and to increasing diseconomies in the core, spread overtakes polarization. Certain peripheral economies grow and industrialize at a more rapid rate than the core. As this happens, the competition between rising peripheral economies and declining core economies intensifies, thereby threatening the stability of the liberal economic system.[6]

The centralization of the world market coincided with the polarization of power. In this polarization period, economic concentration in one or two specific countries and the vertical divisions of global labour ensured that high-wage jobs would be occupied by developed countries, while conflicts primarily happened on the margins of capitalism. But in the period of decentralization, capital and technology flowed and covered more countries/regions, and powers were transferred. Rivalry between states became intense, former dominant countries lost their competitive edge, domestic problems became acute and the gap between poor and rich widened. This was labelled by Lenin as imperialism, a situation in which the power of the state is diluted and social and economic resources are controlled by a very small group. In order to solve these serious social problems, all countries entered into fierce competition and those who had no capacity to export faced tremendous domestic crises. In this sense, social problems were converted into political issues. Just as described by Kondratieff, the polarization of the world market often occurred in Phase A, when hegemony was newly established and the world system was well-ordered. Decentralization has usually occurred in Phase B, when the world system was chaotic because of the decline of hegemony and all-round competition in economy, the military sphere and in politics were intensified.

The period from the First World War to the 1970s was a period of polarization in the world economy. The subsequent decades have been a period of decentralization. During the period of decentralization, Western Europe, Japan and the United States transferred a large number of industries outward and hence enlarged the space for their capital flow. This linked the external industries with their own domestic ones and therefore formed a new economic flow. The transferred industries were domestically replaced by high-tech industries such as information technology and finance. This was the context for the European and American industrial transition, which is continuing. Additionally, Europe experienced tensions which attached equal importance to economic liberalization and social welfare.

Since China's reform and opening-up, China and Europe have tried to develop common interests in three areas. First, in the current international political structure, the two sides have tried to cooperate to counterbalance the dominance of the US. Secondly, the two parties are economically mutually beneficial. For China, at the beginning of its reform and opening-up, a large amount of foreign capital and technology was needed and primary industrial products were offered to export. Meanwhile, Europe needed to transfer its capital and technology abroad as well as export its capital goods. Lastly, in terms of the division of global labour, China showed no unwillingness to accept the transferred low value-added industries from Europe. Therefore, it can be said the Chinese and European common interests since 1978 have been multi-dimensional, highly complementary and mutually beneficial.

However, this relationship has changed not only because of the internal changes on both sides but also because of the transition of hegemonic power. Sino–European relations are not only determined by their bilateral relations but also by the influences of external strategic forces, including the changes of state-to-state relations.

Immanuel Wallerstein grouped these system changes into three stages. First, a rising power achieves overwhelming advantages in production. Then follows prominence in commerce, and, finally, dominance in the financial sector. However, these advantages have usually been associated with victory in war, as in the case of the establishment of US hegemony after the two world wars.[7] After the Second World War, the reshaping of the international structure was greatly influenced by liberalism. Liberal principles, however, in turn became a vital weakness due to the continuous transnational flow of capital and technology. This process eroded the US domestic basis. At the international level it pushed states to intense competition and reshaped their relative advantages in production, commerce and finance.[8] To address this phenomenon, Giovanni Arrighi developed his hegemonic cycles model, which highlighted the role of social forces in the transfer of hegemony.

In Arrighi's model, past hegemons such as the Netherlands or Britain face increasing competition due to other states emulating a hegemon's policies. Thus hegemonic deficits appear. In the subsequent crisis phase, the struggle among countries/enterprises becomes tense and social conflicts intensify. This ultimately leads to the collapse of the hegemonic state, and the systemic leadership to a successor.

In particular, Arrighi stresses that severe rivalries among states, intense social conflicts and the transition of hegemony are related to a process of expansion of the global financial system.[9] He points out that this 'systemwide financial expansion' is 'the outcome of complementary tendencies: an overaccumulation of capital and the intense interstate competition for mobile capital.'[10] The first tendency created the supply conditions for financial expansion, while the latter created their demand conditions.[11] This brought the large-scale redistribution of wealth from various groups to capital operation organizations, which to a large extent separated the financial transaction from trade or manufacture and guaranteed its high profit margin. This global financial expansion brought tremendous political and social consequences. It deepened international competition and triggered social conflict, thus redistributing capital to those organizations that promised better security and higher returns.

We can summarize the above process as follows. After the establishment of a state's dominance in the world system, the centre-oriented flow of capital, knowledge and technology offered new opportunities for the development of the outer regions. But, with their development, competition inside the system was greatly intensified and gradually caused the hollowing of the dominant state, thus increasing the wealth gap among states and intensifying domestic social conflicts.

When reviewing the triangular relationship between China, the United States and Europe from the global system perspective, it may be seen that, in the early stage of financial expansion since the 1970s, China has entered the global development system. Consequently, on the one hand, China obtained billions of foreign funds and localized numerous industries. On the other hand, China entered the global market, especially the markets of developed countries.

In this situation, Chinese and European mutual interests were clear. During this period, despite ideological conflicts in the context of the Cold War, the bilateral relationship on the whole was very stable. But, with further global financial expansions, it seems that the mutual interests of China and the EU began to weaken. And when China entered the development stage of industrial upgrading, the surge of made-in-China products greatly affected the European market. Along with it came the challenges posed by the so-called China model, in which party, state, market, civil society, and civilization interrelate in a unique way and thus cannot be copied by other countries.

The European paradox and Sino–EU relations

In *Capitalism against Capitalism*, Michel Albert, the French economist, put forward the Rhine model of capitalism – now known as the Rhineland model. He thought that, following the collapse of the USSR, there were only two models for capitalism. One is the 'neo-American model' – now commonly referred to as the Anglo-Saxon model – which is based on the success of the individual and short-term financial profits. The other is the Rhineland model, which emphasizes collective success, referendum and long-term interests, as in Germany and Japan.[12] Compared with the Anglo-Saxon model, the Rhineland model values the establishment of a sound welfare system, using tax and welfare policies as the lever to achieve social harmony and justice. It could be said that, like most post-Cold War theories, Albert's theory was overly optimistic.

The end of the Cold War did not mean the end of history, but instead the beginning of a new historical era. Regarding the financial expansion since the 1970s, Arrighi pointed out that the system-wide expansion deprived the working classes in core countries (such as the US) of their privileges and power due to the continuous flow of capital and the emerging financial globalization.[13] From the 1950s until around 1972, the income gap between the rich and the poor in developed countries had narrowed significantly. However, since 1972, the world-wide income gap has been expanding both within and between states.[14] As reported by the BBC, from 1988 to 1993 the average world per capita real income increased by 5.7 per cent. while the growth rate for the richest 20 per cent populations could be as high as 12 per cent. But the gains went to the top 20 per cent of the income distribution, an increase of 12 per cent, while the income of the bottom 5 per cent actually declined by 25 per cent.[15] The middle class has been withering away globally. This survey raises concern about the lack of a 'middle class' at the global level, with most people concentrated at the bottom or at the top of the income scale. The huge gap between rich and poor – with 84 per cent of the world receiving only 16 per cent of its income and with the richest 10 per cent receiving 114 times the income of the poorest 10 per cent – has become more worrying and might continue to exist.[16]

From 1946 to the late 1960s, the gap between rich and poor households in the US narrowed significantly, but since then the gap has been gradually widening.[17] As in the US, the income difference of Western European countries decreased during the early post-war period, while from the 1970s the gap began to expand and continued to enlarge. In Germany, for example, in 2007, the average income of the richest 20 per cent was 4 times of that of the lowest 20 per cent while in 2005, it was 3.1 times and, in 1995, 2.8 times.[18] This shows that the income gap in Germany has been widening and will continue to accelerate. It is estimated that, up to 2009, there were more than 3 million German children living in poverty; in Berlin alone, up to 36 per cent of all children are poor.[19] According to a report from Xinhua News Agency in China, today's Britain under Gordon Brown is a more unequal country than at any time since modern records began in the early 1960s.

> During the 3 years of Brown's administration, deprivation and inequality in the UK rose for a third successive year and overall, the poorest 20% saw real income fall by 2.6% in the 3 successive years. The poorest 10% of households have seen weekly incomes fall by £9 a week to £147 once inflation is accounted for, while those in the richest 10% of homes have enjoyed a £45 a week increase to £1,033. About 15% of pupils in state schools are now entitled to free school meals because their parents receive welfare payments or earn below £15,575 a year.[20]

One main reason for the increase in poverty in 2007–2008 was the minimal income growth for the low-paid. At the same time, rising inflation had also eroded the real value of state benefits and tax credits. It can be seen that, in the context of global economic changes, the Rhineland Model has been fading away.

The Rhineland model, which can be characterized by three 'highs' (high welfare, high taxes and high budget) and once was a source of pride for Europeans, was actually difficult to work with in practice. Under the pressure of globalization, it was difficult for Europe to, on the one hand, compete with the United States in high-tech R&D, and, on the other, to meet the challenges from East Asia in automobiles, clothing and other traditional industries. As for EU internal integration, there have not been many substantial achievements since the mid-1970s. Despite the fact that the establishment of a unified market brought great achievements in economic integration and expansion, the EU, as a union of sovereign states, could not avoid major contradictions and conflicts between national interests and EU interests.

The year 2007 marked the 50th anniversary of the EU, and just prior to that moment there was a change in leadership in three key European countries – Germany, France and the United Kingdom (also called the Troika for European economic development). In 2005, German Premier Schröder gave way to Angela Merkel; British Prime Minister Tony Blair in 2007 was replaced by Gordon Brown; and in France Nicolas Sarkozy became president. After taking office, these new leaders unexpectedly adopted the Anglo-Saxon model and abandoned the Rhineland model. Chancellor Merkel conducted dramatic reforms on tax and education, which caused the German economy to grow greatly. The *Financial Times* said the German economy had finally got rid of the side effects of post-unity traumas, and that it had exceeded the growth rate of France for the first time since 1994 and become the economic engine of Europe again.

Europe does need deeper reforms. But, no matter how popular the concept of post-nationalism has become, nation-states still remain nation-states. The EU cannot adjust its industrial policies so dramatically as a sovereign state can. Research by Paul Krugman has shown that internal flows of resources in Europe are much weaker than in the United States.[21] On the one hand, there are many invisible trade barriers in the member states. On the other, Europe as a whole controls new markets strictly and most member states are greatly subject to public politics, and therefore it has been difficult to realize a breakthrough.

For the EU, the most urgent task is to change the excessive welfare system, to adjust the economic development model, to transfer the less competitive industries outside Europe and to upgrade high-end services. Protectionism will make the EU less competitive in the global economy. In the current period of hegemonic decline, the greatest common strategic interest for Europe and China is to maintain the global political and economic order.

In practice, China and Europe share important common interests for maintaining global currency stability. The 1944 Bretton Woods system set a fixed exchange rate system and pegged other currencies to the US dollar, and consequently linked to the gold standard. This actually required the US to keep a long-term trade deficit so that dollars would flow around the world and guarantee the supply of dollars.

This inevitably affected people's confidence in the dollar and thus caused a dollar crisis. If the United States maintained its balance, international reserves would be short in supply. This was known as the Griffin Problem. The world economy had experienced more than 20 years of steady growth under the Bretton Woods system, but this model had no potential to support the flood of dollars with equivalent gold. On August 1971, the Nixon administration in the US was forced to announce the separation between the dollar and the gold price and to conduct a floating exchange rate, which meant the collapse of the Bretton Woods system.

After this collapse, the alternative Jamaica system did not actually bring a more stable international financial system because of the poor implementation of some provisions. The basic idea of the Jamaica system is that the US dollar was linked to the IMF's Special Drawing Rights (SDR). The idea was good, for it combined a basket of major currencies for trade settlement. But the United States persuaded the Arab oil-exporting countries to use the US dollar for clearing, which subsequently formed a triangular global trade between petroleum, China-made products and American service sectors.

In the triangular trade based on American dominance, the United States provided a large number of industry transfers, technologies, services and currency. China provided low-cost industrial products and the Arab countries supplied oil with US dollar clearing. The Arab countries then invested their surplus in the US capital markets, while most of China's industrial foreign exchange also stayed mainly in the American capital market. Finally the United States provided high value-added services and financial operations to maintain this triangular flow between the US, China and the Arab countries. Europe was at the periphery in this system. Although the launch of the euro helped Europe itself to integrate further, it lacked the power to integrate the whole world. Not only that, even to the extent that the euro-zone and Russia were integrated into the global cycle, they were actually more stakeholders rather than beneficiaries.

Both China and the EU share a common interest regarding the stability of the global currency. The predominance of the US in the world and the deficiencies of the SDR kept the dollar as the main international reserve. Without the counter-balancing of gold, theoretically the amount of US dollars in circulation was mainly dependent on US self-discipline. In order to maintain global circulation, the US had to expand credits and in the long run this resulted in the devaluation of the dollar. In this context, the US government and consumers regarded borrowing as a rational choice. This was the underlying cause of the financial deficits and was also an important element of global financial imbalances.

In the current period of hegemonic decline, Europe and China need to cooperate for their involvement in the international mechanisms that emerge in the post-hegemonic era. The G-20 is a good example. After the financial crisis, which was triggered by American deficits, European countries urged the US to enter into multilateral dialogues. Although no substantive proposals were achieved from the 2008 Washington summit and the 2009 London summit, the G-20 may be able to play a greater role as a mechanism even if it is not the world economic government as described by some media. Despite the G-20 being just a forum, and not an international organization, nor equipped with a permanent secretariat, it did reflect the changes of international power which have continued to have strong momentum.

Secondly, China and Europe share a huge potential for cooperation in keeping political stability in the world. The emergence of non-traditional security threats is closely related to the social changes that are due to hegemonic decline. Gilpin pointed out that,

> intense conflict over resources and markets usually exists between expanding and declining sectors. Labor and capital in declining sectors resist being displaced by labor and capital in expanding sectors and become proponents of protectionism and nationalist policies. Political conflict ensues between declining and rising sectors over the control of economic policy.[22]

This was a cyclical process; this cycle repeated itself over and over again in modern history. Given the recurrent nature of this process, how different societies respond deserves further study.

As Arrighi points out,

> on the expansion phase of the system, the size and the destructive power of those social groups and classes who have been excluded from the benefits deriving from a social contract was on the rise. The fights triggered by these groups for the expansion of their rights were the main causes for competition between states and among enterprises.[23]

In the so-called expansion phase of the system, namely, the Phase B,

> the growing internal conflicts of elite group were the typical characteristics of hegemony transferring at various stages. On one hand, it was the response to the intensifying competition between states and enterprises. On the other hand, it increased the following social unrest.[24]

With the development of the world market, the changes of different actors' capability to act led to changes in power structure. When the hegemon's position is stable, its capital, technology and market, which pose a great attraction for other states, become important goods for dealing. During a hegemony's decline, rival countries acquire certain transferable resources which they are able to use to challenge the hegemonic power.

Intense rivalry between countries and within societies are thus undermining today's global power structures.

Currently, conflicts in the power structures were mostly relieved by some small-scale conflicts. According to Paul Rogers' studies, new forms of conflicts mainly concerned three new areas: the first, 'potential sources of conflict stem from a greater likelihood of increased human migration arising from economic, social and especially environmental desperation'.[25] The second area of conflict 'concerns environmental factors, especially the control of physical resources'.[26] The last relates to 'anti-elite violence, because an economically polarised and increasingly constrained global system will result in competitive and violent responses by the disempowered, both within and between states.'[27] To some extent, the Somali civil strife, the unrest in Algeria, the Passat peasant movement in Mexico and the Shining Path in Peru are all related to these new forms of conflict. It is true that reasons for violent conflict are varied, but the diminishing ability to control violence shows the declining capability for governance at the national level. Therefore, how a potential chain reaction of conflicts are managed and how current global imbalances are adjusted will determine the future of human society. This demands strategic insights and comprehensive cooperation at the global level to effectively manage the international political and economic system during hegemonic decline.

From a wider perspective, China and the EU have very important encompassing interests. Previously the China–EU relationship was to some extent subordinate to each side's respective relations with the US as the hegemonic power. Now, with the decline of hegemonic power and increasing instability of the world, the EU and China have become more focused on each other, overall and globally. With regard to the fluctuations in the global political-economic system, given the relatively simple conditions that in the past brought huge disaster to modern society, it is impossible to predict the full political, economic and social consequences caused by the current cycle of capital expansion. However, we may presume that mankind is facing an uncertain future. At this moment, we need to hope and believe that human beings have the ability and wisdom to improve the current situation. In this context cooperation between the major powers, in particular in-depth cooperation between China and Europe, is crucial.

In order to conduct multi-dimensional global cooperation between Europe and China, both should respect each other's culture, to understand different development models and to rationally deal with the relationship between domestic and international politics. Only with these strategic visions can Sino–European relations develop further and become healthier.

Notes

1 Mancur Olson, *Power and Prosperity: Outgrowing Communist and Capitalist Dictatorships*, New York: Basic Books, 2000.

2 Encompassing interests are sufficiently broad to include the key interests of other party. The term applies in a situation in which positive outcomes of the interaction between the involved parties will benefit all while negative results of interaction jeopardize all. For more about the definition of encompassing interests and evidence of its importance, see Olson, *Power and Prosperity*.
3 Samir Amin, *Shijie yitihua de tiaozhan* (Les défis de la mondialisation), trans.Ren Youliang with others, Beijing: Social Sciences Documentation Publishing House, 2003, p. 118.
4 Wang Zhengyi, *World System Theory and China*, Beijing: Commercial Press, 2000, p. 133.
5 Ibid., p. 313.
6 Robert Gilpin, *The Political Economy of International Relations*, Princeton: Princeton University Press, 1987, p. 97.
7 Giovanni Arrighi and Beverly J. Silver, with others, *Chaos and Governance in the Modern World System*, Minneapolis: University of Minnesota Press, 1999, p. 23.
8 Ibid., p. 23.
9 Ibid., p. 31.
10 Ibid.
11 Ibid.
12 Michel Albert, *Capitalism against Capitalism*, trans. Paul Haviland, London: Whurr Publishers, 1993, pp. 17–18.
13 Arrighi and Silver, *Chaos and Governance*, chapter 3.
14 Su Jingxiang, 'Pinfu chaju jiashen nanbei duili' available at:http://www.cpirc.org.cn/yjwx/yjwx_detail.asp?id=3530.
15 http://news.bbc.co.uk/chinese/simp/hi/newsid_1770000/newsid_1770500/1770507.stm.
16 Ibid.
17 Ibid.
18 http://news.xinhuanet.com/newscenter/2008-01/22/content_7468656.htm.
19 Tristana Moore, 'New Report Reveals the Depth of German Poverty', *Time*, 25 May 2009, available at:http://www.time.com/time/world/article/0,8599,1900649,00.html.
20 'Yingguo pinfu chaju he shehui bugong wei jin bange shiji zhizui', *PhoenixCNE*, 8 May 2009, available at:http://www.pcne.tv/index.php?option=com_content&task=view&id=6946&Itemid=98.
21 Paul Krugman, *Dili he maoyi* ('Geography and Trade'), trans. Zhang Zhaojie, Beijing: Beijing University Press, 2002, p. 74.
22 Gilpin, *Political Economy*, p. 99.
23 Arrighi and Silver, *Chaos and Governance*, p. 164–5.
24 Ibid., p. 165.
25 Paul Rogers, *Losing Control: Global Security in the Twenty-First Century*, London: Pluto Press, 2002, 2nd edn, p. 96.
26 Ibid.
27 Ibid., p. 96–7.

6 US–China–Europe security relations

Global security structure and order in the twenty-first century

Chu Shulong and Chen Songchuan

Introduction

We live in a changing world in the early twenty-first century, and, with the relative decline of the US, the rise of China, and European integration, the US has to share with China and Europe the role of major global actor. Thus, as Zbigniew Brzezinski remarked in 2004, 'In the coming 20 years, China–US–EU relationship will decide the trend of international relations.'[1] The global security structure, too, is undergoing a transformation from singlepolar to multipolar. In some global security fields, China and Europe are starting to share responsibilities with the US. This will lead to the remaking of the role of the US–China–Europe triangular relationship role in international security.

But the world is facing more major common challenges, especially in security areas, than ever before. In the words of the US National Intelligence Council (NIC): 'We now [2009] assess the potential for conflict – both interstate and intrastate – over the next 15–20 years to be greater than we anticipated in [2004].'[2] China, the US and the EU have very considerable influence; it is therefore critically important for all three to act as responsible stakeholders. However, the existing security relations between the US, China and Europe are primarily bilateral and focused at the regional level. This situation does not meet the demands of the international security reality. At the same time, there remains a vast lacuna in the knowledge and mutual understanding between the Chinese and Westerners and between Americans and Europeans. So, how to define and establish a new trilateral US–China–Europe security relationship at the global level is a challenge for us to think about.

The changing role of the major international security actors

There are four major international security actors in the world security system today: the United States, China, Russia and the European Union. In recent years, the power of the major international security actors has been changing greatly. The US still keeps its unique superpower position, but the realization of its global security responsibility depends more and more on its regional allies. By means of NATO, Europe plays a more and more important role in many regional security issues, such as in Kosovo and Afghanistan. At the same time, the EU plays a major role in the Middle East. China also plays an increasingly active role in international security affairs. The Chinese government hosts the Six Party Talks about the North Korean nuclear issue, and it also attends the meetings with other great powers on the Iranian nuclear issue. Compared to other the three actors, Russia's influence is declining.

The US: the only, but decreasing, superpower

Owing to the relative decline of its economy, and, to a lesser extent, its military power, the US is losing some of its flexibility in choosing among policy alternatives. But among the major international security actors, the US with its unmatchable military might undoubtedly remains as the only superpower. The US is unique in terms of having the capability to undertake military activities in any part of the world. It still has a greater impact on international security than any other actor in the twenty-first century. This was clearly demonstrated by the Iraq war and the Afghanistan war. While its Iraq escapade has led to a substantial decline in its security influence, the US continues to play an inevitable and dominant role in all kinds of international security affairs. In the Middle East, the US has been the most important driver behind any progress made since the peace process started. The US security umbrella still has a primary role in Europe and the Asia-Pacific area. Apart from regional security, the US retains its leadership role in other international security issues, such as proliferation and arms control.

However, the dramatic changes in international security relations, and the complexity of the current international security situation, have made it more difficult for the US to shape the international order and the direction of global affairs all by itself. In global and regional security arenas, the US demands its allies share more security responsibilities. Just as Vice President Biden said, 'America will do more, but America will ask for more from our partners. Here is what we will do and what we hope our partners will consider.'[3] That is why NATO is taking on new strategic missions in Kosovo and Afghanistan, outside the territory of its member states, and why it is drawing up a new Japanese–American security guarantee guideline. During the Cold War, the US shouldered the greatest strategic responsibilities in the West and the Asia-Pacific. The US guaranteed the security of Europe and of various Asia-Pacific countries. But now, although the US is still in a dominant position in security, it needs more assistance from its allies than before. The security relations between the US and its allies are undergoing a transformation from dependent to interdependent.

Europe: growing actor in global security

Since the 1990s, two great developments have taken place in the European security arena:

- NATO, the Cold War security regime, far from disappearing with the ending of the Cold War, actually showed a new vitality by increasingly expanding its strategic scope.
- The EU common foreign and security policy (CFSP) has made some progress.

These two great changes, especially the latter, have promoted Europe's position in the world security system, and made Europe an emerging global security actor. Nowadays, Europe plays its role in international security in two forms. One is as a part of NATO, the traditional military ally, by following the US leadership. The other is as an independent actor. As part of NATO, Europe undertook military deployments beyond the territory of its member states, first in Kosovo and subsequently in Afghanistan. As such, Europe engaged in a major military conflict outside its own borders for the first time since the end of the Cold War.

In the Middle East peace process, as one of the four parties involved, Europe plays a secondary role alongside the US. Still, it has repeatedly made its voice heard independently from Washington. Europe has a huge influence in the realm of nuclear non-proliferation. Not only in regard to the Iranian issue, but even in the North Korea nuclear issue, European exerts have exerted some influence now and then. In some key international security issues, we can conclude that Europe's global security influence is partly based on NATO's expanding influence, and partly relies on the common foreign and security policy progress. NATO and CFSP have become the two mechanisms by which Europe plays a more important role as a major global security actor.

NATO and the CFSP face several problems that constrain European influence in international security. Within NATO, any security action needs to follow the American leadership. If there are divergences between Europe and America or between different European countries, or both, the role of NATO in international security weakens. During the Iraq War, differences existed not only between America and some Europe countries (such as France and Germany), but also within NATO's European membership (which prompted the US to divide Europe into 'new Europe' and 'old Europe'). Moreover, Europe is facing difficult domestic challenges in its common foreign and security policy that could constrain its ability to play a larger global role, especially in the security realm. How it deals with these problems will determine the European role in global security. If the EU could complete its eastward enlargement to incorporate all eastern European countries, including Russia, this would be helpful for its role as a global security actor. Due to the common values shared by both sides of the Atlantic, Europe has become the inevitable assistant of America in international security. Of course, the most urgent problem is for the European nations to have a more substantial military capability. In addition, NATO and the European Union should have a common force planning and operational planning system with a single staff and location. Indeed large portions of the NATO and European Union strategic military staffs could be integrated.

China: moving from a regional to an inter-regional actor

After 30 years of reform and opening up, China has achieved great progress in its economic development. By the end of 2009, China had become the third largest economic power, just behind the US and Japan. Furthermore, China is regarded as a driver behind the global economy, together with the US. As Niall Ferguson said: 'Now that the age of leverage is over, 'Chimerica' – the partnership between the big saver and the big spender – is key.'[4] In the current economic crisis, along with the US, China is even supposed to lead the world economy away from recession. China's purchasing managers' index (PMI) rose to 53.5 in April from 52.4 in March.[5] This 'suggests that managers are cautiously optimistic in their outlook, following signs that the Chinese economy has bottomed out'. These data suggest that Chinese economy is starting to turn around. At the same time, it means the Chinese economy has the capability to survive the world economic crisis test, and has embarked on the way of stable development. China's sustainable and stable economic growth appeals to neighbours, and is a powerful demonstration that the main focus on the global stage is shifting from the West to the East. 'Few countries are poised to have more impact on the world over the next 15–20 years than China.'[6]

Since the Seventeenth National Congress of the Communist Party of China (CPC) in 2007, China has formed a certain and clear national strategy, known as the 'peaceful development road.' This term has two main meanings. The first is that China's foremost task is the long-term development of its economy. The second is that China' has chosen a peaceful development mode. China not only promotes cooperation with any type of country, but also enhances its neighbours' trust in itself. Furthermore, this approach is helpful to remove misunderstandings and fear about China's rise.

China is beginning to play an active role in international and regional security. As it is willing to take greater international and regional responsibility, China takes part in the building of regional security mechanisms. In North-East Asia, China is the host of the Six Party Talks about the Korean nuclear issue. These talks are regarded as North-East Asia's security mechanism. Meanwhile, China co-founded the Shanghai Cooperation Organization (SCO), which is developing into an important international organization for Central Asia's stability and development. At the same time, China is playing an active part in multilateral security initiatives. For instance,

China participates in the Iranian nuclear talks. Furthermore, China recently sent naval ships to carry out escort missions in the Gulf of Aden. China's influence in the international security is expanding from its neighbouring areas to regions much further away. China is growing into a global security actor.

Russia: the shrinking regional security actor

At the end of the Cold War, Russia, as the successor of the former Soviet Union, was the world's second great power after the US. But two factors are causing Russia's position to decline rapidly. The first is that its economic power has been diminishing greatly. Russia is now only the tenth largest economy in the world. The recent growth of the Russian economy was based on the export of energy, which depends on the international market. This means that Russia's economy fluctuates along with global economic trends. Recently, in order to strengthen its international influence, Russia began to use its oil and gas exports as strategic tools in its relations with the West. This stimulated the European countries which depend on Russian energy to turn towards other energy-producing countries. This, in turn, is weakening the Russian economy.

The second factor is the gradual shrinking of Russia's strategic scope. In 1991, when the Soviet Union collapsed, the Commonwealth of Independent States (CIS) was founded. After that, the CIS provided the main platform for Russia's strategic relations with the other parts of the former Soviet Union. But the decrease in Russia's economic power and the increasing demand of the other members for more engagement with other parts of the world such as the West and China induced many former parts of the Soviet Union to move away from the CIS and to come close to the EU and NATO. As a result the reach of Russia's influence has greatly diminished.

Russia's weakened economic power is just one element in the decline of its international influence. Equally significant is the eastward-expansion of NATO. In January 1994, NATO formally announced its plans for eastward expansion. Since then not only did all former East European members of the Warsaw Pact transform into NATO members, but also the three Baltic countries of the former Soviet Union entered NATO. And more countries are striving to obtain NATO membership. Furthermore, Moscow was also troubled by the European-based missile-defence system which the US was considering establishing. Although Russia has nuclear weapons and rich energy resources as strategic tools, its lack of a strong economic capability and the loss of a broad and deep strategic sphere of influence is limiting the Russian role in international security.

Apart from the Iranian nuclear issue, the Middle East peace process and the Six Party Talks on the North Korean nuclear issue, Russia plays only a limited role. Recently, the EU launched a new effort – the 'Eastern Partnership' – in an attempt to draw half a dozen countries that Moscow views proprietarily as its 'near abroad' away from its orbit. Senior Czech officials involved in organizing the summit where the Eastern Partnership was launched openly acknowledged that this EU initiative was aimed at countering Russia's influence in its backyard.[7] Under the then president Vladimir Putin Russia manifested a new assertiveness and attempted to reclaim its great power status, but the effects of this have been very limited.

The current state of US–China–Europe security relations

Current US–China–Europe security relations are characterized by regional security regimes or arrangements, although NATO's expansion gave the US–EU relationship a greater inter-regional character. Meanwhile, the existing US–China–Europe security relations are essentially three bilateral relationships, which have very different characteristics. The US–European security relationship (as NATO) has the longest history and is the closest and the most stable. It has clear goals and a mature organizational mechanism. US–China security relations are less direct and more complex, and contain some major elements of uncertainty. These make US–China security relations unstable. This bilateral security relationship comprises several effective mechanisms at the regional and national level, but requires further improvement. With regard to China and Europe, there are no direct security interests shared by these two actors. Their security relations have developed slowly in the past and the pace has only recently started to pick up.

None of these three bilateral relationships has close interaction with other bilateral security relationships. The security activities of these three actors are a part of several multilateral settings, such as the Association of Southeast Asian Nation's Regional Forum (ARF), and the Six Party meetings on the Iranian nuclear issue. Currently, cooperation coexists with competition in these three bilateral security relations. For instance, if NATO takes military action in the name of safeguarding human rights throughout Eurasia, this will naturally lead to Chinese concerns. There is the possibility of US–China or EU–China security relations deteriorating as a result of the traditionally strong transatlantic relationship.

The Atlantic Alliance: mature US–Europe security relations

Among the three bilateral security relationships, it is the US–European relationship which has been in existence for the longest time and which has produced the most mature organizational system. NATO was essentially a traditional political and military alliance for the West in dealing with the emerging military threat from the Soviet Union during the Cold War. From its inception until the early 1990s, NATO functioned as a classic collective security organization, by definition and in practice. The end of the Cold War and the demise of the Soviet Union deprived the military alliance of the reason and prerequisite for its existence.

Yet it did not resign itself to the prospect of becoming extinct. NATO retains its vitality as the main embodiment of US–Europe strategic relations through its eastward expansion and by enhancing European military capabilities within the NATO system. NATO was joined by several former Warsaw Pact states in 1999 and 2004. On 1 April 2009, its membership reached 28 when Albania and Croatia joined. At the same time, NATO's New Strategic Concept showed that the development of an European Security and Defence Identity within NATO is an essential element of NATO's ongoing adaptation. This process enables the European allies to make a more effective contribution to Euro-Atlantic security.[8] Furthermore, the Berlin Plus agreement is a comprehensive package of agreements between NATO and the EU that was concluded on 16 December 2002. With this agreement the EU was given the possibility of using NATO assets in order to act independently in an international crisis, on condition that NATO itself does not want to act – the so-called 'right of first refusal'. So only if NATO refuses to act will the EU have the option to do so. The most important reason why the US–Europe security relationship could remain stable is that NATO is based on common values, including democracy, human rights and the rule of law. The alliance has worked since its inception for the establishment of a just and lasting peaceful order in Europe. This objective remains unchanged.

In order to meet the new strategic environment of the post-Cold War era, NATO increasingly needs to be able to respond to new and unpredicted crises for either collective defence or crisis operations beyond the territory of its members borders. As a result NATO has renewed its security concept in 1990 and 1999. This suggests that the US–Europe security relations are undergoing a transformation from a regional focus towards a global focus. NATO's essential purpose set out in the Washington Treaty and reiterated in the London Declaration is to safeguard the freedom and security of its members by political and military means, in accordance with the principles of the United Nations Charter.[9] However, NATO has taken on several new missions, such as addressing regional conflicts, for example in Kosovo and Bosnia, the proliferation of weapons of mass destruction and their means of delivery, and transnational threats such as terrorism.[10]

In theory, the alliance's strategic concept of 1999 provides a workable roadmap for what these specific capabilities should be, and what particular threats and risks they will mostly have to deal with. Unfortunately, this pre-9/11 document does not provide a genuine threat and risk assessment, and therefore does not provide an adequately prioritized roadmap for expected NATO missions and objectives, and the possible ways of meeting them militarily.[11] After 11 September 2001, caution became no longer an option for the US. The enemy was located and the new role of NATO was clearly stated as to fight terrorism. So there was broad agreement that the 60th Anniversary Summit should launch a new Strategic Concept for the Alliance. The 'Defining the Military Dimension of the New Strategic

Concept', which the Military Committee recently presented to the Secretary General, provides a military framework for the New Strategic Concept and contributes to a common understanding of the new global strategic threats. This entails a revision of NATO's mission towards a global role. The NATO roles in Yugoslavia and Afghanistan indicate moves in this direction. Furthermore, another long-term role for NATO is combating piracy. The North Atlantic Council is currently preparing a political directive to NATO's military authorities for a long-term role in counter-piracy activities off the Horn of Africa.

Multilevel US–China security relations: semi-mature strategic relations

As US General Scowcroft stated recently, the US–Chinese economic relationship is probably the most important in the world, and China may be able to help, at least a little, in easing dangerous situations in North Korea and Pakistan.[12] While the economic side is the most stable part of the relationship, US–China security relations are more sensitive and fragile. Military ties have long been an indicator of the overall state of US–China relations. While realizing the common interests in the domestic and international security realm and the demands for cooperation with each other, US–China security relations have gradually been improving at bilateral and multilateral levels since the beginning of the twenty-first century, when the US viewed the rapidly developing China as a 'potential threat'. The 9/11 incident changed US understanding of the threats to its security and the terrorist threat to US became the No.1 issue in terms of its new security concept. The headquarters and main bases of global terrorist activities were in Afghanistan, next door to China. China has close relations with Pakistan and the Central Asian neighbour Afghanistan. China accordingly takes up a special position. As cooperation in the war on terror became an important common interest for China and the US, their security relations took off in a new direction.

Regarding regional security, the North Korean nuclear issue which emerged in 2003, led to the Six Party Talks in which US–China regional security cooperation plays a crucial role. Although the Six Party Talks have not prevented North Korea from obtaining nuclear weapons, the goal to denuclearize the Korean Peninsula has been agreed upon by all six countries, including North Korea. More important is that the talks have brought five of those countries (North Korea is the odd one out), closer in terms of dealing with regional security. The Six Party Talks will probably develop into a multilateral security cooperation mechanism in North-East Asia in future. At the same time, the US and China engage in security cooperation in the framework of APEC (Asia-Pacific Economic Cooperation). In bilateral security relations, after nearly three decades of development, the Chinese and the US militaries are now carrying out exchanges in many fields and at various levels. Institutionalized exchange modes have also been established, including defence consultations, working-level meetings between either side's defence ministry/department, maritime military security consultations, etc. Recently, the opening of the direct phone lines ('hotline') between the defence ministry/department) was a concrete expression of the enhancement of mutual trust.

In US–China security relations, multilateral security cooperation is developing more rapidly than bilateral security cooperation. This suggests the latter's complexity and uncertainty. It is the consensus in the international community that China's rapid rise as a regional political and economic power with growing global influence has significant implications for the Asia-Pacific region and the world.[13] Therefore, although there are many disputes between the US and China, economic and political cooperation continues to deepen. As pointed out by Wu Xinbo, 'security issues, emerging in the mid-1990s, now appear to be the most important factor affecting bilateral relations'.[14] Among these, the Taiwan issue is the most crucial one, especially US arms sales to Taiwan. As long as the current US Taiwan policy continues, Washington will remain unable to stabilize its relations with a rising China. At the same time, there are many misperceptions and conceptual differences between China and the United States. Chinese and US security interests in Asia both converge and diverge, and, as the US begins to contemplate China as a latent adversary, such divergence will become even more conspicuous. Hence, to enable durable, peaceful coexistence, both sides will have to make certain shifts in their current security policies. In the words of Henry Kissinger,

> The Sino–American relationship needs to be taken to a new level. This generation of leaders has the opportunity to shape relations into a design for a common destiny, much as was done with trans-Atlantic relations in the postwar period – except that the challenges now are more political and economic than military.[15]

China–Europe security relations: low-level with an uncertain potential

There have been no direct security links between China and Europe for a long time: compared with US–Europe and US–China, Sino–European security relations at a much lower level. They are less well-established, not clearly defined and there is no clear common understanding between Europe and China about the nature of their security relations. In all aspects of the China–EU relationship, security relations are linked to economic and political relations. The dialogue on security issues is a part of the annual EU–China summit. Along with the US, China and the EU participate in the ARF, while the Asia–Europe Meeting (ASEM) is another platform for China and the EU to communicate. In addition, China has also established formal bilateral counter-terrorism and defence consultation dialogues with France, the United Kingdom, and Germany. Europe and China, especially since the mid-to-late 1990s, have seen a steady overall convergence of interests. In the broader sense, neither side views the other as a main strategic threat.

To the degree European policymakers see 'threats' emanating from China, they tend to be either on questions of 'soft security' or on 'hard security' issues that have only an indirect impact on European security, such as arms proliferation by China.[16] To some extent, differences over the US approach to the global war on terror and the war in Iraq has promoted EU–China relations to develop in all aspects, so EU–China security relations in past few years have reflected the intention to balance US power, and push forward a multipolarized world. Currently, China–EU security relations are still in a relatively underdeveloped state. Two European observers stated in early 2008, that 'China is now one of the European Union's two main external partners, second only to the United States.'[17] This may refer to economic and certain political issues, but not to military or security issues.

Sino–European security relations appear more in specific security-related exchanges including global and regional security concerns, non-proliferation and arms control, peacekeeping, military transparency and defence exchange, military technology transfer and the arms embargo, and issues related to Taiwan. In recent years, the security- and military-related ties between the EU and China have also intensified. The bulk of EU–China security and military relations are largely in such 'soft' activities as strategic dialogue, military-to-military diplomacy and educational exchanges, port visits, peacekeeping training and some basic joint military exercising. The Council of the European Union has stated that the EU has 'a significant interest and stake in East Asian stability, security and prosperity'.[18] Thus, China and EU have a joint commitment to realize the peaceful stability and effective denuclearization on the Korea peninsula. Of course, if they intend to enhance their cooperation deeply in East Asia, China and EU need to better define their common ground on East Asia security interest. Now one task for both sides in security is a joint commitment to combat terrorism in Afghanistan and Pakistan. At the same time, there is a new chance for the EU and China to take on security cooperation through their respective existing mechanism with Africa. Non-proliferation and arms control takes a very important position in China–EU security relations. The EU and China signed the Joint Declaration on Non-Proliferation and Arms Control at the 2004 EU–China summit, which acknowledges the need to work together as 'strategic partners in the area of disarmament and non-proliferation'.[19] Hence, both sides have taken some steps to promote cooperation in such fields, especially in Iranian nuclear issues.

In peacekeeping, military transparency and defence exchanges, European and Chinese soldiers and experts have already been working alongside one another in support of several UN missions, including Kosovo, Darfur/ Sudan, Liberia and the Democratic Republic of the Congo (DRC).

There are many problems existing in China and European security relations too. Over the past decade, they have also had a fair share of controversy, especially related to the EU embargo on the sale of arms to China. The EU's position, as well as some individual EU member states, towards the Tibetan and Xingjiang issues, are seen by the Chinese government and people as a serious threat to China's national sovereignty, unity and territorial integrity. In addition, one of the major challenges for the EU–China relations is that the EU has been lacking in a unified position on its China policy.

The possible future development of US–China–Europe security relations

Now, cooperation is the main catchword in US–China–Europe relations, not only in the economic field, but also in the security arena. Because the world has been faced with more major common challenges than ever before, a renewed global governance system is a pre-condition to successfully meeting these challenges. And the three sides all confront the common long and urgent to-do list, especially in world security issues, including the traditional security and non-traditional security problems. That reflects a wide security cooperation scope. The US, China and Europe have been using current bilateral and multilateral mechanisms and establishing new mechanisms to cope with these problems too. In the regional security field, concerning the Afghanistan issue, the US–EU's security mechanism – NATO – is the main actor, while China plays only a supporting role. On the Iranian nuclear issue, US–China–Europe security consultation plays a balancing role through the meeting of foreign ministers of six countries plus Iran (US, China, Russia and three EU countries: the United Kingdom, France, and Germany). In the Six Party Talks about the North Korean nuclear issue, the US and China are the major players, while the EU plays a supporting role. And the US, China and Europe all participate in the ARF. In the non-proliferation field, China, the US and the EU have founded bilateral consultation mechanisms. In non-traditional security, apart from anti-terrorism, the US, China and the EU have started the consumer product safety cooperation. In sum, although the three parties' security relations are not as comprehensive and deep as their economic relations, the US, China and Europe have all realized that security cooperation is in their common interests and have started to enhance their security relations in bilateral and multilateral settings, preparing the ground for establishing trilateral cooperation further at the strategic level.

Although US–China–Europe security relations are developing at the more comprehensive level, there are still many difficulties. First, what role EU will play depends on its progress of 'the common voice'. While the EU has advanced very much in this process, it is still having great difficulty in forging a common foreign and security policy. Secondly, NATO is facing a new strategic environment. NATO leaders' voice strong desires to launch a new strategic concept to define its task. Thirdly, there are increasing transatlantic political tensions, because of a strong sense of disagreement between the

US's unipolar and the EU's multipolar approaches. And, finally, there is the potential for hostilities between the West and China, especially due to mutual distrust. A socialist China which is rapidly developing is a difficult fact for the US and the EU to accept. Just as the Pew Global Attitudes Survey of 2007 suggested, in the US and Europe, the public have negative views toward China (see Table 6.1). After all, they see themselves as enemies during the Cold War and remain wary of each other. Thus, how to resolve those problems and shape new US–China–Europe trilateral security relations in order for these to contribute to global peace and stability is a crucial strategic issue.

The prospect for US–China–Europe: the emerging world security structure (G-3)?

As China's influence in the world increases, the US carries on with its world leadership role, and the EU is strengthening its position as a more cohesive and effective voice in international affairs (it is important not to neglect the possibility of Russia integrating with the EU in the future), so in the perspective of the capabilities and geo-strategic situation, the US–China–Europe grouping will reflect the world power structure, not only in economic and political terms, but also in security terms: their security relations will form one important part of the new world order or arrangement. But existing US–China–Europe security relations appear more in bilateral relations and multilateral security mechanisms, and do not have a clear trilateral nature. So we need to consider their trilateral cooperation in a global perspective. The three powers have already realized the importance of US–China–Europe security relations in the world community. Daniel Fried, US Assistant Secretary of State for European and Eurasian Affairs,

Table 6.1 How China's growing power affects your country (%)

| | Growing military power | | Growing economic power | |
	Good thing	Bad thing	Good thing	Bad thing
United States	15	68	41	45
Spain	15	58	35	44
France	15	84	35	64
Britain	12	66	45	55
Sweden	9	61	62	18
Italy	7	70	19	65
Slovakia	10	75	33	44
Bulgaria	10	42	34	36
Poland	8	72	33	44
Czech Rep.	8	83	34	56

Source: Pew Attitudes Project, http://pewglobal.org/reports/display.php?ReportID=256.

said recently that 'NATO is a trans-Atlantic organization, but Article 5 now has global implications. NATO is in the process of developing capabilities and political horizons to deal with problems and contingencies around the world. That is a huge change.'[20] Henry Kissinger pointed out that

> to promote [Sino–US cooperation on addressing security issues in various parts of the world] we need an informal G2. The relationship between the US and China has to be truly a comprehensive global partnership, parallel our relations with Europe and Japan. Our top leaders should therefore meet informally on a regular schedule for truly personal in-depth discussions regarding not just about of bilateral relations but about the world in general.[21]

In Robert Francis Cooper's opinion, the type of global leadership which Europe envisages is one in which the US, Europe and China jointly play a leading role, that is, a collective leadership in global governance.[22] These voices may present some major trends in the global development and need us to think about.

In general, security cooperation between the US, China and Europe would need to be made more concrete, increasing trilateral ordinance step by step, and at last forming the perfect trilateral mechanism on the basis of existing bilateral and multilateral mechanisms to promote the new world order.

Currently, less emphasis is placed on security issues than on economic ones, but the outcome of the misperception and misunderstanding which result from the 'security dilemma' is more serious than that of the economic friction. So, the US–China–Europe grouping should shape up as 'stakeholders' to manage their security relations more systematically and promote the greater development of trilateral cooperation.

First, all three need to take a more global and comprehensive strategic view of the US–China–Europe triangle. It demands a trilateral approach to justify its role in international security responsibility, and to emphasize the cooperation and coordination in international and regional security areas initiatively, so its aims could be realized by the new strategic environment in future.

Secondly, in order to account for the increasing international responsibility of China and Europe, the US should make room for them in global security, not only through drawing up new NATO strategic concepts, but also through promoting the EU's participation and accepting and encouraging China as a active actor in regional and international security affairs.

Thirdly, the three parties need to form a more effective security coordinating mechanism. In coping with emerging security challenges, such as denuclearization on the Korea peninsula, Afghanistan, the Iranian nuclear issue and proliferation and arms control, the US, China and Europe have already taken up a joint commitment. But they should also develop a more mature trilateral cooperation mechanism. Moreover, trilateral security relations need to strengthen the cooperation mechanism in the UN as well as beyond the UN system.

Fourth, to get rid of misunderstandings and suspicion between the West and China is another important task for the three actors. China must make its strategic aims clear and provide understanding of what kind of country it is becoming. The US and the EU should jointly reduce their hostility towards China, and narrow their differences about whether the world should be unipolar or multipolar. At the same time, the US and the EU should understand China's serious concern over its core national interests, such as Taiwan, Tibet and Xingjiang. On these internal and national security interests China will not compromise.

Finally, how to deal with relations between NATO and the EU is a challenge for the trilateral security relations. NATO is determined to expand its membership circle and to expand its mandate. Ultimately NATO is likely to become a global military force. Meanwhile the EU is advancing in terms of an integrated defence policy, and will eventually complete its integration process. So NATO's and the EU's different responsibilities need to be made clear.

In the future, as a stable structure in international relations, the US–China–Europe security mechanism will probably take on a more active role. The following are possible trends:

- The power of the US, China and Europe will be more balanced, but also the balance of trilateral security relations will appear. The balanced strength can already be seen in economic and political fields, and it will also happen in the military power. Along with US–China and China–Europe bilateral security relations, trilateral security will eventually also be more in balance.
- Although disagreement still exists, the consensus on the main security issues will surpass the dispute among the trilateral powers. The increasing common challenges which countries cannot deal with alone will strengthen the consensus that the international community demands greater cooperation. Thus, along with the acknowledgement of the global problems and challenges in the world, and the increasing need for the trilateral parties to work together in their security relations, trilateral coordination can develop and become a more mature one in the long-term future.
- Certainly, the security mechanism between the US, China and Europe is a blend of bilateral and multilateral, but it will be more flexible and diversified. In different regions and on different issues, the three parts will have different levels of cooperation and coordination. At the same time, the trilateral security mechanism will be involved in more international security activities, and will have a stronger influence on world security.

- In the trilateral cooperation, China will play a more active role in the world security activities and take more international responsibility, thus becoming a 'stake-holder' in international security. Through participating in international security activity, China's military policies will become more transparent, enhancing the mutual understanding between the West and China.
- The trilateral cooperation and coordination will be beneficial in forming new methods to deal with international security affairs. Because of their different strategic cultures, the US, China and Europe in dealing with international security problems are different in some sense. The core of China's strategic culture is to find the golden mean and to refrain from dominating other countries. It thus focuses on the non-aggressive and flexible patterns. Europe's focus is on institution-building and values; while the US pays attention to power/strength and also values. Through three-party cooperation, it would be possible to bring in a more reasonable approach to international security problems.

Conclusion

Currently the priority of the three powers is with political and economic relations rather than with security relations. The US, China and Europe have become established powers in the international security arena, and their growing mutual interdependence in the post-Cold War era calls for new concepts, new fields and new ways of cooperation. It is time to review the state of the three bilateral relationships and advance their trilateral relations. As we all know, treating someone as your enemy is frequently a self-fulfilling prophecy. We must together look at the global context and the potential of common ground. Therefore, it is necessary to transform US–China–Europe security cooperation – which currently lacks a mechanism – into a new trilateral security cooperation mechanism. We may call this a drive for 'neo-trilateralism'. In our view, US–China–Europe security relations will become the most important force for international peace and security. It would be helpful for constructing a new global security regime or arrangement. Of course, this 'neo-trilateralism' would not be a traditional alliance as currently exists between the US and Japan, or the US and Europe. It would be a working relationship. Through establishing both formal and informal mechanisms to discuss common problems that confront the international community, there would be greater opportunities for contact and communication. As such both US–China–Europe security cooperation and global peace and stability would benefit.

Notes

1 Brzezinski quote according to Stanley Crossick, 'China, EU & US: Holy trinity or ménage à trois?', *Blogactiv*, 18 June 2006, available at: http://crossick.blogactiv.eu/2008/06/18/china-eu-us-holy-trinity-or-menage-a-trois/.

2 'Global Trends 2025: A Transformed World', Washington DC: US National Intelligence Council, 2009, p. 61, available at: http://www.dni.gov/nic/NIC_2025_project.html.
3 Joe Biden, speech at the 45th Munich Security Conference, available at: http://www.securityconference.de/konferenzen/rede.php?menu_2009=&sprache=en&id=238&
4 Niall Ferguson, 'Team 'Chimerica'', *Washington Post* , 17 November 2008.
5 'China Posts Increase in Manufacturing Activity', *Wall Street Journal*, 4 May 2009.
6 'Global Trends 2025: A Transformed World', Washington DC: US National Intelligence Council, 2009, p. 29, available at: http://www.dni.gov/nic/NIC_2025_project.html.
7 Ian Traynor, 'EU Pact Challenges Russian Influence in the East', *Guardian*, 7 May 2009, available at: http://www.guardian.co.uk/world/2009/may/07/russia-eu-europe-partnership-deal.
8 'Fact Sheet: Nato's New Strategic Concept', 24 April 1999, available at: http://ftp.fas.org/man/nato/natodocs/99042450.htm.
9 NATO, 'The Alliance's New Strategic Concept', available at: http://www.nato.int/docu/comm/49-95/c911107a.htm - 57k.
10 Ibid.
11 Pavel Necas, 'Beyond Tradition: A new strategic concept for NATO?', Rome: NATO Defense College, 2004, available at: http://www.isn.ethz.ch/isn/Digital-Library/Publications/Detail/?ord516=OrgaGrp&ots591=0C54E3B3-1E9C-BE1E-2C24-A6A8C7060233&lng=en&id=14523
12 Gerald F. Seib, 'A Policy Shaper Sees Improvement in US Ties with China, Russia', *Wall Street Journal*, 4 May 2009.
13 'Annual Report to Congress: Military Power of the People's Republic of China', Washington DC: US Department of Defense, 2009, p. I, available at: http://www.defense.gov/pubs/pdfs/China_Military_Power_Report_2009.pdf.
14 Wu Xinbo, 'US Security Policy in Asia: Implications for China–US Relations', September 2000, available at: http://www.brookings.edu/papers/2000/09northeast asia_xinbo.aspx?p=1.
15 Henry Kissinger, 'The World Must Forge a New Order or Retreat to Chaos', *Independent*, 20 January 2009.
16 Bates Gill and Melissa Murphy, 'China–Europe Relations: Implications and Policy Responses for the United States', available at: http://www.csis.org/index.php?option=com_csis_pubs&task=view&id=4498.
17 Francois Godement and Mark Leonard, *China Analysis*, 17, January–February 2008, available at: http://www.centreasia.org.
18 Gill and Murphy, 'China–Europe Relations', p. 16.
19 'Joint Declaration of the People's Republic of China and the European Union on Non-Proliferation and Arms Control', Beijing: Ministry of Foreign Affairs of the People's Republic of China, 9 December 2004, available at: http;//www.chineseembassy.org/eng/wjdt/2649/t173749.htm.
20 Press roundtable, 17 April 2007, available at: http://prague.usembassy.gov/md704-fried.html.
21 Henry Kissinger, 'Moving Toward a Reconciliation of Civilizations', *China Daily*, 16 January 2009, available at: http://www.chinadaily.com.cn/opinion/2009-01/15/content_7399816.htm.
22 Zhang Xinghui, 'Europe Strives for US–China–Europe to Govern World in "Collective Leading" Form', *Zhongguo Qingnian Bao*, 16 October 2008.

7 Russia–China–Europe security relations

Feng Feng

The EU, Russia, and China are the three most important strategic forces on the Eurasian continent. Their triangular relations are currently the most significant strategic combination in international politics and perhaps even in the foreseeable future. The reasons are that:

- four permanent members of the UN Security Council are included in this triangular relationship, whose political influence plays a very important role;
- the three parties are composed of Russia, with its military power, China, ancient civilization and rising power, and major long-standing powers such as the UK, France and Germany;
- their territories extend from the Atlantic to the western rim of the Pacific, amounting to 56 per cent of the total area of Europe and Asia;
- competition among big powers for international influence in modern times has been deeply connected with this area.

Security relations between China, the EU and Russia therefore have a significant influence on the global security environment. However, compared with other combinations of the great powers, such as the US–EU–Russia, China–US–Russia and China–US–Japan etc, the triangle relations between China, Russia and the EU attract little attention. In this chapter, the character and status quo of the Russia–China–EU security relations are discussed from three perspectives: notion, interests and interaction.

Multilateralism as a shared security notion

The framework of security relations is decided initially by the security notions of the three parties, of which an important commonality is that each party tends to pursue multilateralism, which entails resolving contradictions and differences among nations by peaceful ways of negotiation and dialogue. The security notion of multilateralism is not only essentially different from unilateralism and pre-emption pursued by previous US policies, but also deviates from traditional security thinking which emphasizes the build-up of power by individual states to deal with the military threat of enemy states and potential enemy states. The latter often leads to a security dilemma and an arms race.

Member states of the EU, reflecting on early twentieth-century European experiences, realized the great significance of multilateralism. Europe was the main battlefield of the two world wars and European states and people suffered much from them. The European Economic Community, the predecessor of the EU, started from difficult circumstances after the devastation of the Second World War. The member states of the EU abandoned unilateralism and stepped forward in the direction of integration of economy and politics. The foundation, expansion and integration of the EU are actually the adoption and employment of multilateralism, which is one of the most important methods of resolving the great powers' struggle for hegemony, maintaining the prosperity and long-term peace after the Second World War. So it can be said that EU is the biggest beneficiary of multilateralism. As one of the internal principles of EU, multilateralism gradually became an important rule in dealing with international affairs.

After the latest expansion to the east, the GDP of the EU, whose economic and political influence is increasing day by day, almost equals that of the US. The EU not only endeavours to obtain the decisive power of stipulating the rules of international trade, but also tries to possess the power of establishing the norms of international monetary relations. In international affairs, the EU is growing as an important strategic force that is evidently different from the US, which pursues the establishment of a unipolar world order. Although allies of the US, Germany and France have quite different views on such issues as missile defence, the Kyoto Protocol and so-called rogue states. The EU opposes the US policy of realpolitik and unilateralism, and insists on solving international issues by way of communication, dialogue and cooperation. At the same time, the EU advocates the establishment of a world order of multilateralism on the basis of international law and within the framework of the UN and other international agencies, an obviously different approach from the idea of unilateralism plus the coalition of the willing and the military strategy of pre-emption pursued by the US.

The EU's understanding of international politics and national security is coincident with that of China. In the course of its thousands of years of history, China has realized that great power struggles for hegemony are not the best way of obtaining and prolonging prosperity. From the foundation of the PRC, the Chinese government has been emphasizing that, when it is pursuing its own security, the security of other states must also be taken into consideration. Since the 1990s, China has consistently advocated a new security concept, the core of which is mutual trust, mutual benefit, equality and cooperation, and has the aim of accelerating common security through dialogue and cooperation.

The new security concept is based on the Chinese worldview, which values harmony while allowing for differences between nations. China and the EU are jointly against unilateralism and put emphasis on multilateralism to maintain democracy and the rule of law in international politics, emphasizing the effects of the UN and other international organizations in global affairs and opposing arms abuse. Both sides also share some common grounds on the establishment of a new order of international politics which embodies demands for human progress. The Russian approach is similar to that of France and Germany, in that Russia also emphasizes the UN mechanism and holds that international organization should play a more important role in international affairs. At the same time, Russia recognizes the value of forming partnerships with other great powers in order to improve its own international position.

In the traditional security sphere, the principles of multilateralism advocated by the EU, China and Russia display mainly in stressing collective security and common interests, highlighting the core part of the UN in international system. Firstly, the three parties do not pursue the military advantage over the other two as the basis of self security. In the nuclear arms era, it is not a reliable security concept for one's security to be established by having a military advantage over the opponent. And, secondly, the three parties share similar grounds on the series issues as the prevention of weapons of mass destruction (WMD) proliferation, arms- and armament-control, peacekeeping, etc. For instance, on the denuclearization of the Korean peninsula, the three parties prefer to solve the issue by way of negotiation, not by force. Thirdly, after the Cold War, the EU and Russia build up the security space between them, which is a security cooperation mechanism as a systematic plan. On the Iraq war, a temporary alliance was composed by France, Russia and Germany, which emphasized the role of the UN, so as to contain the unilateralism and the coalition of the willing advocated by the US.

In the non-traditional security sphere, starting from multilateralism, China, the EU and Russia share similar standing and policy on a number of important issues. Firstly, they recognize that many non-traditional security issues cannot be resolved by military force. Secondly, the cognition of most EU member states on the security threat was different from that of the US, while being similar to China and Russia. They considered that the US exaggerated the threat from terrorism, and anti-terrorism cannot be called a war; the solution to terrorism depends on the combination of different ways and treatment of both symptoms and root causes. The EU high representative for common foreign and security policy and former NATO Secretary-General Javier Solana wrote that Europeans 'view terrorism as the most extreme and reprehensible symptom of a broader and deeper political dysfunction', and tend to see it as 'one of several threats, alongside poverty, unresolved regional conflicts, pandemic diseases, and climate change'.[1] Thirdly, the three parties realize that the continuous development of economy, society, environment protection and global climate change should be treated strategically. However, the resolve of these issues depends on the participation of every nation and within the framework of multilateralism.

Naturally there exist some differences between the three actors' security notions, but these do not amount to structural contradictions. Especially in regard to security relations, the notion of multilateralism takes up a dominant position.

Security interests

The security interests of China, the EU and Russia determine the characteristics of their mutual security relations. Generally speaking, the three actors share extensive common security interests. At the same time, there also exist differences that cannot be ignored.

Common interests

The common interests of the three parties of China, the EU and Russia have been increasing daily since the end of the Cold War, especially since entering the twenty-first century. As great power centres of Eurasia, the maintenance of stability and prosperity of the continent and the balance of global strategy is conforming to their common concerns.

Firstly, on the aspect of world structure, with the US becoming the only superpower after the Cold War, the strategic circle of the US was full of confidence and expectation to establish a unipolar world order dominated by America. On the unipolar world order, owing to different reasons, the three parties do not counterbalance US power policy, whereas historically, counterbalancing the hegemonic state is the usual way taken by other powers. Even so, the three parties have unanimously agreed that the unipolar world order was not in accordance with their own strategic interests. States such as France and Germany did not follow the steps of the US to establish a unipolar world centred on the US. According to former president of France, Jacques Chirac, the unipolar world is essentially unbalanced and the world must be rebalanced by a multipolar world order where a variety of powers balance or offset the power of the US.[2] After a meeting with former Italian Prime Minister Romano Prodi in the Russian resort of Sochi in January 2007, President Vladimir Putin said that, since the end of the Cold War, the US has had the illusion that the world is unipolar and that all problems can be resolved from one centre. But, in fact, a unipolar world order cannot solve the mounting crises on the globe and Russia therefore advocates a multipolar world. Putin also said that Russia will independently determine its place in the world and seek a balanced and multipolar world order.[3]

Secondly, in the field of traditional security, China, the EU and Russia do not constitute threats to each other. Traditional security issues refer mainly to geopolitics and military security. Although in the domain of traditional security, the main attention is paid to military security, the relations between China, Russia and EU had surpassed zero-sum game thinking after the end of the Cold War. At the same time, as permanent members of the UN Security Council, the three parties share extensive common grounds in regional security, WMD proliferation, disarmament and armament-control, peace-keeping, etc. The effort of maintaining the stability of international situation from each side was supported by the other; and they all try to avoid the tension of regional and global confrontations. None of the three states wants to see the proliferation of WMD globally and they coordinate with each other to prevent such a phenomenon. For example, after the India and Pakistan nuclear weapon tests in May 1998, China, Europe, and Russia took the same stance in the UN Security Council. On the issue of the American invasion of Iraq, Russia, France, Germany and China actually formed an alliance with each other and thwarted American's attempt to get UN permission to invade Iraq. On the method employed in Iraq war, some EU member states such as France and Germany shared the same views with China and Russia.

However, in the field of traditional security, the common interests of the three are not an equilateral triangle. Those shared by China and Russia are larger than those of EU–China and EU–Russia:

1 *Maintenance of territorial integrity.* China and Russia both face the great task of safeguarding the integrity of sovereignty and territory. It is considered by many scholars that, for instance due to economic problems, the possibility of a Russian collapse similar to what happened to the Soviet Union cannot be precluded. Henceforth, China and Russia share the same concern regarding the threat of regional independence movements, and focus on maintaining national territorial integrity. EU member states do not have this concern.

2 *Maintenance of peace and stability of domestic and foreign situations.* As far as China is concerned, it has put most of its effort into domestic construction in order to realize peaceful development and finish the process of modernization as soon as possible. China believes that global peace and stability, especially peaceful surroundings, is a must for the smooth undertaking of modernization construction. The significance of the peace and stability in Eurasia is as important as that of the Asian-Pacific region for the security and economic development of China. Since the breakdown of the Soviet Union, Russian power cannot parallel that of the Soviet Union as a superpower. And, after the chaos and economic recession in 1990s, Russia is paralleling China in adopting an opening-up policy to the outside world. They all expect a favourable situation, both internally and externally, which is suitable for domestic development. So far as the EU is concerned, for the predictable future, the situation that threatened EU security and stability is not about to come into being.

3 *Common interests in the non-traditional security field.* In recent years, the security threat from non-traditional fields has become more prominent

and caused the diversity of security needs for each state. The common concerns shared by China and Russia in this field are the acceleration of economic development, the stabilization of the international financial system, environmental pollution, global climate change, combating terrorism, drug trafficking, piracy, international crime and such threats from communicable diseases as SARS, Avian influenza and A influenza. It is against the globalization background that communication of people and economy become more frequent and a single country cannot deal with such a non-traditional security threat. In dealing with such threats to human beings, both China and the EU are willing to strengthen cooperation. For example, on the solving of the current international financial crisis, although the financial strength and financial status of the three are different, they share some basic interests in restoring the stability of international financial system, regaining economic growth and even reforming the international financial system.

On the issue of terrorism, although Chinese and Russian definitions of 'terrorism' are different from that of EU, the aim of eradicating terrorism is almost the same between the three parties. Combating terrorism and eliminating threats of terrorism are common interests. China and Russia share extensive common interests in combating the three disruptive forces of terrorism, separatism and extremism, and the maintenance of the stability of mid-Asia. The EU and Russia are interdependent in non-traditional security issues. Russia and the EU share some common ground in anti-terrorism and dealing with organized international criminal groups. Therefore, the three parties need to strengthen their cooperation and make efforts with other countries with the aim of making progress in the battle to resolve these threats.

Differences of interests

Although the three parties share extensive common interests in the security field, it is inevitable that some contradictions and differences exist.

Russian interests are quite different from those of China and the EU in strategic objectives. Traditionally, Russia is an expansionist nation. Since the foundation of Russia in the mid-fifteenth century, Russia expanded its territory continuously for over 500 years, increasing its size from a small dukedom to a great empire extending over Europe and Asia. In its expansion history, Russia has suffered many setbacks. The breakdown of the Soviet Union is the latest one. Its weakened power has forced Russia to take a defensive policy. Once Russia regains its power, the possibility of great powers contending for hegemony may occur again.

Both China and the EU lack the internal impetus for hegemony. Although two of the main countries involved in EU integration, a feud had existed between France and Germany since at least the Napoleonic Wars and the Franco-Prussian War; they had been conquered by each other during both

World Wars. However, after the end of the Second World War, France and Germany realized that the catastrophe had been caused by striving for hegemony, so they got rid of that centuries-old policy. It is the traditional culture of China that sculptures the introvert character of Chinese people, which also stipulates that China did not expand or possess the liability for hegemony. Some scholars put this peculiar and unique phenomenon into the Chinese tradition of its 'no-soldier' culture.[4] That's why China is the most resolute one in resisting unipolar world order; China is against any nation which may become hegemonic power and does not want to be a hegemon itself.

The second is the issue of anti-terrorism. China and Russia are for cracking down on any form of terrorism in any place. However, double standard exists in this respect in EU member states and the US. Military actions of the Irish Republican Army are regarded as terrorism, while terrorist actions in the Xinjiang Autonomous Region are regarded as activities for national liberation or freedom and human rights actions by the EU and America. Similarly Russia considers Chechnya as an inseparable part of Russia and the activities of Chechnyan terrorists did harm to the federation; once again, the EU considered these activities to be for national independence, not terrorism.

The third is in the field of traditional security. Although there is no security contention in mid-term for the three parties, and common grounds are greater than the differences, a series of differences in interest still exist. Generally speaking, differences between the EU and Russia are greater than those between China and the EU, and China and Russia:

1 *China–Europe.* Geopolitically speaking, China and the EU do not threaten each other; and there is no security contention. However, the EU arms embargo impairs China's security interests and is politically discriminatory. As for Tibet, China considers this issue relates to the principle of sovereignty and integrity of territory, which is in the domain of national security, whereas the EU considers the issue of the Dalai Lama as a matter of human rights and religious freedom, which is not as serious as China had thought. In the field of regional security, differences also exist between China and the EU. Supported by the EU, NATO bombed Yugoslavia in 1999, which was against the national security interests of China. China advocates resolving international conflicts by peaceful means and is against arms and arms threat. Armed interference under the pretext of humanitarianism is not acceptable to China.

2 *China–Russia.* Since the end of the Cold War, China's and Russia's common interests are becoming increasingly greater. On the signing of the supplementary agreement on their eastern border, China and Russia have eradicated a potential point which might have led to conflict. But, even so, the differences between the two cannot be neglected. Differences between them are not the same as differences between other

countries; their differences are mainly on understanding and cognition. The boundary between China and Russia stretches for several thousand kilometres; and Russia has in the past seized several million square kilometres of land from China, although the land has been stipulated by several agreements, Russia is concerned about a possible retaliation by China when she regains her power. In the past ten or twenty years, their comparative strengths have been reversed for the first time in modern times. The Russia has powerful nuclear weapons, but in terms of economic power, Russia cannot compare with China. This is the root cause for the notion of a 'China threat' that exists in Russia. Alexander Sharavin, director of the Moscow-based Institute for Political and Military Analysis and a member of the Russian Academy for Military Sciences, wrote that the relationship between China and Russia is a point of destiny: China is a threat to Russia whether it is strong or weak.[5] The worries in Russian strategic circles are the result of misunderstandings not only of Chinese traditional culture and history, but also of the status quo of China. China when weak pursues peaceful development, and, will stick to the diplomatic and security policy of peaceful development even when stronger in the future. These are not mere diplomatic words, but determined by the tradition of Chinese history and culture and national characteristics. Therefore the so-called conflict in security interests does not exist. China, as the victim, has scrapped its historical antipathy towards Russia to pave the way for an improved relationship; but Russia is unable to match China's repositioning.

3   *EU–Russia.* Although structural contradiction does not exist between Russia and the EU in traditional security areas, the conflict of interests was not halted by the end of the Cold War. Differences between the EU and Russia are complex, due not only to the lack of confidence caused by historical resentment, but also actual geo-political concerns and the reflex of 'new Europe' and 'old Europe' on EU–Russian relations, even with some elements filtered by the US. The lack of mutual trust between Russia and the EU is deeply rooted and its influence is persistent,[6] due to the historical entanglement and actual disputes of interests. The EU has expanded to Russia's western border since the end of Cold War. For Russia, this eastward expansion is not a serious problem, and it is not the reason for EU and Russian tension. But new Eastern European member states have shown their anti-Russian attitudes since entering the EU. Therefore, the former hostility between Russia and Eastern Europe countries has developed into tension between Russia and the EU. Generally speaking, new EU member states such as Poland and the Czech Republic are more favourable to the US than previously existing member states and against Russia. In many cases, these new member states have 'hijacked' the EU to harm Russian interests. US-led NATO's transatlantic security issues is the main fuse for EU and Russia tensions.

In the early part of 2007, Poland and the Czech Republic allowed the US to establish anti-missile systems in their countries, which led to strong Russian reactions. On receiving no active reply after a series of warnings, Russia declared in July 2007 that it would no longer adhere to the Treaty on Conventional Armed Forces in Europe, and officially suspended this treaty in December 2007. In August 2007, Russia also resumed routine long-range fighter-bomber flights after a 15-year suspension. The EU's interference in the 'colour revolution' of CIS (Commonwealth of Independent States) countries was interpreted by Russia as an infringement of its geopolitical space, which is a new point of friction between Russia and the EU. And, further, on the Kosovo and South Ossetia issues, Russia and the EU are in a stalemate.

But, generally speaking, the common interests of the three parties are larger than the differences in the field of non-traditional security; while in the domain of traditional security, differences and common interests combine together. And differences between the three parties in the traditional security field are greater than those in the non-traditional field.

Security interaction

After the end of the Cold War, China, Russia and the EU established three sets of bilateral relations: the EU–Russia strategic partnership, the China–EU comprehensive strategic partnership and the China–Russia strategic partnership of cooperation, which is one part of security interactions. The security interactions of the three parties are not only a manifestation of the essence of security relations, but they also accelerate the formation of those security relations.

The security interactions of the three parties feature the following two characteristics. In the first place, a trilateral mechanism has not yet been established. Since the end of the Cold War, bilateral security relations of the three parties have increased continuously. China and Russia have good cooperative security relations; with the support of SCO (Shanghai Cooperation Organization), the two share benign interactive security relations, covering almost every aspect of security, from military exercises to weapons and technical facilities and anti-terrorism. What's more, the Treaty of Good Neighbourliness and Friendly Cooperation between China and Russia signed in July 2001 is beneficial not only for the national interest of the two countries, but also in promoting global peace and stability. The treaty specifies that, if one party is threatened by invasion, the two sides should contact and communicate instantly, which indicates that mutual support and reliance form part of their security strategy.

The security interaction between the EU and Russia is relative mature, too. Besides the interaction at the level of the Russia–NATO Council, there is also the security dialogue mechanism especially established by EU and Russia. Therefore, all kinds of joint actions are taken and information communicated with each other in the domain of anti-terrorism, transnational crime, prevention of environmental pollution and the prevention of WMD proliferation in traditional and non-traditional security issues. Of course, EU and Russian cooperation has its limits, as there are certain tensions surrounding some security issues. What should be stressed is that the security interaction of the two sides is frequent, which is indicative of maturity in the security relations.

Compared with the Russia–EU and China–Russia security interactions, the security interaction of China and EU is relatively weak. Even so, there have been rapid developments in this field in recent years. The fixed meeting mechanism of different levels was set between main EU member states and China, and the leaders of the two sides hold regular summits. The interaction between China and EU relates to such global issues as joint anti-terrorism, prevention of WMD proliferation, drug-trafficking, transnational crime, global climate change and vicious communicable diseases.

However, it is surprising that the security relations of the three parties are limited to three sets of bilateral interaction. Compared with other trilateral relations with an obvious feature of security interaction, such as US–EU– Russia, China–US–Russia, US–EU–Japan, US–Japan–Russia, China–US–Japan, the security interactive mechanisms between China, Russia and EU have not been formed. The security interactive mechanism of the three parties should be a comprehensive body with such features as conflict management and coordination of interests. In such a body, the security interactions of two sides would probably affect the interest of the third – whether positively or negatively – so the activity of each party may draw the attentions of the other two. It is unfortunate that, whether nominal or factual, there is no tripartite security interactive mechanisms, not even a security forum involving experts from the three. Nor has cooperation by the three on terrorism resulted in a unique global interactive security mechanism. And, what's more, although their policies on the rebuilding of Afghanistan and Iranian nuclear issues are similar, the three still depend on the coordination of a more extensive temporary international organization. So, although the three sets of bilateral relations are relatively mature, the tripartite security interactive relations lag behind.

In the second place, the security interaction of China–EU–Russia is seriously influenced by the US. China, Russia and the EU are the three most important indigenous strategic forces in the Eurasian continent and each has far-reaching influence outside its own region. However, none of the three are the leading power in Asian and European security affairs: their security interaction is contained by the power of the US. In spite of their bilateral security relations and the relations between the three parties together, they all are under the long shadow of the influence of the US.

Since the end of the Cold War, America became 'the neighbour of every country'; and, behind each bilateral security relation, the US became the invisible third party. Each bilateral security relationship of China–EU, China–Russia and EU–Russia is influenced heavily by the US. In the relationship between the EU and Russia, the omnipresent shadow of the US and NATO – which is dominated by the US – can be seen. EU–Russia security relations depend on the Russia–US and EU–US relations to some extent. As for the EU, Russia is not only the largest neighbouring country, but also a nuclear power; therefore, the safety of the EU is inseparable from Russia. Since the Cold War, the EU has strengthened the role of the Organization for Security and Cooperation in Europe (OSCE), but the EU was concerned that Russia had the veto on European safety, so the EU turned to the US for security support. The process of eastward expansion of NATO was almost monopolized by the US; member states of EU had lost the ability to judge independently. With the continuing expansion of NATO, including the admission of former CIS states, it is impossible to maintain a benign interaction of security relations between Russia and the EU.

Moving into the twenty-first century, China and Russia developed full-scale security communication and cooperation without becoming formal allies. The interactions are frequent and the security relations develop smoothly. Facing America's hope to establish a unipolar world, however, China has no intention to check the US; and Russia also has no strategy to counterbalance the US by allying with China. It is striking to note that Sino–US relations and Russia–US relations take priority over China–Russia relations. The premise of China–Russia relations is that these should not harm Sino–US or Russia–US relations. During the period of Chirac as the president of France and Gerhard Schröder as German chancellor, the EU arms embargo on China was almost lifted. However, because of US interference, this issue has been postponed indefinitely. The fact that EU–China security relations are heavily influenced by the US is self-evident. And the EU's security policy on China often refers to that of the US.

Conclusions

China, Russia and the EU form a new mode of interactive security relations between great powers. The pattern of the three parties bypasses the traditional ways whether in alliance or in conflict, and is developing into a new tripartite interaction of non-alliance, non-conflict and no card-playing, and therefore makes new contributions to great powers' security relations.

First, there is no structural tension between the three parties in security interaction. Generally speaking, bilateral or combination relations of great powers pertain to structural conflict of geopolitical factors. For example, the issue of Diaoyu Islands between China and Japan is a conflict of territory; in the relations of the US–EU–Russia, the EU is allied with the US, leaving Russia isolated; while in the EU–US–Japan relations, the EU and Japan are both allied with the US and depend to some extent on US protection. The contradiction between China and the US on Taiwan is structural; under the current framework of each party's politics and law, no intrinsic concession can be made to the other. It is encouraging to note that, although there are different stances and interests on a series of issues between China, Russia and the EU, these contradictions are not structural or antagonistic. In the predictable future, there appears to be little possibility of security dilemmas and security contention between the three parties.

Second, the fixed pattern of enemy or ally has been discarded by the three parties, as has the traditional framework of balance of power thinking. After the rise of the West, alliance or contention became a basic pattern of great power relations, and the balance of power became an important feature of great power security interaction. Since the end of the Cold War, China, the EU and Russia have surpassed such kinds of cognition and diplomatic practice. China does not play any other country as a card and will not allow other people to play the China card. Neither does China ally itself with Russia opposing the EU or vice versa; equally China does not ally itself to Russia and/or the EU in opposition to the US, Japan or any other country. None of the three parties are allied with or strategic opponents of each other. Their security interactions have become an innovation of great power security relations.

Third, China, Russia and the EU have become a model for countries of different kinds. The three parties represent different political systems (although Russia considers itself to be a democracy, the EU and the US do not recognize this), different culture inheritance and different stages of economic development; the formation of strength and the demands of interest differ greatly among the three. However, such kinds of difference do not impede the development of their security relations. For example, tensions have occurred often in trade, economy and politics between China and the EU; there are differences between China and Russia in arms and technology transfer, and cooperation in gas and petroleum; the contentions between Russia and the EU ranges from the EU's and NATO's eastward expansion, to Yugoslavia Federation and Kosovo, from organized crime to illegal immigrants, from natural gas pipeline to 'colour revolution', which has never stopped. But none of this has affected the field of security. The three parties communicate and cooperate smoothly in the rebuilding of Afghanistan, the Iranian nuclear issue, etc.; even on Iraq the three parties formed a united front.

Fourth, in the process of the tripartite security interactions, a mode of maintaining peace and stability by way of multilateral cooperation, not by hegemonic order, has been created, what has been called a mode of 'soft security coordination'.[7] The mode in formation will exert far-reaching influence on the future of the world. For hundreds of years, the world has followed the pattern of a certain hegemonic order; a multipolar pattern with the Concert of Europe after the Napoleonic Wars; a bipolar system with the Soviet Union and the US after the end of the Second World War; the unipolar system dominated by the US since the end of the Cold War.

In recent years, according to the principles of multilateralism, and through multilateral organizations and international institutions, extensive cooperation has been conducted by China, the EU and Russia in traditional and non-traditional security fields. If the coordinating effects of international institutions such as the UN can be strengthened and great powers increase their security dialogues on an equal basis, seeking common grounds while acknowledging their differences, this will contribute to global stability and development.

Notes

1 Javier Solana, 'The Transatlantic Rift: US Leadership after September 11', *Harvard International Review*, Winter 2003, 24(4), pp. 63–4.
2 Derek Kelly, 'Unipolar and Multipolar World Orders Are Unworkable', available at: http://www.lewrockwell.com/orig6/kelly1.html.
3 'Putin says Russia Advocates Multipolar World', *People's Daily Online*, 27 January 2007, available at: http://english.peopledaily.com.cn/200701/24/eng 20070124_344216.html.
4 Liang Shuming, *The Principal Characteristics of Chinese Culture*, Shanghai: Shanghai People's Publishing House, 2005, pp. 23, 142.
5 See Jiang Yi, 'Security Dilemma and China–Russia Relations', *Russian, East European & Central Asian Studies 5*, 2008, p. 29.
6 Chen Xinming, 'On the Three Major Factors that Influence Russian and European Relations', *International Forum*, November 2008, 10(6), pp. 16–17.
7 Tang Yongsheng, 'To Activate the Sino–Russia–EU Relationship', *World Affairs 13*, 2008, p. 12.

8 The European Union and East Asian security

Prepared for the future?

Gudrun Wacker

Introduction

The European Union (EU) and its member states have become economically and politically engaged in East and Southeast Asia, but neither of them is playing a significant role when it comes to security arrangements in the region. The most important actor in that respect since the Second World War has been the United States, which has been maintaining a close-knit web of security relations. At its centre are five bilateral military alliances with Japan, South Korea, Australia, the Philippines and Thailand, and military and security agreements with other countries as well as military bases and a substantial military presence. Neither the EU nor any of its member states possess even a fraction of the US's material and political power in the region. The EU has been a commercial power here, but in terms of providing security in the traditional sense ('hard security') it has been mostly a free rider.

Most observers agree that there is a global power shift underway.[1] The centre of gravity has been moving in the direction of Asia, with China as the major rising economic power, which also implies growing political influence and weight, and – to a lesser degree and somewhat slower – military capabilities. The global economic and financial crisis which started in 2008 might even accelerate the rise and global influence of China.[2] Despite the officially displayed 'modesty' of the Chinese leadership which has been insistent that China is first and foremost still a developing country with very limited capacities, the dictum of Deng Xiaoping for China's foreign policy – 'keep a low profile'[3] – seems less and less applicable and appropriate.

What characterizes the security situation in East Asia? How is the EU involved in the region, and what are the main features of its relations with China and other actors? Which factors have been limiting the European role? How would the EU be affected by open conflict and/or instability in this region? Is it prepared for negative scenarios such as a military conflict over Taiwan or on the Korean peninsula? Such scenarios will most likely involve the United States. Has the EU thought through the transatlantic implications of a major crisis in East Asia? And what would such a development imply for the relations with China? Can and should the EU contribute more to peace and stability in the region?

The security situation in East Asia: hot spots and relevant actors

East Asia and the Asia-Pacific region as a whole are characterized by great diversity in every respect: the spectre ranges from highly industrialized countries such as Japan to subsistence economies such as Laos, politically from established and consolidating democracies, South Korea and Taiwan, to authoritarian states, China and Singapore, and even a Stalinist country, North Korea. In terms of security the region features a mixture of traditional problems and conflicts and a whole range of new ('non-traditional') security challenges such as environment, energy, natural disasters, fragile or failing states. Among the traditional challenges are unresolved legacies of the Second World War and the Cold War, territorial conflicts between several states, and conventional and nuclear military build-up. Aside from all this, there is a very fundamental lack of trust, most notably between Japan and China. Two hot spots, the Korean peninsula and the Taiwan issue have been considered as the most likely sources of open conflict and military escalation. Both cases concern divided nations,[4] both constitute a situation of no peace, and in both the US is deeply involved – in stark contrast to the EU.

The North Korean nuclear programme first became virulent in the 1990s. The 1994 Agreed Framework signed in Geneva was supposed to address North Korea's energy demand in return for freezing and dismantling the nuclear programme, but in the end failed to resolve the issue. In 2003 the DPRK restarted uranium enrichment and declared its withdrawal from the Non-proliferation Treaty (NPT). Since then, efforts have been made to convince North Korea to give up its programme and return to the NPT. While the DPRK would have preferred to negotiate with the United States on a bilateral basis, Washington refused such a setting. On the initiative of China, negotiations since August 2003 have been taking place mainly within the framework of the Six Party Talks (6PT), with the two Koreas, China, the US, Japan and Russia participating. After several rounds of these talks, agreement was thought to have been reached, in September 2005 and February 2007, which foresaw a phased, 'action for action' approach. But due to failures to meet obligations by the various participants, all of which pursue specific interests and have different domestic constraints, the process stalled again in 2008. Many experts on Northeast Asia express the hope that the 6PT could develop into some sort of security arrangement or architecture beyond the nuclear issue.[5] However, with the denuclearization process not going forward and the basic issue unresolved, progress in this direction is difficult to achieve. In spring 2009, it was not clear whether the 6PT could be put back on track at all. The ill health of the North-Korean leader, Kim Jong-il, created further complications leading to a greater lack of transparency in the DPRK's domestic situation.

The Taiwan issue is considered by China as a 'domestic affair', since Beijing claims that Taiwan is an integral part of China (despite the fact that the island has been *de facto* independent since 1949). Most governments in the world basically accept this view and accordingly don't maintain formal diplomatic relations with Taiwan. When Washington switched diplomatic recognition from Taipei to Beijing, the US Congress passed the Taiwan Relations Act in 1979 committing the United States to help Taiwan defend itself. At the time, the island was under the one-party rule of the Kuomintang (KMT), which also claimed that mainland China was rightfully a part of the 'Republic of China'. In the 1980s and 1990s, Taiwan successfully (and peacefully) went through a democratization process. The presidential elections of the year 2000 were won for the first time by a representative of the opposition. The new president Chen Shui-bian's Democratic Progressive Party (DPP) advocated Taiwan's independence from China. During his two presidential terms from 2000 to 2008, cross-strait relations deteriorated in spite of growing economic interdependence between the two sides. The leadership in Beijing deeply mistrusted Chen Shui-bian and saw his activities to strengthen Taiwan's identity as a provocation and a challenge to the status quo. The Taiwan issue is the only problem where China has been threatening the use of force, should Taiwan overstep a (not clearly defined) red line in the direction of formal *de jure* independence. China's military modernization in part is geared to a conflict over Taiwan. The US is not interested in such a scenario, nor are other countries. With the election in March 2008 of a KMT president, Ma Ying-jeou, the atmosphere between China and Taiwan has improved and progress has been made in establishing direct transport and communication links across the Taiwan Strait. Despite these positive developments, escalation and military conflict cannot be ruled out; military conflict between China and Taiwan would probably involve the United States.

Another constant source of security concerns in the region, though not a 'hot spot', are Sino–Japanese relations. Here, too, strong economic interdependence is coupled with political friction and a deep mutual distrust. Legacies of the Second World War, territorial (and resource) conflicts in the East China Sea and implicit competition over the leading role in East Asia all complicate Sino–Japanese relations. The atmosphere was particularly strained during Junichiro Koizumi's tenure as Japanese Prime Minister, by his regular visits to the controversial Yasukuni Shrine, where convicted war criminals are included among the nation's honoured war dead. After a new Prime Minister was elected, the atmosphere improved somewhat, but the problematic issues have not vanished or been solved. The US is involved indirectly in this constellation, since it maintains a close security alliance with Japan (though the US would like Japan to take over more responsibility) and China is seen by the US as the most likely challenger to US predominance in the region. The strained relations between China and Japan have also been a constraint for regional integration in East Asia.

While US bilateral military alliances in the region shape and give direction to the basic security architecture in East Asia, several regional organizations with overlapping memberships and overlapping agendas have also formed over time, mainly around the grouping of Southeast Asian countries, the Association of Southeast Asian Nations (Asean). One of the organizations intended to address security issues is the Asean Regional Forum which was founded in 1994. These regional organizations and security arrangements have been criticized – mainly by Western industrialized countries – for their lack of institutional depth and of formalization, and they have been denounced as mere 'talk shops',[6] especially by the US. However, there have been no major military conflicts in the region for the past three decades. Perhaps Asian regional organizations are better and more effective in preventing the outbreak of open conflict than their reputation would imply.

The EU is certainly concerned about the 'hot spots' and security issues outlined above, because, in none of these cases, can a military escalation be completely ruled out, even if the likelihood of worst case scenarios is currently rather low. The EU would be affected by any of the issues developing in the wrong direction, with grave consequences in the economic realm, but also for Europe's security (migration, etc.). And it would mean a grave setback for the EU's global security goals. But, when it comes to contributions beyond goodwill and money, the EU has played at best a marginal role.

Europe's interest in East Asian peace and stability and the limitations of its role in the region

The EU has declared many times that it has a significant stake in stability and peace in East Asia. This has been stressed in all recent 'strategy papers' concerning the region as well as individual countries such as China. With the EU being one of China's most important economic partners, but also of other countries in East Asia, any destabilization or military conflict would have a negative impact on its interests. Europe depends on the unobstructed flow of goods to and from the region; major domestic unrest and social destabilization in China, for example, would affect European investments and trade relations. Moreover, the EU sees its own security as influenced by a set of global issues including climate change, energy security, the proliferation of weapons of mass destruction, smuggling of drugs and arms, and illegal migration. Finding solutions for these global issues will not be possible without the active cooperation of Asian countries. Should there be a disruption to peace in the Asia-Pacific region, these global challenges have no chance of being tackled.

However, the EU's contributions to security in the region have been limited, especially in Northeast Asia, where traditional 'hard' security issues have been dominating the security agenda. This is basically due to four factors, two internal and two external.

First, in contrast to the United States, the EU and its member states do not have any security commitments or military alliances with Asian countries, nor do they have any substantial military presence in the region. France and the UK maintain a symbolic presence and the UK is still an active member of the Five Power Defence Arrangements,[7] but this is no match for the forward deployment of the US and its military bases in Japan, South Korea and Guam. The EU does not have its own military forces, only those of its member states, and the battle groups the EU decided in 2005 to set up will certainly not be based in Asia. They are intended to improve European capacities in crisis- and conflict-intervention and will mainly be deployed in missions of the European Security and Defence Policy (ESDP),[8] preferably under UN mandate.

In general, the EU would like to be seen as a 'civil power' and a 'normative power', although there is some debate over whether the ESDP will over time lead to a 'militarization' of the EU's foreign policy.[9] The image of the civil and normative power is difficult to reconcile with the capability and willingness to deploy or use military force in order to reach certain goals.

Secondly, EU member states are divided about what kind of international actor the EU should be and what role it should play. This was amply demonstrated by the debate about and ultimately the failure of the Constitutional Treaty in spring 2005. The Common Foreign and Security Policy (CFSP) is still very young and a construction site at best. The enlargement of the EU from 15 to the present 27 member states has introduced an even broader range of different interests, opinions and approaches, which – in the absence of institutional reform – has complicated decision-making processes even more. Different groupings of member states pursue their own preferences, including the geographical focus of their foreign policy orientation.[10] Moreover, the EU remains very much focussed on its own problems with the integration process and enlargement as well as on its immediate neighbourhood. It seems that EU external relations – perhaps with the sole exception of the transatlantic partnership – are structured in concentric circles around the EU: the greater the geographic distance, the more declaratory and symbolic the policy. This fundamental fact applies not only to East Asia, but also to other regions: for almost every part of the world, the EU has formulated lofty goals, but failed to set clear priorities or to define a roadmap how to achieve them. Nor are there mechanisms to monitor effectively what has been achieved. Under these circumstances, it is hardly a surprise that there has been no definition of what qualifies the EU's strategic partnerships (in Asia with Japan, China, India and perhaps in the near future also with Korea) as 'strategic'.[11]

Until now, common positions and actions of the EU have to be based on consensus among member states. And due to the differing views and interests among the 27 governments (plus their respective domestic debates) this consensus – if one is found – usually represents the lowest common denominator. For a decision on joint action, the initiative has to come from one or several member states and sustained support has to be forthcoming. This makes taking political action in a geographically distant region such as East Asia, where economic links and interests are still predominant, not very likely.

A third factor limiting a stronger European role is the United States. Washington has been disinterested at best in a European security involvement in East Asia. Its main concern seems to be that the EU or its members do not get in its way or do anything perceived as detrimental to US interests. As long as the EU more or less follows the US lead in the region, it is largely irrelevant from Washington's perspective. The first time the US really took notice of European activities in East Asia was in 2003 when several EU member states, most prominently Germany and France, started to lobby for lifting the European arms embargo against China. This move was widely seen in US political circles, and especially in US Congress, as opportunistic, greedy and irresponsible behaviour of the Europeans who were apparently willing to compromise the safety of US and their allies' troops for profits from arms sales.

On the 'positive' side, the indifference of the United States implies that there are no high expectations about what can be contributed by or expected from Europe. In case of military escalation in one of the East Asian conflicts, the US will turn to their military allies, first and foremost Japan, for support.[12] Europe could be indirectly affected if the US in such a case had to withdraw troops from other theatres and ask EU or NATO partners to take over their tasks, at least temporarily.

Fourthly, it is far from clear whether all countries in East Asia would welcome a more pronounced security profile of the EU. Like the United States, China basically wants the EU to take a supportive stance on issues that China considers as its 'core national interests' (see below). The same applies to other states in the region as well: a stronger EU involvement is welcome as long as it is in line with their own respective positions.

This situation poses a dilemma for the EU and its member states: on the one hand, it is only noticed (and consulted) by the US as an actor in East Asia if it does something that, from Washington's perspective, is assessed as unacceptable and against US interests. On the other hand, it will be hard for the EU to raise its profile in the region if it just follows and supports the US positions.[13] How can the EU be accepted as a credible actor under such conditions?

> European states must find a balance between the reality of US regional influence and the necessity of acting independently for their own interests. Unfortunately, there are differing perspectives within Europe on the degree to which European policies should be coordinated with Washington.[14]

In the aftermath, and as a result of, the arms embargo debate, the UK (under their EU presidency) initiated 'Guidelines for the EU's Foreign and Security Policy in East Asia'. This document was completed in late 2005. At the time, member states would have insisted on watering down the text if it had been published,[15] so it was decided to use it internally as a frame of reference. In December 2007, the Guidelines were finally published in a revised and updated version.[16] Moreover, a formal transatlantic dialogue on East Asia ('EU–US Strategic Dialogue on East Asia') was established in 2005 that also addresses security and military issues and the implications of China's rise.[17] While the relevance attributed to this dialogue by the US side might have decreased since the embargo issue has been shelved, the 'Guidelines' can be seen as a real step forward, since they provide an agreed frame of reference which makes it easier for the EU (normally the current Presidency on behalf of all member states) to formulate statements on events and developments seen as contributing, or doing the contrary, to stability and peace in the region without starting discussions on a shared European position. This has facilitated official statements or demarches by the EU, for example on the Taiwan issue.

The 'Guidelines' state that security and stability in East Asia are important to the EU as a precondition for the continued economic success. The security challenges listed above (Korean peninsula, Taiwan and 'competitive nationalism' in East Asia) are listed as threats to regional security with 'a direct bearing on the interests of the EU'. And the special position of the US is explicitly acknowledged:

> The US's security commitments to Japan, the Republic of Korea and Taiwan and the associated presence of US forces in the region give the US a distinct perspective on the region's security challenges. It is important that the EU is sensitive to this. Given the great importance of transatlantic relations, the EU has a strong interest in partnership and cooperation with the US on Foreign and Security policy challenges arising from East Asia.[18]

However, the 'Guidelines' do not argue in favour of a stronger military engagement of the EU in the region. The approach is generally to 'deepen dialogue' with partners in the region and to provide assistance in certain fields. Since the promotion of 'effective multilateralism' is one of the declared global goals of the EU, regional integration is also high on the European agenda for East Asia. The measures advocated by the 'Guidelines' are generally intended to lower the risk of open conflict. They do not address the question what the EU would do if such preventive measures failed.

EU–China Relations: in search of a strategic approach

Resulting from growing trade and economic relations with China, the EU and its member states, especially the bigger ones, step by step deepened and broadened their contacts with China. During the 1990s, cooperation with China first intensified in the economic field. Bilateral trade went up by more than 2,000 per cent to over US$350 billion between 1990 and 2007, and China became a popular destination for European investment, especially when it finally joined the World Trade Organization in 2001. The negotiations on China's WTO entry which were conducted by the European Commission might also have been the first time the Chinese leadership and government started to see the EU as a serious actor on the international stage. Political dialogue developed gradually in the 1990s, and in 1998 the EU and China held their first formal summit meeting.

In 2003–5, EU–China relations reached a peak when the High Representative of the CSFP, Javier Solana, in the first ever European Security Strategy, listed China among the three countries in Asia that Europe wants to build a 'strategic partnership' with.[19] A few months later, China also published a strategy paper focussing on the EU. This latter document demands the lifting of the arms embargo, but also contains some passages in which the EU is admonished on its policy concerning Tibet and Taiwan,[20] which suggest that China welcomes European engagement only as long as it is supportive to Chinese core positions.

The period of 2003–5 can be characterized for both sides as one of almost euphoric mutual perception and, consequently, great expectations: China expected the EU to become an important actor on the global political stage, a supporter of the multipolar world and a counterweight to the US. The EU expected China to stay on its trajectory of convergence with Western democratic market economies, not only economically, but also politically.

However, disillusionment and frustration set in on both sides when it became clear that the basic assumptions underlying these perceptions and expectations might not be correct or not go forward as smoothly as expected. Friction and conflicts in the economic field, the failure to deliver on certain issues such as the arms embargo, lack of progress on vital questions such as human rights, Chinese activities abroad, most importantly in Africa, have made recent Sino–European relations more complicated and multidimensional.

This trend of more complex relations notwithstanding, EU member states pursue their own interests and approaches vis-à-vis China. A study conducted in 2008 by the European Council on Foreign Relations came to the conclusion that these national China policies can be roughly divided in four groups: 'assertive industrialists' (Poland, Czech Republic and Germany under Chancellor Angela Merkel), 'ideological free-traders' (Netherlands, Sweden, Denmark and UK), 'accommodating mercantilists' (Slovenia, Finland, Bulgaria, Malta, Hungary, Portugal, Slovakia, Italy, Greece, Cyprus, Romania, Spain) and 'European followers' (Belgium, Ireland, Austria, Luxemburg and the three Baltic States). France under President Sarkozy has not clearly fitted into any of the four categories.[21] These differences between member states help to explain why a unified approach to a strategic European China policy will be hard to bring about. The categories also reflect the two topics dominating the European agenda with China: economics and trade, and the Chinese political system. Security issues have not been taking centre stage.

Even though there is an ongoing debate about whether China should still be considered a developing country, the EU and its member states have not stopped providing support in capacity-building, law-making and implementation and offering technical cooperation. Underlying this continued support is also a concern about the domestic, regional and global implications should developments in China lead to major unrest and perhaps destabilization and loss of political control. Here, again, the EU and its member states have been trying to contribute to transformation and modernization in China, but they have no contingency planning should these processes lead to a less desirable scenario.

In the security field, some of the bigger member states within the EU over recent years have initiated and expanded military relations and exchanges with China. France, the UK and Spain have each held joint maritime exercises with China. Officers from European countries have been invited to observe Chinese military manoeuvres. Regular meetings have been held between militaries at the ministerial level as well as the working level, and Chinese officers have attended training courses in European countries. These contacts mainly serve the purpose of exchanging information and improving transparency, and thereby reducing mistrust.

Since the early 1990s, China has become more active in participating in peace-keeping and monitoring missions mandated by the United Nations.[22] Within this context military personnel from China and from European member states have been cooperating with and working alongside each other. The latest example for such joint activities is the anti-piracy mission off the coast of Somalia.

Finally, despite the arms embargo, which had been decided at a summit of the European Community as a reaction to the events in 1989 and despite the European existing Code of Conduct on Arms Transfers,[23] several European states in the late 1990s started exporting military equipment to China. The governments of France and the UK each at some point provided their own interpretation of the arms embargo and started selling arms-related material such as helicopter engines and radar equipment to China. Moreover, European member states and the EU have been more forthcoming than the US in exporting high technology goods to China and also invited China (together with India) to participate in high-tech projects like the European satellite positioning system Galileo.

The Taiwan issue: is there a European position?

All member states of the EU officially endorse in one way or other a one-China policy, which basically means that diplomatic relations with the

Republic of China (Taiwan) were cut off when diplomatic relations with the People's Republic of China were established. The government of the PRC is recognized as the sole legal government of China.

However, below the formal level, lively economic, trade and cultural relations between EU member states and Taiwan have been kept up. In 2007 Taiwan was the EU's 13th largest trading partner, and European member states were the largest source of foreign direct investment on the island. Almost all EU member states maintain an unofficial representative office in Taiwan (and vice versa), and, on the European level, a European Economic and Trade Office was opened in March 2003.[24] In spring 2009, the EU Centre in Taiwan was established to facilitate exchanges with universities in Taiwan.[25]

During the 1980s, when China had not yet become such an important trading partner, France and other European countries such as Italy were still willing to sell military equipment to Taiwan. France sold several La Fayette class frigates and Mirage fighter planes to Taiwan in the early 1990s.[26] China protested strongly against this decision, and further attempts of the Taiwanese side to purchase, for example, submarines from Germany or the Netherlands were not successful. China effectively used its growing economic clout to put political pressure on European governments.

Within European publics, Taiwan enjoys much support. In most European member states, there are groups of parliamentarians who sympathize with Taiwan's situation and make Taiwan a topic in parliamentarian debates. This is also the case in the European Parliament which has several times passed China-critical and Taiwan-friendly statements and resolutions. This has not changed the official positions of governments in Europe, but the fate of the young democracy on Taiwan is nevertheless a matter of concern.

Yet in practically all joint statements between the EU or one of the member states and China, the European side reiterates the one-China policy, and China normally expresses its appreciation for this position.

The EU's overriding interest concerning the situation in the Taiwan strait is the preservation of peace and stability, which in practical terms means to support the status quo.[27] After Chen Shui-bian was elected president in Taiwan in 2000, the EU gradually became more outspoken on cross-strait relations – not, as one would have expected, in defending Taiwan's position vis-à-vis China, but rather in appealing to both sides to refrain from activities challenging the status quo in cross-strait relations. Thus, the European Council's presidency made several public statements expressing concern about steps by Chen Shui-bian's government which could be interpreted as provocative by Beijing. In the second term of Chen Shui-bian's presidency especially, Beijing managed quite successfully to 'enlist' the Europeans (and Washington, for that matter) to support China's understanding of the status quo. On the other hand, the EU also reacted when the Chinese National People's Congress passed the so-called anti-secession law in spring 2005, which threatened Taiwan with the use of non-peaceful means should all hopes for peaceful unification be lost.[28]

Since Europeans tend to believe that (economic) interdependence between countries will lower the risk of conflict escalation, it is only consistent if they welcome all developments that point to deeper interdependence between China and Taiwan. This also explains the EU's positive reactions when Ma Ying-jeou was elected president in Taiwan in March 2008. He stood for a less confrontational approach and for the willingness to deepen cooperation with mainland China by opening direct communication and transport links and other measures. Since Ma took office in May 2008, developments between China and Taiwan have pointed in a direction welcomed by the EU: more dialogue and more practical cooperation. The EU responded with a positive statement acclaiming the decision of China's political leadership to allow Taiwan to be invited as an observer to the World Health Assembly in 2009.[29]

In the 'Guidelines' cited above, the EU acknowledges 'the sensitivity' of the issue for both sides of the Taiwan Strait and for China's relations with the US and Japan. However, in the passages describing the steps the EU should be ready to take in order to support peace and stability in cross-strait relations, all measures listed are on the level of welcoming positive developments and expressing concern over negative ones. The need to get a better understanding of the military balance involved in the issue is also stated:

> The EU should also, in consultation with all partners, deepen the understanding of the military balance affecting the cross-strait situa-tion; of the technologies and capabilities which, if transferred to the region, could disturb that balance; of the related risks to stability including the risk of miscalculation; and factor that assessment into the way that Member States apply the Code of Conduct in relation to their exports to the region of strategic and military items.[30]

In sum, the EU hopes for the best, does not want to contribute inadvert-ently to the risk of destabilization, but otherwise has not thought of going beyond the issuing of statements. The readiness to come out with such statements has improved over recent years, and this is certainly a result of the 'Guidelines'. However, it cannot be assumed that a debate has taken place among member states how the EU should react in case of open conflict. It can hardly be expected that such a possibility will be discussed in times when a confrontation becomes less likely due to a process of alleviation of tension in cross-strait relations.

The Korean peninsula: a role for Europe?

As a result of the first nuclear crisis on the Korean Peninsula, the Agreed Framework was signed in 1994 in Geneva for freezing and ultimately dismantling North Korea's nuclear programme and the Korean Peninsula Energy Development Organization (KEDO) was established in 1995 to help implement the Agreed Framework's provisions (mainly by supplying heavy oil to North Korea). The EU joined KEDO in 1997 and became a member of its executive board, but mainly contributed financially. Some European member states such as Germany even opened diplomatic relations with the DPRK when the US under the second Clinton administration also seemed to be willing to move towards normalizing its relationship with North Korea. However, the US in the end did not recognize the DPRK diplomatically and KEDO became defunct when it became clear that North Korea had returned to uranium enrichment and announced its intention to leave the Non-proliferation Treaty (NPT) in early 2003.

The EU is of course in favour of a nuclear-free Korean peninsula and is particularly concerned about the possibility of proliferation from North Korea to other countries, such as in the Middle East. However, unlike the negotiations on the nuclear programme in Iran, the EU has not been invited to join the Six Party Talks (6PT),[31] nor did it openly express the wish to join the negotiations. In light of the diversity of interests among the six participants of the 6PT and the stalemate within the then Bush administration on how to deal with the issue, the EU's position as a bystander providing humanitarian aid to the people in the DPRK seems prudent. It is doubtful whether the EU or member states could have contributed anything substantial to the talks themselves.

Once again, the EU generally favours a solution through negotiations and would be ready to provide material and technical assistance if such a solution were to be found. But it is not prepared for any role in the event of a military escalation.

Conclusion: the EU's security engagement – limited, but useful

It has become clear that the EU and its member states are marginal players when it comes to hard security challenges in East Asia and the hot spots that could develop in the direction of a military confrontation. The EU is not and does not aspire to become another United States. A strong military presence in East Asia which would underpin the EU's desire to project power in the region has not been on the agenda in Brussels or any of the capitals in Europe. The EU has, however, indirectly contributed to stability and peace in the region. The problem with these measures is not that they have no effect, but that most of them (with the exception of arms transfers) are generally not acknowledged by the US or Asian countries as genuine contributions to security and stability.

The EU's strength has been in the field of preventive measures, assistance for domestic transformation processes through financial and technical assistance and (ideational) support for regional integration. In the past two decades, the EU has participated in several UN-mandated peace-keeping and monitoring missions in Asia, especially in Southeast Asia (Cambodia, Aceh), and it is ready to offer assistance as facilitator and also to provide experience and a 'tool box' with instruments if it is invited to do so. Post-conflict reconstruction, nation-building, institution-building, security sector reform, police training – these are the fields for which the EU and its members have provided assistance and funding. The means and instruments the EU is willing and able to bring on the table should be 'advertised' more pro-actively. And they should be acknowledged as different from, but possibly complementary to, the US approach.[32] Looking back at the past eight years and the difficulties encountered in Afghanistan and Iraq, the new US administration might be more prepared to see some merit in the EU's more comprehensive security concept. At the same time, European governments have become more aware of the transpacific dimension of US power and of the security interests of the US and its allies in the Asia-Pacific region over the last years. But Europe's contribution to peace and security in this region will probably remain in the field of prevention and confidence-building.

However, Europe should provide a more realistic picture of what can and cannot be expected from it. The EU may have formulated regional and country strategy papers for all parts of the world and global security goals, but in terms of political and military power it is a regional actor concentrating mainly on its own neighbourhood. On the global level, it is focussed on issues of global governance in order to close the gap between growing global challenges on the one hand and the capabilities and capacities to address these challenges on the other.

Notes

1 See for example Kishore Mahbubani: *The New Asian Hemisphere: The Irresistible Shift of Global Power to the East*, New York: Public Affairs 2008; James F. Hoge Jr: 'A Global Power Shift in the Making', *Foreign Affairs*, July 2004, pp. 2–7.
2 See for example Tom Engelhardt, 'Tomgram: Dilip Hiro, The Next Superpower', 3 May 2009, available at: http://www.tomdispatch.com/post/175067/dilip_hiro_the_newest_superpower (5 May 2009).
3 See for example Willy Lam: 'Beijing's New "Balanced" Foreign Policy: An Assessment', *China Brief*, 4, 20 February 2004, p. 4.
4 Even though in the case of Taiwan part of the population and the Democratic Progressive Party (DPP) which ruled the island from 2000 to 2008 see Taiwan as a separate and independent country that does not wish to be united with China.
5 One of the five working groups established as a result of the 6PT addresses this issue, namely the one on a 'Northeast Asia peace and security mechanism'.
6 See for example Dick K. Nanto, 'East Asian Regional Architecture: New Economic and Security Arrangements and US Policy', CRS Report for Congress, RL 33653, updated 4 January 2008, p. 38.
7 The other four participants are Australia, New Zealand, Singapore and Malaysia. On the role of the FPDA cf. Carlyle Thayer, 'The Five Powers Defence Arrangements: The Quiet Achiever', paper presented at the 1st Berlin Conference

on Asian Security (BCAS), September 2006, available at: http://www.swp-berlin.
org/common/get_document.php?asset_id=3563.

8 Cf. on battlegroups in more detail: Gustav Lindstrom, 'Enter the EU Bat-
tleegroups', Chaillot Paper 97, February 2007, pp. 17ff., available at: http://www.
iss.europa.eu/uploads/media/cp097.pdf (24 August 2009).

9 On this discussion, see Annegret Bendiek and Heinz Kramer, 'Die EU als globaler Akteur: Unklare 'Strategien', diffuses Leitbild', SWP-Studie, April 2009,
Berlin, p. 12, available at: http://www.swp-berlin.org/common/get_document.
php?asset_ id=5898 (24 August 2009).

10 The French proposal for a Mediterranean Union ('Club Med') in 2008 was a
good example of a regional initiative which was – understandably – not supported with the same enthusiasm by all EU member states.

11 For a critical look at the EU's regional policies and strategic partnerships, see
Bendiek and Kramer, 'Die EU als globaler Akteur'; on CFSP see Christos Kat-
sioulis, 'European Foreign Policy on Trial: Global Actor in the making?',
International Policy Analysis, Friedrich-Ebert-Stiftung, March 2009, available
at: http://library.fes.de/pdf-files/id/ipa/06157.pdf (14 August 2009).

12 Bernt Berger and Heather Gilmartin, 'The Quiet Europeans? Appraising Europe's
Commitment to East Asian Security', in Hans J. Giessmann (ed.), *Emerging
Powers in East Asia: China, Russia and India*, Baden-Baden: Nomos, 2008,
p. 231.

13 See Adam Ward: 'The Taiwan Issue and the Role of the European Union', in
Bates Gill and Gudrun Wacker, *China's Rise: Diverging US–EU Perceptions and
Approaches*, Berlin: SWP, August 2005, available at: http://www.swp-berlin.
org/common/get_document.php?asset_id=2402, p. 47.

14 Berger and Gilmartin, 'Quiet Europeans?', p. 231.

15 Information from a member of the European Commission delegation to Beijing,
Spring 2006.

16 Full text available at: http://www.consilium.europa.eu/ueDocs/cms_Data/docs/
pressdata/en/misc/97842.pdf (4 March 2008): Council of the European Union:
'Guidelines on the EU's Foreign and Security Policy in East Asia'.

17 Ibid. p. 4.

18 Ibid. p. 3.

19 'A Secure Europe in a Better World: European Security Strategy', December
2003, available at: http://www.iss-eu.org/solana/solanae.pdf (3 January 2008).
The other two were Japan and India.

20 The EU did not respond to these passages on Tibet and Taiwan. The full text of
the document 'China's EU Policy Paper', 13 October 2003, is available at: http://
www.china-un.ch/eng/ljzg/zgwjzc/t85896.htm.

21 John Fox and François Godement, 'A Power Audit of EU–China Relations',
European Council on Foreign Relations, April 2009, available at: http://ecfr.eu/
page/-/documents/A_Power_Audit_of_EU_China_Relations.pdf (13 Aug. 2009).

22 China provides more personnel to UN-mandated peace-keeping missions than
the other four Permanent Members of the UN Security Council. On China's
growing engagement in this field see Bates Gill and Chin-hao Huang, 'China's
Expanding Peacekeeping Role: Its significance and the policy implications',
SIPRI Policy Brief, February 2009, available at: http://books.sipri.org/files/misc/
SIPRIPB0902.pdf (13 August 2009); International Crisis Group, 'China's Growing Role in UN Peacekeeping', Asia Report 166, 17 April 2009, available at:
http://www.crisisgroup.org/library/documents/asia/north_east_asia/166_chinas_
growing_role_in_un_peacekeeping.pdf (13 August 2009).

23 This Code of Conduct has been in force since 1998. It aims at harmonizing arms
exports from EU countries and provides eight criteria which have to be considered before national governments can grant an export licence for military

equipment to non-European countries. Member states provide details of the export licences granted and refused due to one or more of the criteria to a database. A report has been published on an annual basis. A revision of the Code was conducted after 2005, and in December 2008 the revised and strengthened 'Code' was published as a 'common position' of the European Union. More information including links to the text of the Common Position and Annual Reports is available at: http://ue.eu.int/showPage.aspx?id=1484&lang=en (16 May 2009).

24 This was after Taiwan had successfully joined the WTO under the name 'Separate Customs Territory of Taiwan, Penghu, Kinmen and Matsu' (or Chinese Taipei) in January 2002 one day after the PRC. More information on the European office on Taiwan is available at: http://www.deltwn.ec.europa.eu/.

25 See website at: http://www.eutw.org.tw/index-e.html (13 August 2009).

26 See Jean-Pierre Cabestan, 'Taiwan's Challenge to China and the World: Part I', *Yale Global Online*, 12 March 2004, available at: http://yaleglobal.yale.edu/display.article?id=3504 (13 August 2009).

27 Of course, the status quo is not stagnant, but continually in flux. 'Status quo' therefore means that no side openly challenges the present state of *de facto*, but not *de jure* independence of Taiwan.

28 The passing of the anti-secession law also provided the EU with a welcome excuse to refrain from lifting the arms embargo.

29 'Declaration by the Presidency on behalf of the European Union on the occasion of the participation of Taiwan as an observer in the 62nd session of the World Health Assembly', Council of the European Union, 8 May 2009, 9486/09 (Presse 123), available at: http://www.consilium.europa.eu/uedocs/cms_data/docs/pressdata/en/cfsp/107600.pdf (11 May 2009).

30 Council of the European Union, 'Guidelines', p. 8.

31 The 6PT were started in 2003 to address the nuclear issue; its members are the two Koreas, the United States, China, Japan and Russia.

32 Berger and Gilmartin, 'Quiet Europeans?', p. 239.

9 Cooperation and competition on the Iran nuclear dispute

The role of the European Union and China

Willem van Kemenade

Introduction

Alireza Jafarzadeh, US representative for the exiled Iranian ('terrorist') opposition group 'National Council of Resistance of Iran' (NCRI), the political wing of the Mujahideen-e-Khalq guerillas, made a startling revelation in Washington on 14 August 2002, that the disputed Iranian *peaceful* nuclear programme was not limited to the neverending construction of the Bushehr nuclear plant, which was initiated under the Shah by a German company in 1974.[1] There were two other top secret nuclear sites under construction: a partly underground uranium enrichment facility in Natanz, and a heavy water facility, destined to produce plutonium in Arak.[2]

The International Atomic Energy Agency (IAEA), the United Nations' nuclear watchdog moved in for intensive inspections and reported in November 2003 that,

> it is clear that Iran has failed in a number of instances over an extended period of time to meet its obligations under its Safeguards Agreement with respect to the reporting of nuclear material and its processing and use, as well as the declaration of facilities where such material has been processed and stored.[3]

Iran was required to inform the IAEA of its importation of uranium from China – pre-1997 – and subsequent use of that material in uranium conversion and enrichment activities. It was also required to report experiments with the separation of plutonium, but had failed to do so.

Jafarzadeh's 2002 announcement was the trigger for a major EU initiative, the launching of a coordinated diplomatic effort to submit Iran's nuclear programme to closer international scrutiny. The United States had no part in this and did not even support it; they just did not oppose it openly. President George W. Bush ostensibly believed his own 'Mission Accomplished' propaganda (1 May 2003) after the 'opening' battle in the Iraq War had been won and Under-Secretary of Defense Douglas Feith was briefing his colleagues in the State and Defense Departments about 'continuing the Iraq war into Iran and Syria'.[4] Feeling threatened by the serial wave of American military adventurism, the Iranian government of then reformist President Mohammed Khatami sent through Swiss diplomatic channels a comprehensive proposal for a US–Iran 'Grand Bargain' in which all outstanding issues –nuclear programme, missiles, weapons of mass destruction, Hezbollah, Palestine, even an end to confrontation with Israel – would be on the table. In return Iran wanted its security concerns to be addressed and there were many and serious ones: Iran was surrounded by American troops in Afghanistan and Iraq, nuclear armed naval forces in the Indian Ocean and the Persian Gulf, a strategic bombing force of B-52s on the British Indian Ocean Territory of Diego Garcia, US/NATO bases in Uzbekistan (until 2005) and Kyrgyzstan, and a military presence in Georgia on Iran's north-western border. Then there was Israel with a bombing force with 200 nuclear warheads and nuclear submarines. President Bush did not initiate any debate about the Iranian proposal and allowed Vice-President Dick Cheney to torpedo it with the ominous one-liner 'We don't speak to evil.'[5] This was contrary to the truth. In August 2003 the first session of the 'Six Party Talks on the North Korean Nuclear Programme' convened in Beijing, after North Korea, a comrade-in-arms of Iran in Bush's 'Axis of Evil' had withdrawn from the Nuclear Non-Proliferation Treaty on 10 January 2003. Why did Washington engage the one 'evil' and not the other?

The international community was deeply divided over the alleged 'emerging Iranian nuclear threat'. On the one hand there were hardliners such as Dick Cheney and the civilian leadership of the State Department and Pentagon (Bolton, Feith, Perle) and Israel's military and intelligence establishment. They were unwavering in their conviction that Iran was secretly making a bomb. The Bush administration basically echoed the same themes during the critical period of 2003 to 2007.

China and Russia have been major players in Iran's nuclear programme as suppliers of technology and raw materials, China from 1985 to 1997 and Russia since then. China believed that Iran's nuclear programme was for peaceful purposes, but in recent years it has become more sceptical and called on Iran to reassure a suspicious world more strongly about the veracity of its claims that it aims only to produce civilian nuclear energy. The Russians are not – yet – convinced that Iran is building a bomb and are happy to be the main suppliers of the current Iranian programme as long as it is properly inspected by the IAEA.

The Europeans were wary of a confrontational approach, not least because they believed that Iran, unlike undeclared and/or unrecognized nuclear powers such as Israel, India and Pakistan, as a signatory of the Nuclear Non-proliferation Treaty could argue that it had the right to enrich uranium for use in nuclear power plants. It was with this mindset that Britain and France as the two European permanent members of the Security Council, plus Germany as Iran's second largest trading partner – after China – embarked on the marathon of arduous negotiations with Iran to persuade Tehran to first suspend, then fully terminate its uranium enrichment and eventually shift to international cooperation in a fully transparent, truly civilian multilaterally supplied nuclear energy programme.

This chapter focuses mainly on the competitive roles of China as an early major supplier in Iran's nuclear programme (1985–1997) and currently leading trading and investment partner and of the EU as an aspiring guardian of the civilian character of the programme. The Iranian nuclear programme under the Shah was initiated by the US and assisted by the Europeans and others. After the Islamic revolution in 1979 there was a five-year lull in the programme, but then China took over as the main supplier until it bowed out in 1997 under American pressure. After Iran's history of concealment, with the connivance of China and Pakistani nuclear rogue trader A.Q. Khan, was exposed in 2002, the EU-3 (the UK, Germany, France) negotiations with Iran started and so its struggle with the IAEA over the Additional Protocol to its Safeguards Agreement, which would authorize the IAEA to demand access for *extemporaneous* inspections almost anywhere. Iran signed this agreement but never ratified it in retaliation for being referred to the Security Council in 2006. Then there was the Paris Agreement of November 2004 which reaffirmed Iran's willing cooperation with the IAEA and the EU-3 until it broke down in August 2005 over Iran's refusal to extend suspension of uranium enrichment. During 2006–07, the main themes were referral to the Security Council and sanctions-diplomacy, reinforced by Bush–Cheney–Rumsfeld-style threats of military strikes, possibly jointly with the Israeli Air Force. Another dispute chronicled is that between the intelligence services of the US, Russia, France and particularly Israel, who over the years offered many contradictory accounts, most of them incriminating for Iran but some exonerating and according to the experts without solid factual basis.

The conclusion of this chapter is a discussion of the 'trilemma' that the world is facing in Iran. Until the exit of the Bush administration it was a 'dilemma': hardliners in Washington, and more recently President Nicholas Sarkozy of France, believed Iran was deviously hoodwinking the world and close to completing its bomb. The Russians and Chinese, although critical of Ahmadinejad's confrontational style, in the end still believe that an Iranian bomb is far from imminent. Since the Obama administration has entered the White House 'nuance' has broadened the American Iran debate. Like any random contention can be true, untrue or half true, so there is a third option to Iran's nuclear programme apart from 'peaceful or military': achieving *nuclear capacity*, that is, mastering all the technology, including the full fuel cycle but stopping short of industrial manufacturing of the bomb.

China protector of Iran against US pressure and threats, 1985–97

China and more recently Russia had and have nuclear and defence technology supply relationships with Iran and were supportive of Iran's nuclear programme as long as it was properly supervised by the IAEA. China had been Iran's major supplier of arms during its war with Iraq (1980–88), of nuclear and missile technology from 1985 until 1997, and had protected Iran against American threats and pressure at the United Nations and had also acted as a substitute supplier for goods that were under Western sanctions. As a gradually normalizing revolutionary state, post-Mao China was not yet playing by international rules and it was US policy to bring China within the global non-proliferation regime and nudge it away from its arch-enemy, Iran. In 1985, China and Iran concluded a secret agreement on the peaceful use of nuclear energy, which was only disclosed to the IAEA in 1992.[6] During 1991, China delivered 1,600 kg of uranium products to Iran, which went unreported to the IAEA until discovered by investigators in 2003. In October 1991, US intelligence determined that Iran was attempting to develop nuclear weapons and that China was assisting Iran in this effort.[7] During the first Clinton term (1993–7) there were escalating tensions with China over human rights, Taiwan and trade issues, aggravated by regular showdowns over China's nuclear aid to Iran. By 1996–7 there was mounting, but not conclusive evidence of Iran's covert and possibly weapons-oriented programmes.

The US believed that China had to halt all nuclear cooperation with Iran, and it had to go beyond the letter of the law. Even cooperation that might technically be legal under the NPT had to stop. This was hegemonic arrogance at its bluntest, but China in the end yielded. President Jiang Zemin concluded that China could not risk a major crisis in US–China relations over accumulating tensions over human rights, plus Taiwan plus support for Iran's nuclear programme. Yielding to US pressure on human rights might jeopardize the continuation of Communist rule and softening on the Taiwan issue (i.e. allowing Taiwan to remain a military protectorate of the US) might undermine China's rise as a regional and global superpower. As China's relations with Iran were of secondary importance and not an indispensable core-interest, Beijing committed to forgo all nuclear cooperation with Iran, which included cancellation of the supply of a heavy water reactor, the hexafluoride plant and nuclear power plants.

In exchange, the US would then finally implement the US–China Nuclear Agreement, signed by President Reagan in 1985 and stalled ever since over China's nuclear aid to Iran and others. It was further agreed that human rights issues had to be downgraded on the US agenda towards China, and Washington would act with more restraint on Taiwan-related issues.[8]

Khomeini denounced nuclear weapons as 'un-Islamic'

After the Islamic Revolution in 1979, the new regime had abandoned the civilian nuclear programme started by the Shah in the early 1970s and Ayatollah Khomeini himself had denounced nuclear weapons in his theological writings as 'un-Islamic'. Due to energy-shortages in the mid-1980s, the regime reconsidered the need for civilian nuclear energy and, during the final days of the war with Iraq in 1988, Khomeini himself lamented that Iran would need vast quantities of laser and nuclear weapons to win the war.[9] Iran wanted to resume work on the Bushehr complex, but potential European partners were under American pressure not to engage in nuclear cooperation with it. Thus, Iran turned to the Soviet Union and China. In 1991 China proposed to complete the Bushehr plant but it soon expressed scepticism for technical reasons and pulled out in 1993, probably under American pressure. The Atomic Energy Organization of Iran (AEOI) and the Russian Ministry of Atomic Energy signed a new agreement for the construction of two Russian reactors at Bushehr, but it was not implemented as Iran was facing major financial problems. In a speech in 2001, the former Iranian President Rafsanjani, a so-called moderate pragmatist, clearly indicated, like his late mentor Khomeini, that Iran should become a nuclear power and linked Iran's nuclear development to the nuclear power Israel:

> If a day comes when the world of Islam is duly equipped with the arms Israel has in its possession, the strategy of colonialism would face a stalemate, because the exchange of atomic bombs would leave nothing of Israel while only damaging the Muslim world.[10]

In other words, Iran was seeking to introduce the Cold War doctrine of mutually assured destruction (MAD) to the Middle East. On the question of whether Iran had a hidden nuclear weapons programme, the IAEA reported in 2003 that it had found 'no evidence' that the previously undeclared activities were related to a weapons programme, but also that it was unable to conclude that Iran's programme was exclusively peaceful. In such inconclusive cases, the IAEA requires an Additional Protocol to the Comprehensive Safeguards Agreement that a state signs when acceding to the NPT. Iran joined the NPT in 1968 as a non-nuclear state, and the Shah initiated a civilian nuclear energy programme in the early 1970s in cooperation with American, German, French and South African firms, which ended with the Islamic Revolution in 1979. What role China has played – directly or indirectly – in the concealed military components of Iran's programme may never be fully known. Beijing has been a wholesale lonterm supplier to Pakistan's nuclear weapons programme – with which it had a comprehensive strategic partnership to keep India down – and as such China contributed to the proliferation bazaar of nuclear rogue trader A.Q. Khan who in his turn had extensive military nuclear dealings with Iran.[11]

The biggest Iranian smoking gun were traces of bomb-grade uranium that had been found by IAEA inspectors two years earlier, news of which was seized upon by the Bush administration as conclusive evidence that Iran was close to having the bomb. Iran had acquired centrifuge materials and equipment from A.Q. Khan.

With Pakistan's assistance a group of US government experts and scientists from France, Japan, Britain and Russia pored for nine months over the evidence, collected by IAEA inspectors and concluded in August 2005 that the traces of bomb-grade uranium in Iran came from contaminated equipment, acquired from Pakistan and were not evidence of a concealed nuclear weapons programme in Iran.[12]

Nevertheless, on 4 February 2006, the 35-member Board of Governors of the IAEA voted 27–3 (with five abstentions: Algeria, Belarus, Indonesia, Libya and South Africa) to report Iran to the Security Council. The measure was sponsored by Britain, France and Germany, and it was backed by the United States. Two permanent members of the Security Council, Russia and China, agreed to referral only on condition that the council take no action before March. The three members who voted against referral were Venezuela, Syria and Cuba. IAEA and European compromises were rejected because the Bush administration made clear that it would not accept any enrichment at all in Iran.

Three 'Wise Men' from Europe fly to Tehran

The first public event in the EU-3 Diplomatic Marathon was a visit to Tehran on 21 October 2003 by foreign ministers Jack Straw of Britain, Dominique de Villepin of France and Joschka Fischer of Germany for intensive talks with the Iranian government. In a joint statement Iran agreed to measures aimed at settlement of all outstanding IAEA issues with regard to the Iranian nuclear programme and at boosting confidence for peaceful cooperation in the nuclear field. The Iranian authorities reaffirmed that nuclear weapons had no place in Iran's defence doctrine and that its nuclear programme and activities had been exclusively in the peaceful domain. Iran further agreed to sign and implement an 'Additional Protocol' to its accession agreement to the Nuclear Non-Proliferation Treaty and, as a voluntary, confidence-building measure, to suspend all uranium enrichment and reprocessing activities as defined by the IAEA. The EU-3 in return agreed to recognize Iran's rights to a civilian nuclear programme under the NPT and believed that this would open the way to dialogue on longer-term cooperation which would have provided all parties with satisfactory assurances relating to Iran's nuclear power generation programme. Once international concerns, were fully resolved Iran could expect easier access to modern technology and supplies in a range of areas. The three foreign ministers further informed the Iranian authorities that they would cooperate with Iran to promote security and stability in the Middle East including the establishment of a zone free of weapons of mass destruction in accordance with the objectives of the United Nations.[13]

The Additional Protocol and the Paris Agreement

Iran signed the Additional Protocol on 18 December 2003, granting the IAEA authority to conduct more rigorous, short-notice inspections at undeclared nuclear facilities to ferret out secret nuclear activities. The EU-3 and Iran then signed a separate agreement in Paris on 14 November 2004 to reaffirm the implementation of the Protocol. One of the EU-3 commitments in this agreement was the recognition that Iran's suspension of uranium enrichment was a voluntary confidence-building measure and not a legal obligation. Here the trouble started. The Iranians meant the suspension to be only a temporary measure, but the EU's intent was to recast it into permanent cessation upon completion of negotiations on a long-term settlement. The suspension applied not only to uranium but also to manufacturing of gas centrifuges, plutonium separation and other components. In the context of this suspension, the EU and Iran agreed to begin negotiations, with a view to reaching an agreement on long-term arrangements.[14] However, before the Paris text was signed, the Iranian negotiator, Mullah Hassan Rohani, emphatically told the EU-3 that they should be committed neither to speak nor even to think of cessation any more. The ambassadors delivered his message to their foreign ministers prior to the signing of the Paris text, that 'The Iranians made it clear to their European counterparts that if the latter sought a complete termination of Iran's nuclear fuel-cycle activities, there would be no negotiations.' The European response was that they were not seeking such a termination, but an assurance on the non-diversion of Iran's nuclear programme to military ends. During negotiations in early 2005, the EU-3 continued to insist on permanent cessation of uranium enrichment in exchange for incentives in the form of the supply of a light water reactor to replace its heavy water reactor – for eventual production of weapons grade plutonium – under construction in Arak. Iran rejected both.

In response to the EU3's unremitting insistence to terminate enrichment indefinitely, Iran threatened to end suspension and resume nuclear activity, unless the EU3 came up with new proposals. This they did in early August without making them public; in any case, Iran rejected them because the temporary character of the suspension was not adequately addressed. Then, on 8 August 2005, Iran removed the IAEA seals and cameras from its uranium conversion facilities in Isfahan, and began feeding nuclear fuel into centrifuges. UK officials termed this a 'breach of the Paris Agreement' although it was obvious that the EU had 'misinterpreted' the Paris Agreement by assuming that Iran after a temporary suspension would abandon nuclear enrichment unequivocally. The essence of the breakdown of the Paris Agreement appears to be a significant philosophical gap between the two sides. The Europeans took a 'maximalist' approach, based on the self-perceived moral high ground. The EU3 officials argued that

> the only 'objective guarantee' of the exclusively peaceful nature of Iran's nuclear program (to use the terms of the November 15, 2004 agreement) is the effective cessation of all activities leading to the production of nuclear materials (i.e. enrichment, reprocessing and heavy water technologies). If there were other measures that are as

effective – and objective – as cessation, we would be ready to consider them, but we, for our part, cannot conceive of any such measures.[15]

Iranian officials took a 'minimalist' approach and argued that Tehran was ready to 'present everything necessary to prove that [it] will not produce an atomic bomb'.[16]

IAEA votes for sanctions but then 'lowers the pitch': from EU-3 to P–5+1

By early 2006 Iran was emboldened by the US deadlock in Iraq and by soaring oil prices, and, with intractable President Ahmadinejad firmly installed in power, Tehran was fully determined to develop full nuclear fuel cycle capability. On 10 January 2006, IAEA inspectors confirmed that the Iranians had broken UN seals for the second time, on enrichment-related equipment and material at Natanz and two other locations.[17] The EU-3 issued a statement, calling Iran's position a rejection of the two-year process of engagement with the EU-3. The IAEA board then voted with a majority of 27 votes out of 35 to report Iran to the Security Council. Iran responded by suspending its implementation of the Additional Protocol and end prospects for a compromise on uranium enrichment. Russia and China and even India had voted in favour of the resolution, the latter two on condition that it did not contain any immediate threat of sanctions and India despite intense domestic pressure to stand by Iran. Only Venezuela, Cuba and Syria had opposed the resolution. In late February 2006, IAEA Director-General Mohammad El-Baradei raised the suggestion of a deal, whereby Iran would give up industrial-scale enrichment, instead limiting its programme to a small-scale pilot facility, and agree to import its nuclear fuel from Russia. The Iranians indicated that while they would not be willing to give up their *right* to enrichment in principle, they were willing to consider the compromise solution. The P–5+1 (Permanent Five Members of the Security Council plus Germany[18]) then met in Berlin in late March, but failed to agree on what next steps to take. Russian Foreign Minister Sergei Lavrov said sanctions could not be used 'to solve' the Iranian nuclear dispute, adding that the IAEA had yet to provide 'decisive evidence' that Iran was developing the capability to make nuclear weapons. El Baradei seconded Lavrov at a separate meeting in Qatar: 'Sanctions are a bad idea. We are not facing an imminent threat ... We need to lower the pitch.'[19] The P–5 + 1 then offered Iran a package of incentives aimed at getting the country to restart negotiations, but Iran refused to halt its nuclear enrichment first. An avalanche of criticism descended on Tehran from all directions, the White House, the EU, the IAEA and the UN Security Council which was now ready to impose new sanctions.

The European position was one of taking the middle-road between the American demand for surrender, or even US military action, and the

Russian and Chinese stand of opposing further sanctions without giving up the eventual goal of accepting Iran to go nuclear. The Europeans wanted the US to join them in direct talks with Iran, but on 31 May 2006 Secretary of State Condoleezza Rice declared: 'As soon as Iran fully and verifiably suspends its enrichment and reprocessing activities, the United States will come to the table with our EU-3 colleagues and meet with Iran's representatives'.[20] Demanding from Tehran that it concede the key issue before even agreeing to talk was tantamount to unconditional surrender, and Iran resolutely rejected the demand, calling it just a propaganda move. The P–5+1 were now ready to move towards referring Iran to the Security Council, which they agreed on 12 July, two days after investigative reporter Seymour Hersh had published a very sobering *New Yorker* article, revealing that a military attack on Iran would be too risky for the United States. According to one of Hersh's sources, Flynt Leverett, a former National Security Council aide for the Bush Administration, 'The only reason Bush and Cheney relented about talking to Iran was because they were within weeks of a diplomatic meltdown in the United Nations. Russia and China were going to stiff us', that is, prevent the passage of a UN resolution.[21] With the military option discredited, the EU-3 worked now with the US in assembling a broad coalition that voted for Iran's referral to the Security Council.

Three rounds of UN sanctions

On 31 July 2006, the Security Council adopted Resolution 1696 under Article 40 of Chapter VII of the UN Charter, giving Iran until 31 August to 'suspend all enrichment-related and reprocessing activities, including research and development' or face potential economic and diplomatic sanctions. The resolution was approved by a vote of 14 to 1, Qatar, representing the Arab world at the Council. It was the first legally binding resolution on Iran and included the threat of sanctions for non-compliance. The Council called on the Director-General of the IAEA to report by 31 August whether Iran had 'established full and sustained suspension of all activities mentioned in this resolution' and if not, that appropriate measures would be taken, that is, a detailed package of sanctions.[22]

On 22 August 2006, Iran delivered a 21 point counterproposal to the P–5+1 with a fresh approach, expressing readiness for serious negotiations. However, three days later, President Ahmadinejad announced the formal opening of a heavy water production plant at Arak, which according to experts will eventually be able to produce enough plutonium for two bombs a year. While EU foreign ministers concluded during a Luxembourg summit on 17 October that 'Iran's continuation of enrichment-related activities has left the EU no choice but to support consultations on United Nations sanctions', Iran expanded its nuclear programme by starting a second cascade of centrifuges in Natanz, doubling its enrichment capacity. Tehran said it planned to install an additional 3,000 centrifuges by the end of 2006. Some 54,000 centrifuges would be required to produce enough nuclear fuel for a reactor. The US and its European allies were circulating a draft UN Security Council resolution that would ban the sale of missile and nuclear technology to Iran and deny the country certain assistance from the IAEA. China and Russia, with their veto powers were reportedly pushing for continued dialogue with Iran instead of punishment.[23]

The Bush administration wanted stronger sanctions than the Europeans and Iran wanted to alleviate Western criticism by phased, piecemeal concessions, but the IAEA still had a whole list of demands, namely that Iran restore wider-ranging inspections of sites not declared to be nuclear under the Additional Protocol that Iran signed in 2003 but stopped observing in 2006 as retaliation for the first sanctions.

Having concluded that Iran had failed to halt uranium enrichment, the Security Council on 23 December 2006 adopted resolution 1737, blocking the import or export of sensitive nuclear material and equipment, and freezing the financial assets of persons or entities supporting its proliferation sensitive nuclear activities or the development of nuclear-weapon delivery systems. The halt to those activities would be verified by the IAEA. This time the Council requested a report within 60 days on whether Iran had suspended all activities mentioned in the resolution.

The interim US ambassador John Bolton expressed hope that the resolution would convince Iran that the best way to ensure its security and end its isolation was 'to end its nuclear weapons program [sic!] and take the steps outlined in today's text... which provided an important basis for action, and it was not open to interpretation'.[24] Solid evidence that Iran had an active nuclear weapons programme had never been submitted by any intelligence agency, the IAEA or Iranian defector, but for Bolton there was no doubt. The one who three years later finally hit the nail on the head on the basic legitimacy of Iran's nuclear programme was George Bush's opponent in the 2004 US election, Senator John Kerry, now Chairman of the Senate Foreign Relations Committee, who told the *Financial Times* in an interview: 'The Bush administration [argument of] no enrichment was ridiculous ... because it seemed so unreasonable to people', said Mr Kerry, citing Iran's rights as a signatory of the nuclear non-proliferation treaty. 'It was bombastic diplomacy. It was wasted energy. It sort of hardened the lines, if you will', he added. 'They have a right to peaceful nuclear power and to enrichment in that purpose.'[25]

Upon publication after 60 days of the new IAEA report, the Security Council again deplored Iran's non-compliance with the earlier resolutions 1696 and 1737. Then, on 24 March 2007, the Council adopted resolution 1747, which widened the scope of its December 2006 sanctions by banning the country's arms exports and freezing the assets and restricting the travel of additional individuals engaged in the country's proliferation-sensitive nuclear activities.[26]

On 3 March 2008, the Security Council adopted another resolution 1803, for Iran's continued refusal to suspend uranium enrichment, tightening restrictions on proliferation-sensitive nuclear activities, increasing vigilance over Iranian banks and having third states inspecting cargo heading for Iran. It called upon all countries to exercise vigilance over the activities of financial institutions in their territories with all banks domiciled in Iran, in particular with Bank Melli and Bank Saderat. States were also called upon to inspect cargo to and from Iran of aircraft and vessels owned or operated by Iran Air Cargo and Islamic Republic of Iran Shipping Line, provided 'reasonable grounds' existed to believe that the aircraft or vessel was transporting prohibited goods.[27] Since another report found conclusively that Iran was continuing along its path of non-compliance unperturbed, the Council adopted a final resolution 1835 on 27 September 2008, reaffirming all previous resolutions and urging Iran once more to comply. As before, Iran dismissed the resolution, saying that its uranium development was for peaceful purposes and that it would not stop its enrichment programmes.

That was the end of the UN efforts to impose sanctions. Was it all wasted? Russian Foreign Minister Sergei Lavrov stated that it was Russia's belief that the resolution helps further 'the primary goal' of the P–5+1, which is 'to help the IAEA ascertain that there is no military dimension to the nuclear programme in Iran'.[28] The glaring disparity was that Russia was looking for evidence that Iran was 'innocent'. The Bush and Sarkozy administrations were certain that Iran was guilty, without being able to provide evidence.

Therese Delpech, Director of Strategic Studies at the French Atomic Energy Commission and a leading French hardliner in dealing with Iran, lamented in a debate at the Brookings Institution in Washington in October 2008:

> We – Europeans – have negotiated during five years with the Iranians, different teams, and we came to the conclusion that they are not interested at all in negotiating, but in buying time for their military programme. And this is in writing in a number of newspapers. It's in Farsi, not in English, but sometimes we translated it in French. So we know.

She told the audience that, in June 2008, the Europeans were joined for the first time by an American, Under-secretary of State William Burns.

> Our view is that the Americans have not negotiated with the Iranians since 1979, meaning that perhaps you have something to learn from what we have acquired in terms of knowledge about the Iranians... At no point the Iranians during those five years told us, well, if the Americans would be involved; if only we would get – *non regime-change* [my italics] –security guarantees from the Americans; if only we

would get investment from the Americans. They never made any of those statements. So, if you want to try another deal, a big deal, believing that this will be a new departure and that you will succeed where we failed, good luck![29]

By November 2008, communication between the IAEA and Tehran had completely broken down.[30] Since Russia and China were unwilling to impose hard-hitting UN sanctions on Iran, Britain and France adopted a new strategy to increase pressure on Teheran, that is, use 'moral suasion' with financial and energy companies to stop doing business with Iran. The *Financial Times* quoted a senior European diplomat as saying: 'We won't get sanctions at the UN because the Russians and Chinese don't want them … So we have to work together with like-minded countries.'

Confusion about the National Intelligence estimate

United States policy towards Iran stumbled into disarray with the disclosure in December 2007 of a new assessment by American intelligence agencies that Iran had halted its (parallel, secret) nuclear weapons programme in 2003 and that the programme remains frozen, contradicting a judgment two years earlier that Tehran was working relentlessly toward building a nuclear bomb.

The assessment, a 'National Intelligence Estimate' (NIE) that represented the consensus view of all 16 American spy agencies, stated that Tehran is probably keeping its options open with respect to building a weapon, but that intelligence agencies 'do not know whether it currently intends to develop nuclear weapons'. The estimate did not say when American intelligence agencies learned that the weapons programme had been halted, but it was being made public 'since our understanding of Iran's capabilities has changed'. Some intelligence officials said that the spectre of the botched 2002 NIE on Iraq hung over their deliberations over the Iran assessment, leading them to treat the document with particular caution.[31]

America's allies in Europe expressed puzzlement about the December 2007 intelligence estimate, and some suggested its timing – and the IAEA report – were intended to reduce the chances that Bush could take military action against Iran's nuclear sites during the remainder of his term. Bush had entered his final year of 'misguided Middle East policy of strengthening Israel and marginalizing Iran', and was now rallying other nations to impose harsh financial sanctions for continuing to produce uranium fuel. Russia and China, both with deep strategic and economic relationships with Iran, indicated they would not go along with severe sanctions, but then, unexpectedly, both joined the West in demanding Iran suspend its uranium enrichment, without specifying new harsh sanctions. The IAEA also stepped up its criticism of Iran, saying its attempts to get Tehran to clear up allegations that it militarised its nuclear programme had reached a 'dead end'.[32] The agency said that Iran was enriching uranium at such a pace, that by early 2009 it could reach break-out capacity, one step away from producing enough fissile material for a crude nuclear bomb.

The great paradox is that American intelligence agencies, compromised by the Bush/Blair directed forged intelligence about Saddam Hussein's alleged weapons of mass destruction had become more reticent and on several occasions had given evidence almost to the defence of Iran. The British and German secret services have done the opposite and produced more damning evidence against the mullah-regime. The Bundesnachrichtendienst (BND), the German foreign intelligence agency, challenged the 'politicized' US NIE of December 2007, in concluding that Iran had suspended its nuclear weapons programme in 2003. The BND had amassed evidence of a sophisticated Iranian nuclear weapons programme that continued beyond 2003. This usually classified information came courtesy of Germany's highest court, the Bundesverfassungsgericht (Federal Constitutional Court) in Karlsruhe. It concerns a case against a German-Iranian businessman illegally acquiring high tech nuclear equipment and materials from Germany for Iran's military nuclear programme. In a 30-page legal opinion on 26 March and a 27 May 2009 press release in a case about illegal trading with Iran, a special national security panel of the Supreme Court cites from a May 2008 BND report that the agency 'showed comprehensively' that 'development work on nuclear weapons can be observed in Iran after 2003' and even in 2007. All the incriminating data were allowed as evidence by the German Supreme Court. The BND accuses American intelligence not just of ignoring the findings and documentation of the German investigators ahead of the NIE, but of sabotage of the international campaign to take stronger action against Iran.[33]

The Obama presidency

President Barack Obama ordered an Iran Policy Review early in his presidency and the first details became public in early April (2009). During the Bush era the sound-bite was 'No uranium-enrichment under any conditions' and under Obama it was slowly evolving towards: 'Don't make a nuclear weapon.'[34] This might leave open the option that Iran would in the end, within the context of détente with the West, be satisfied with not going all-out for the bomb, but having 'nuclear capability' instead, that is, having an increasingly sophisticated nuclear fuel cycle programme, with part of the enrichment facilities within its borders, carefully safeguarded to manage proliferation risks, without moving to the final stage of the industrial production of nuclear weapons. This is called the 'Japanese formula', that is, the non-possession, non-production and non-introduction of nuclear weapons, but mastering all the technology, including the full fissile cycle and possibly, in case of a national security emergency, making the bomb at short notice.

In August 2009 the US State Department's Bureau of Intelligence and Research (INR) published the latest estimate for Iran's acquisition of nuclear capability which echoed the timeline the Director of National Intelligence Dennis Blair had given to the Senate in February 2009. INR said that Iran is unlikely to be able to produce enough highly enriched uranium (HEU) for a nuclear weapon until at least 2013. Admiral Blair said in February: 'Iran is clearly developing all the components of a deliverable nuclear weapons program: fissionable material, nuclear weaponizing capability and the means to deliver it.' But he added that Iran had not decided to pursue the production of weapons-grade highly enriched uranium (HEU) and the parallel ability to load it on to a ballistic missile. Iran is unlikely to make such a decision for at least as long as international pressure and scrutiny persists. 'Our current estimate is that the minimum time at which Iran could technically produce the amount of highly enriched uranium for a single weapon is 2010 to 2015'. Many in Washington consider the latest estimate, that Iran won't have the technical capability to produce HEU before 2013, as a signal to defuse the crisis atmosphere that has come to characterize discussion of the issue in Washington and Jerusalem and bolster those calling for patience in dealing with Tehran.[35]

Iran's June 2009 disputed presidential election

The prospects for fruitful negotiations on the nuclear issue suffered a serious setback when the re-election of President Ahmadinejad by a landslide was rejected by the opposition as premeditated massive fraud and resulted in huge demonstrations which were violently suppressed by the Islamic militia, the *basiji,* police and revolutionary guards, with dozens of people killed and hundreds arrested. The regime branded the protests a Western conspiracy, aimed at a colour or velvet revolution, a claim eagerly endorsed by Russia and China as a first step towards regime change. European leaders were loudest in their condemnation of the controversial election and repression and President Barack Obama most restrained, while Congress by September had already started work on a new wave of sanctions, the 'Refined Petroleum Sanctions Act (RPSA)', a bill designed to limit Iran's access to gasoline and other refined petroleum products. The Senate Banking Committee held a series of hearings on the economic sanctions on Iran and to evaluate the pros and cons of the RPSA. The Obama administration was aware that the United States was not likely to win support for an embargo on shipments of gasoline or other refined fuel to Iran. The European allies, said French Foreign Minister Bernard Kouchner, viewed this as a 'blunt instrument' that could hurt ordinary Iranians, inflame public opinion and unite the country behind President Ahmadinejad. A much bigger obstacle would be to get Russia and China on board.

As the threat of sanctions was ratcheted up, the stunning revelation came in late September from President Obama himself, flanked by French

President Nicolas Sarkozy and British Prime Minister Gordon Brown at the start of the G20 in Pittsburgh, that Iran was completing a second uranium enrichment facility, hidden under a base of the Revolutionary Guards near the holy city of Qom. Allied intelligence services had been aware of the hidden tunnel-complex for several years already but had kept this under wraps to be made public at the right moment for maximum PR impact on the Iranian regime. The resonance was loud and clear but a far cry from a knock-out blow to Iran. Transatlantic disunity was palpable. Sarkozy had been frustrated for months with Obama's moderation towards the Iranians.[36] He stated that France's intelligence services were convinced that Iran was hiding its programmes to develop nuclear arms and called for 'massive sanctions in the financial and energy sectors' if Iran failed to change its nuclear policy by the end of the year. British Prime Minister Gordon Brown spoke out strongly as well but without any specific threat.[37] American intelligence agencies however, reaffirmed even after the disclosure, that no nuclear feedstock had been moved into the new plant and Secretary of State for Defense, Robert Gates, told CNN that the US and its partners still had 'somewhere between one to three years' to convince Iran to change course before it could make weapons grade uranium.[38] Iran itself claimed that it had not been in violation by not declaring the new plant with the IAEA, because, according to its original accession agreement to the NPT, it was required to do so 180 days before nuclear materials were fed into it. Even the departing chief of the IAEA, Mohamed ElBaradei, who has had his share of wrangling with Iran, argued that the latest clamour for urgent action against Iran had been 'hyped'.

'Historical negotiations'

The first official negotiations in 30 years between senior representatives of the United States and Iran on 1 October 2009 stirred a flurry of optimism when, after seven hours of talks and a tête-à-tête of the Iranian Chief Nuclear Negotiator, Saeed Jalili and his American counterpart, Under-Secretary of State for Political Affairs William Burns, two preliminary major results were announced: a tentative agreement to ship 2,645 pounds, 70 per cent of Iran's low enriched uranium to Russia for further enrichment from 5 to up to 20 per cent for medical isotopes, still substantially less than the 90 per cent required for weapons-grade fuel.[39] Then the uranium would be shipped to France to be processed into fuel rods for use in the old 1960s' era American-supplied Tehran Research Reactor to make medical isotopes.

The other result was the opening of the new uranium enrichment plant in Qom for full inspections by the IAEA before the end of October. By the time the second round of talks started, the Iranians were backtracking, obfuscating and seeking amendments. The main reason was an escalating struggle in which the levers of power were shifting towards the hard-line Revolutionary Guards.

As time passed, internal opposition in Iran against the deal escalated from across the political spectrum. Amidst rough, volatile Iranian politics, Ahmadinejad was now the strongest supporter of the deal, because, if successful, the anti-Western demagogue would paradoxically strengthen his position among Iran's pro-Western younger generations as the 'pragmatist' who ended Iran's isolation. In the West, people preferred to circumvent Ahmedinejad and strengthen the reformist opposition, but they didn't know how. Sarkozy continued to demand harsh sanctions, the American Congress was finalizing legislation towards that end and General James Jones, Obama's national security adviser, restated the zero enrichment option favoured by the Bush administration. At the same time, the IAEA inspection of the reviled underground 'enrichment' plant was carried out. The final result wouldn't be available immediately, but ElBaradei said inspectors had found 'nothing to be worried about. The idea was to use it as a bunker under the mountain to protect things [against Israeli or American attacks]. It's a hole in the mountain.'[40]

By early November, Iran conveyed the firm message that it would only send its LEU out of the country in staggered stages and that it wanted to buy new supplies from elsewhere to replenish its stockpile. This was rejected by the Western allies as this negated the whole purpose of the pact – to remove the uranium and ensure it is not enriched to levels suitable for nuclear weapons.

Since Obama had no interlocutor within the regime, he increasingly expressed support for the democratic aspirations of the Iranian people and protested the violence of the regime, but in a muted way, while keeping the doors open for a nuclear deal. When on 4 November the demonstrating 'Green' Masses in the streets of Tehran chanted in dramatic, eloquent fashion: 'Obama! Obama! You're either with them or with us!', this was becoming more problematic.

On 27 November, the board of the IAEA voted by a wide margin – 25 to 3 (with six abstentions) – to censure Iran for its refusal to accept tighter scrutiny of its nuclear activities. All five permanent members of the UN Security Council – Russia, China, France, Britain and the US – voted in favour. The Western Four of the P–5+1 were hopeful that, now Russia and China had joined them, they would do the same during the much more important Security Council vote in January, but this was far from certain. The most contested issue in Vienna this time was not the 'secret' Qom plant and the regime's backing away from the 1 October Geneva nuclear fuel deal, but Iran's stonewalling of the investigation into allegations that it had been working on nuclear weapons designs, that is, how to shape uranium for nuclear cores, on conventional explosions needed to detonate a nuclear chain reaction and on simulations of a warhead detonation at about 2,000 feet, the height at which the bomb was set off over Hiroshima in 1945.[41]

Iran's bewildering response came within two days. It would build 10 new uranium enrichment sites and look into enriching uranium at higher grade inside the country.[42]

China: less talk and more action

During the second half of 2009, European, especially French, attitudes towards Iran hardened, President Obama's position towards the regime was restrained and non-confrontational, and Russia spoke with two voices: President Medvedev cautiously distancing himself somewhat from Tehran and Prime Minister Putin maintaining his strong opposition to Western policies. China on the other hand had never fully accepted Western suspicions that Iran's nuclear programme is non-peaceful, opposes Western interference in Iranian domestic affairs, favours a negotiated settlement and opposes new and further sanctions. The obvious explanation is that China wants to protect its vital energy-links with Iran, but there is more to it than meets the eye. The rise of Iran as a major player in the highly unstable regions of Central and Southwest Asia is beneficial to China, which is facing instability in its own far western Muslim-majority border region of Xinjiang. The United States and NATO have failed to bring stability to fragile states such as Afghanistan and Pakistan, which share borders with China. In the Persian Gulf, China and Iran share the goal of a reduction of American domination and the introduction of multipolarity in its place.

Between June and November 2009, China signed US$14.5 billion worth of contracts with Iran to help expand two existing Iranian oil refineries to produce more gasoline domestically and to help develop the giant South Pars natural gas field. Iran's national oil corporation has also invited its Chinese counterparts to participate in a US$42.8 billion project to construct seven oil refineries and a 1,600 kilometre trans-Iran pipeline that will facilitate pumping fuel to China.

When French President Nicolas Sarkozy in September called for 'massive sanctions', Jiang Yu, the Chinese Foreign Ministry spokeswoman said: 'China always believes that sanctions and pressure should not be an option and will not be conducive to the current diplomatic efforts over the Iran nuclear issue.' At the same time, Chinese companies had started selling refined oil products to Iran from the Asian spot market, up to 30,000 to 40,000 barrels a day, one-third of Iranian demand. This was all geared towards helping Iran to hoard reserves and busting a possible new wave of harsh sanctions. Iran is dependent on imports for 40 per cent of its refined petroleum and 11 per cent of its diesel – despite the country's status as a big crude oil producer.

Two weeks before his mid-November visit to China, President Obama sent two senior White House officials to Beijing on a 'special mission' to try to persuade China to pressure Iran to give up its alleged nuclear weapons programme. If Beijing did not help the US on this issue, the consequences could be severe, the visitors, Dennis Ross, an Iranophobe former Middle East negotiator and pro-Israel lobbyist, and Jeffrey Bader, China-director at the National Security Council, informed the Chinese. The Chinese were told that Israel regards Iran's nuclear programme as an 'existential issue and that countries that have an existential issue don't listen to other countries'. The implication was clear: Israel could bomb Iran, leading to a crisis in the Persian Gulf region and almost inevitably problems over the very oil China needs to fuel its economic juggernaut.[43] The Chinese side has not – publicly – responded to the Israel–Iran related warning. China would instead support a tough resolution at the IAEA, criticizing Iran for flouting earlier UN resolutions. After his meeting with Chinese President Hu Jintao, President Obama said both had agreed Iran 'must provide assurances to the international community that its nuclear programme is peaceful and transparent'. He added that if Tehran 'fails to take this opportunity, there will be consequences'. But Mr Hu merely said: 'To appropriately resolve the Iranian nuclear issue through dialogue and negotiations is very important to stability in the Middle East.' He did not mention sanctions at all.[44] The wrangling about the uranium swap deal dragged on for weeks with the Iranians floating sometimes contradictory, but unacceptable counter-offers.

The standoff over the nuclear issue and the sanctions got further inflamed when during late December a new wave of 'Green', sometimes violent, street-protests on the Shiite Holy Day of Ashura was again brutally suppressed, killing at least eight people. The regime accused the British and American governments of inciting the protesters, leading to volleys of mutual recrimination back and forth. The Obama administration increasingly questioned the long-term stability of the Islamic regime and pondered whether ways should be found to directly support the opposition.[45] Trita Parsi, President of the National Iranian–American Council, who is regularly advising the White House said:

> We have been putting the nuclear clock at the centre, hoping that all the other clocks will adjust to it. But Iran's democratic development has to be at the centre. Otherwise they are trying to do a deal with a government that might not exist in three months' time.[46]

Speculation of regime change was rife for over two weeks in the international media,[47] followed by some thoughtful commentaries that ruled it out and suggested that significant change within the regime through compromise, possibly the replacement of Ahmedinejad, was more likely. The view of US and European governments that the dynamics of Iran's opposition movement would help in solving the nuclear issue and lead to normalization of relations between Iran and the West was dismissed as naïve wishful thinking.[48] The main opposition leader Mir Hossein Mousavi, who is now advocating compromise with the government, is also an ardent supporter of Iran's nuclear programme.[49]

China consistently opposed to sanctions

Beijing seems unperturbed by the volatility of Iranian politics as long as it does not affect China's energy and strategic interests. China does not agree with the disputable Western notion that Iran is heading towards making the bomb. China's policy towards Iran is not just based on its energy and other trade and investment interests as Western governments usually put it. As a rising power in West Asia, Iran is a relatively stable and cohesive former imperial state that shares with China the strategic goals of stabilization of West and Central Asia and gradual reduction of US domination in the region. Moreover, China wants to integrate West and Central Asia into one regional energy and power grid, linked by a mega-infrastructure from Xinjiang to the Persian Gulf and Indian Ocean, in case Pakistan, China's long-time strategic ally and backdoor to the Indian Ocean, disintegrates.

As a permanent member of the UN Security Council, China has voted in favour of three rounds of mild, partly conditional sanctions in 2006–2008 for not complying with UN resolutions on uranium enrichment, but during the current crisis China has consistently opposed what in American and French lingo is called expanded 'harsh', 'massive' or 'crippling' sanctions. Chinese diplomats and scholars have frequently expressed their disenchantment with the vagaries of Iran's diplomacy, but their fundamental policy is to advance more dialogue, diplomacy and compromise, not further confrontation and inflammation of the situation.

After the expiration of President Obama's 31 December deadline for progress, Iran failed to back down and on 17 January the P–5+1 convened a meeting in New York on how to proceed on a new package of sanctions. China stunned the other five, the US, Russia, Britain, France and Germany, by not sending its vice-minister of foreign affairs, He Yafei as planned, but a secondary ranking official of its UN mission to deliver the message that more diplomatic efforts should be made before embarking on new sanctions.[50] Since China was holding the rotating chair of the Security Council in January, Iran would probably not even be on the agenda anymore.

President Obama's policy of engagement with Iran has proved a failure in the sense that no top-level dialogue with the regime has materialized, comparable to President Richard Nixon's meeting with Chinese Chairman Mao Zedong in 1972 after 23 years of total estrangement between the two countries. The main reason is the serious political upheaval inside Iran, which has rendered the decision-making process of the regime highly dysfunctional. But Obama's outreach has had a major impact on segments of Iranian society, such as the urban middle class and the younger generation of highly educated, secular people who favour the replacement of the clerical regime by a liberal democratic one. This is unachievable for the moment but is probably the inevitable mid- to long-term trend.

Obama's 'Plan B', pressure and sanctions, is probably also doomed to fail. China is highly adverse to UN-authorized sanctions, unless they are 'not crippling, neither massive, nor biting' and leave China's extensive interests in Iran unaffected. The other option is 'Western' sanctions of the United States and like-minded European countries. Hardliners in the US Congress have a tendency to place the reach of US law above international law and impose legislation on the international community interfering with free trade and investment, thereby mightily annoying the US's European allies. President Bill Clinton was aware of the invalidity of American 'extraterritorial' legislation and gave waiver after waiver to international companies to do business in Iran without hitting their US operations and President Obama will probably do the same. If the US Senate passes and implements the Iran Refined Petroleum Sanctions Act, which would ban imports by Iran of refined petroleum products, China is ready to ignore it and so are Iran's other neighbours such as Pakistan, Turkmenistan, the Emirates and even NATO-ally Turkey.

The biggest retrograde impact of sanctions could be that they are likely to produce a new wave of anti-Western nationalism that would heal the rift between the regime and the Iranian people: that might be most detrimental to long-term Western interests.

The next (pen)ultimate phase in the Iran saga has not yet started and the end is not yet in sight, but indications are that US (and European) policies towards Iran have failed irreversibly. The fundamental reason is that the Bush administration stuck obsessively to a highly ideological policy that Iran, regardless of its rights as an NPT signatory, could not be permitted to engage in any uranium enrichment. Tehran fiercely resisted this classical 'imperialist' bullying with the support of Russia and China, the latter a long-time fellow victim of imperialist encroachment. When the 'EU Three' took a major initiative in launching a diplomatic dialogue with Iran in 2003, they basically accepted the constraints of the Bush administration and so did the Western Three of the UN Security Council. This has now backfired after more than three years of fruitless diplomacy, US and European pressure and threats, countered by Iranian foot-dragging and obstruction without yielding an inch. What we may be witnessing here is a shift of diplomatic prowess from West to East. Time will tell.

Notes

1 The original contract for two nuclear reactors at Bushehr was awarded in 1974 by the Shah's government to Kraftwerke Union, a subsidiary of Siemens. The project came to a full stop after the Islamic revolution in 1979. Iran first turned to the Soviet Union and then in 1991 to China. China bolted in 1993, partly under American pressure and the Russians took over, but 16 years later the project is still far from completed.
2 Jafarzadeh maintains, in a book published in 2007, that there has been a military component of the Iranian programme from the very beginning which was separated from the AEOI and became the exclusive reserve of the Revolutionary Guards, the state within the state that was determined to keep this secret from

the outside world. Alireza Jafarzadeh, *The Iran Threat: President Ahmadinejad and the Coming Nuclear Crisis*, New York: Palgrave MacMillan, 2007, p. 126.

3 IAEA Board Report, available at: http://www.iaea.org/Publications/Documents/Board/2003/gov2003-75.pdf.

4 Trita Parsi, *Treacherous Alliance: The secret dealings of Israel, Iran and the US*, New Haven: Yale University Press 2007, p. 249.

5 Ibid., pp. 243–57.

6 John W. Garver, *China and Iran: Ancient partners in a post-imperial world*, Seattle: University of Washington Press, 2006, Chapter 6: 'China's assistance to Iran's Nuclear Programs', pp. 139–65. Inspections then established that it was innocuous, but a more thorough inspection in 2003 revealed that there were secret spaces on a massive scale and it is unclear whether China was aware of these: ibid., p. 143.

7 Ibid., p. 208. Garver refers in the footnote to an article in the *Washington Post* of which the original is not available, but NTI (Nuclear Threat Initiative) carries an excerpt. It is based on another 'National Intelligence Estimate' concluding that Iran is seeking to develop a nuclear weapons capability, indicating concern for Iran's cooperation with China. The report adds that Iran's nuclear programme appears disorganized and in its early stages. R. Jeffrey Smith, *Washington Post*, 30 October 1991, pp. A1, A20, available at: http://www.nti.org/e_research/profiles/Iran/1825_1864.html.

8 Garver, *China and Iran*, pp. 221–2.

9 BBC News, 29 September 2006, available at: http://news.bbc.co.uk/2/hi/middle_east/5392584.stm.

10 Con Coughlin, *Khomeini's Ghost: The Iranian revolution and the rise of militant Islam*, London: MacMillan 2009, p. 298.

11 Mohan Malik, 'A.Q. Khan's China Connection', *China Brief*, 4(9), 29 April 2004.

12 Dafna Linzer, 'No Proof Found of Iran Arms Program: Uranium traced to Pakistani equipment', *Washington Post*, 23 August 2005.

13 Statement by the Iranian government and visiting EU Foreign Ministers, Tehran, 21 October 2003, available at: http://www.iaea.org/NewsCenter/Focus/IaeaIran/statement_iran21102003.shtml.

14 Iran–EU Agreement on Nuclear Programme, as reported on 14 November 2004 by Mehr News Agency.

15 Philippe Errera, 'The E3/EU–Iran Negotiations and Prospects for Resolving the Iranian Nuclear Issue: A European perspective', *Global Security*, 5–6 March 2005, available at: http://www.globalsecurity.org/wmd/library/report/2005/errera.htm.

16 Comments by the secretary of the foreign relations committee of the Iranian Supreme National Security Council Hossein Mousavian. 'Iran Demands More US Concessions', BBC News, 13 March 2005, on: http://news.bbc.co.uk/1/hi/world/middle_east/4344871.stm.

17 'Iran Nuclear Watch: Iran Nuclear Timeline', available at: http://irannuclearwatch.blogspot.com/2006/08/iran-nuclear-timeline.html.

18 Germany preferred the term 'EU–3+3 (the US, Russia and China), because that would reflect equal status. In fact it was just EU–3+2 because the US would not sit down with the Iranians until Summer 2008.

19 'Big Powers Fail to Agree Next Move on Iran', *Financial Times*, 30 March 2006.

20 Rice made the offer because of America's acute discomfort in Iraq but it was not until more than two years later, after Iranian officials had installed more than 3,000 centrifuges in a facility designed to hold 50,000, that Undersecretary of State William Burns joined envoys from France, Britain, Russia, China and Germany in talks with Saeed Jalili – Iran's nuclear negotiator and an

Ahmadinejad confidant – about incentives to give to Tehran. Michael Rubin, 'Now Bush is Appeasing Iran', *Wall Street Journal*, 21 July 2008.
21 Seymour M. Hersh, 'Last Stand: The military's problem with the President's Iran policy', *New Yorker*, 10 July 2006.
22 SC8792, Resolution 1696, 31 July 2006, available at: http://www.un.org/News/Press/docs/2006/sc8792.doc.htm.
23 'Iran Reportedly Takes Another Step in Nuclear Program', Associated Press, 27 October 2006.
24 SC8928, Resolution 1737, 23 December 2006, available at: http://www.un.org/News/Press/docs/2006/sc8928.doc.htm.
25 John Kerry, 'Time for Diplomacy to End the Stand-Off with Iran', *Financial Times*, 30 September 2009.
26 SC8980, Resolution 1747, 24 March 2007, available at: http://www.un.org/News/Press/docs/2007/sc8980.doc.htm:

> ['5. *Decides* that Iran shall not supply, sell or transfer directly or indirectly from its territory or by its nationals or using its flag vessels or aircraft any arms or related materiel, and that all States shall prohibit the procurement of such items from Iran by their nationals, or using their flag vessels or aircraft, and whether or not originating in the territory of Iran; '6. *Calls upon* all States to exercise vigilance and restraint in the supply, sale or transfer directly or indirectly from their territories or by their nationals or using their flag vessels or aircraft of any battle tanks, armoured combat vehicles, large calibre artillery systems, combat aircraft, attack helicopters, warships, missiles or missile systems as defined for the purpose of the United Nations Register on Conventional Arms to Iran, and in the provision to Iran of any technical assistance or training, financial assistance, investment, brokering or other services, and the transfer of financial resources or services, related to the supply, sale, transfer, manufacture or use of such items in order to prevent a destabilising accumulation of arms;']

27 SC9268, Resolution 1803, 3 March 2008, available at: http://www.un.org/News/Press/docs//2008/sc9268.doc.htm.
28 http://www.voanews.com/uspolicy/2008-10-06-voa4.cfm.
29 Therese Delpech, 'Who is Reshaping the World?', Washington DC: The Brookings Institution, 8 October 2008, available at: http://www.brookings.edu/events/2008/1007_aron.aspx.
30 Daniel Dombey, 'Iran Increases Stockpile of Uranium', *Financial Times*, 19 November 2008.
31 Office of the Director of National Intelligence, National Intelligence Estimate, 'Iran: Nuclear Intentions and Capabilites', November 2007, available at: http://www.dni.gov/press_release/20071203_release.pdf; Mark Mazetti, 'US Says Iran Ended Atomic Arms Work', *New York Times*, 3 December 2007.
32 James Blitz, 'Russia Joins UN Move to Condemn Tehran', *Financial Times*, 27 September 2008.
33 Bruno Schirra, 'Germany's Spies Refuted the 2007 NIE Report: "Work on nuclear weapons can be observed in Iran even after 2003"', *Wall Street Journal Europe*, 24 July 2009.
34 Daniel Dombey, 'Flames to Douse', *Financial Times*, 16 April 2009.
35 Daniel Luban, 'New Nuke Report Debunks Iran Hawks', *Asia Times*, 11 August 2009.
36 'French Atomique Pique', *Wall Street Journal*, 29 September 2009.
37 David E. Sanger and Helene Cooper, 'US and Allies Warn Iran Over Nuclear "Deception"', *New York Times*, 26 September 2009.
38 'Iran Test-Fires Long Range Missile', *Financial Times*, 27 September 2009.

39 2,205 Pounds is the commonly accepted amount of low-enriched uranium needed to produce weapons-grade uranium.
40 Roger Cohen, 'Bunkers or Breakthroughs', *New York Times*, 6 November 2009.
41 Alan Cowell and David E. Sanger, 'Iran Censured Over Nuclear Program by UN Watchdog', *New York Times*, 28 November 2009; William J. Broad and David E. Sanger, 'Report Says Iran Has Data to Make a Nuclear Bomb', *New York Times*, 4 October 2009; William J. Broad, 'Iran Shielding Nuclear Efforts in Tunnel Mazes', *New York Times*, 6 January 2010; Con Coughlin, 'Iran Seeks Nuclear Parts Through Taiwan', *Daily Telegraph*, 10 December 2009.
42 Najmeh Bozorgmehr and Monavar Khalaj, 'Iran Plans to Build 10 Enrichment Plants', *Financial Times*, 29 November 2009.
43 John Pomfret and Joby Warrick, 'China's Backing on Iran Followed Dire Predictions; Before Obama's visit, NSC warned leaders of Mideast turmoil', *Washington Post*, 26 November 2009.
44 Helene Cooper, 'China Holds Firm on Major Issues in Obama's Visit', *New York Times*, 18 November 2009.
45 Jay Solomon, 'US Shifts Iran Focus to Support Opposition', *Wall Street Journal*, 9 January 2010.
46 Anna Fifield, 'Washington Grows More Vocal on Iran', *Financial Times*, 28 December 2009.
47 For examples see: 'The Peoples' Revolt in Iran: The regime is losing legitimacy, even as Obama engages it', *Wall Street Journal*, 22 December 2009; 'Iranian Regime Critic Kadivar: "I am convinced the Regime will collapse"', *Der Spiegel*, 26 December 2009; Abbas Milani, 'The Tipping Point in Iran', *Wall Street Journal*, 29 December 2009; 'Iran Protests Turn into Open Rebellion', *Financial Times*, 30 December 2009; Roger Cohen, 'Change Iran at the Top', *New York Times*, 31 December 2009; Najmeh Bozorgmehr, 'Fissures Widen in Tehran Regime', *Financial Times*, 1 January 2010; '2010: Regime change in Iran – engagement didn't work', *Weekly Standard*, 4 January 2010.
48 Flynt Leverett and Hillary Mann Leverett, 'Another Iranian Revolution: Not likely', *New York Times*, 7 January 2010; Dilip Hiro, 'Regime Change in Tehran: Don't bet on it', *Asia Times*, 14 January 2010.
49 Kaveh L. Afrasiabi, 'From Confrontation to Reconciliation', *Asia Times*, 5 January 2010.
50 Harvey Morris, 'China Move Threatens to Delay Sanctions', *Financial Times*, 17 January 2010.

10 Chinese and European engagement in UN peace operations

Janka Oertel

Introduction

Since the establishment of the world body to 'save succeeding generations from the scourge of war',[1] the United Nations system has structured and influenced the post-war international order in various fields of international cooperation. The peace and security realm has often been the most visible (and controversial) area of UN activity. Marking its 60th anniversary in 2008, peacekeeping[2] has been the spearhead of UN engagement in the prevention and overcoming of international crises. The significance of peace operations lies mainly in the actual activities on the ground but also in a mission's capacity to draw attention to and mobilize resources for a specific conflict area.

UN peacekeeping operations depend on the contributions of member states to staff and carry out the respective missions around the globe. Financing for these activities is largely provided by the Western industrialized states, while soldiers predominantly stem from developing countries – especially from Asia.[3]

In its last report the UN Special Committee on Peacekeeping Operations detailed the overstretch of peacekeepers and the necessity to cooperate closer with troop-contributing nations to guarantee efficient and effective deployments.[4] This analysis is underlined by the findings of the recent internal report by the Department of Peacekeeping Operations (DPKO)/Department of Field Support (DFS) 'A New Partnership Agenda: Charting a New Horizon for UN Peacekeeping' (New Horizon Report), which identifies key challenges to UN peacekeeping in the twenty-first century and attempts to develop a 'forward agenda' for crucial change and offer potential solutions.[5]

The current UN-overstretch is not necessarily a result of a general lack of soldiers provided for UN operations. It is rather a lack of *qualified* personnel, as well as basic logistic needs such as transportation and airlift capacity. The largest current troop-contributing nations, such as Pakistan, Bangladesh, India and Nigeria,[6] offer soldiers which are not always capable and equipped to cope with the mounting challenges that Blue Helmets face in

increasingly complex crisis situations on the ground. The report also identifies the need for ongoing capacity building in the assessment, planning and
management of peacekeeping operations as well as the persistent urgency
of clear and practicable Security Council (SC) mandates.[7]

The *Annual Review of Global Peace Operations 2009* also advocates the
observance of a more conservative approach to UN peacekeeping activities,
a 'less might be more' approach, as peacekeeping is not adequate for all
types of international crises, especially when there is no actual peace to keep
and host nation consent is questionable. It states that most major power
doctrines, such as the US, French or Indian, now include peacekeeping as a
strategic dimension, thereby failing to distinctly separate peacekeeping from
fighting wars. According to the authors' assessment, this lack of distinction has
contributed greatly to the various failures and unfulfilled expectations
concerning the conduct of peacekeeping operations.[8]

Due to the fundamental deficits in post-Cold War UN peacekeeping,
demonstrated especially in the devastating failures in Somalia (1993),
Rwanda (1994) and Srebrenica (Bosnia-Herzegovina 1995), Western powers
have been increasingly reluctant to engage their troops in UN operations.
Deployment of personnel has decreased gradually (see Figure 10.1). At the
same time, EU countries have increasingly followed a regional approach in
the peacekeeping sector, acting less often within a UN context, but in
(UN-mandated) EU or NATO operations. Since the beginning of this century,
however, China has steadily increased its engagement in UN peacekeeping
operations and evolved into a significant pillar in the UN's peacekeeping
architecture.[9]

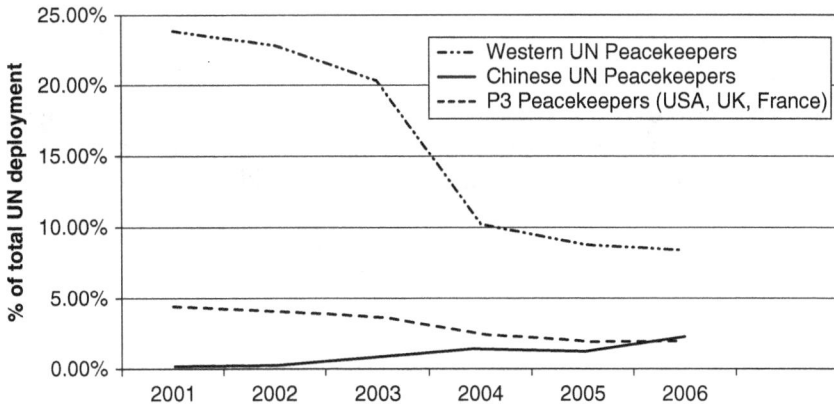

Figure 10.1 Troop contributions to UN peace operations 2001–2006.

Source: Western figures based on Bellamy and Williams, 'The West and Contemporary Peace
Operations', Journal of Peace Research, Vol. 46, No.1, p. 45. Chinese figures based on DPKO
data (of August each year) available at http://www.un.org/Depts/dpko/dpko/contributors/.

The main question guiding the analysis will thus be: to what extent can China complement Europe's recently more limited role in United Nations peacekeeping operations? It will be argued that China's increased activity has the potential to fill an existing void in the UN peacekeeping sector, especially on the African continent. Its pragmatic and 'less ambitious' approach to peacekeeping in comparison to European nations could increase the likelihood of successful (albeit less comprehensive) missions. However, China cannot and will not shoulder international peacekeeping operations on its own. European nations will be responsible for reinvigorating UN peacekeeping operations by recommitting their capacities to the world body. In this respect an increased Chinese engagement could be an incentive for renewed cooperation.[10]

After briefly addressing the current challenges to UN peacekeeping, Chinese and European conceptions of security and sovereignty will be examined, serving as the background for the subsequent analysis of the respective policies regarding UN peacekeeping operations. Actual capacities and the rationale behind the detectable tendencies in Chinese and European policies will be assessed to identify potential challenges to the international peacekeeping architecture.

Between peacemaking, peacekeeping and peacebuilding: UN peacekeeping operations in crisis?

> Legitimacy and consent are, to a peace operation, what body armour is to an infantry soldier: something to reduce the probability of catastrophic system failure.
>
> Source: W. J. Durch and M. L. England,
> *Annual Review of Global Peace Operations 2009*, p. 17.

The international peace and security environment has undergone significant changes over the past decades. UN peacekeeping operations have evolved from classic peacekeeping activities, such as truce supervision, to complex integrated missions, which often include peacemaking or peace-building activities and even the temporary adoption of administrative functions to restore self-governing capacities.[11] The UN's greatest strength and capital in administering global peacekeeping operations lies within the legitimizing force the world body has to offer. The importance of international action in the realm of peacekeeping operations is hardly questioned. However, the scope and the depth of engagement are often contested.

Classic peacekeeping in its current form was established within the context of truce supervision in the Suez crisis in 1956. Since then the so-called Blue Helmets have carried out more than 60 missions worldwide. Despite their special status within the UN system, the Blue Helmets find no mentioning in the UN Charter. The collective security mechanisms, in Articles 43 to 50 of the founding document, have never been resorted to, due to the ideological confrontation and resulting stalemate in the Security Council up to the end of the twentieth century.

When the end of the Cold War enabled a surge of newly deployed missions, making UN peacekeeping the instrument of choice for stabilizing conflict areas, weaknesses in the existing system became ever more obvious. After the devastating failures in the 1990s the entire peacekeeping apparatus was subjected to major reform.

Initiatives, such as the Brahimi Report[12] published in 2000, called for a significant increase in professionalism, personnel and material contributions, and commitment by member states, as well as a sufficient assessment of the situation on the ground to actively strengthen UN peacekeeping capacities when sending peacekeepers to conflict regions. UN peacekeeping operations are still far from being the ideal instrument for conflict resolution – grave challenges remain.

In an attempt to conceptualize UN practices, which have evolved over time the Department of Peacekeeping Operations and the newly established Department of Field Support introduced the Capstone Doctrine[13] in 2008. It outlines the difficulties of modern peacekeeping operations, often dealing with the simultaneity of different phases in the political (and military) process of conflict resolution. Following this operational manual, conflict prevention provides the most effective measure. However, once a situation has deteriorated, *peacemaking* – efforts include third party mediation, diplomatic consultations, inclusion of civil society actors – is an initial step for peaceful conflict resolution. It can eventually be carried out parallel to *peace-enforcement* operations – mandated by the UN Security Council under Chapter VII of the UN Charter, resorting to military efforts of troops deployed either under UN command or UN-mandated regional actors and state coalitions. Once a cease-fire is reached, *peacekeeping* serves as an important instrument for truce supervision or monitoring the observance of a peace agreement. Most likely, however, peace-enforcement or peacemaking efforts prevail in early phases of conflict resolution. To consolidate peace in a fragile post-conflict environment, *peacebuilding* measures have to be established, preventing a country from relapsing into conflict.[14]

Consolidating peace remains the most difficult task, including as it does elements of security sector reform and re-establishment of police forces, as well as the rule of law, but also such difficult tasks as return of internally displaced persons and refugees, disarmament and general state-building responsibilities. In summary, these so-called 'multidimensional operations' can now be required to:

- assist in implementing a comprehensive peace agreement;
- monitor a ceasefire or cessation of hostilities to allow space for political negotiations and a peaceful settlement of disputes;
- provide a secure environment encouraging a return to normal civilian life;
- prevent the outbreak or spill over of conflict across borders;

- lead states or territories through a transition to stable government based on democratic principles, good governance and economic development; and
- administer a territory for a transitional period, thereby carrying out all the functions that are normally in the responsibility of a government.[15]

These tasks, which have emerged from the limited functions of classic peacekeeping can infringe greatly on the sovereignty of the afflicted state and constitute a significant intrusion in its internal affairs.

In comparison to most European nations, which endorse this wider, norm-based UN approach, focusing on the civilian population, human rights and conflict prevention, the People's Republic of China (PRC) favours a traditional concept of peacekeeping: China as one of the permanent members (P5) of the UN Security Council is constantly stressing the triad of host nation consent, neutrality and use of force merely for self-defence. It also regards an SC mandate as a necessary imperative for the deployment of a peace operation. The People's Republic thus acknowledges the classic principles of the early years of UN Peacekeeping, which have been reiterated throughout the decades of peacekeeping's evolution and reform[16] and – as stated above – China can indeed link its approach to recent strategic considerations in the overall evaluation of peacekeeping operations.

Concepts of security and sovereignty

The question thus remains how Chinese involvement in UN peacekeeping operations relates to China's understanding of security and sovereignty in international relations. Mainstream Chinese international relations research remains centred around basic Realist assumptions. The Chinese government can only to a limited degree embrace a broadened concept of security, which currently constitutes the basis for UN activity in crisis scenarios, as it contradicts traditional understandings of national sovereignty and territorial integrity. Non-intervention in another state's affairs is in this respect a central element in the protection of national security. China's traditional 'Westphalian' position concerning issues of state sovereignty occasionally prevents more ambitious Chinese engagement in UN peace and security structures.[17] Despite this rhetoric in its approach to national security, however, China recognizes the fact that the security environment of the twenty-first century has changed significantly and adapts its policies flexibly.

To grasp the ongoing processes, new concepts of understanding security have been promoted especially by the UN system. They all rest on the overarching dimension of 'human security', introduced by the Human Development Report of the United Nations Development Programme (UNDP) in 1994. The concept as such is subject to debate and at least two readings with different emphases exist.[18] The term itself, however, has become a keyword in the discussions about multilateral crisis prevention and peacekeeping operations – especially when discussing the elimination of root causes of conflicts and in peacebuilding contexts. It establishes the individual as the main referent object for security.

The EU has stressed the human security approach towards international conflict resolution.[19] It includes various forms of 'threats', which endanger an individual's 'physical safety, economic and social well-being, respect for dignity and worth as human being' and calls for the 'protection of human rights and fundamental freedoms'[20]. Human security (individual well-being) is thus detached from national security (state survival).

The EU's understanding of security is formally summarized in the European Security Strategy of 2003. It states that security is the necessary precondition for development, which fosters stability. It is the EU's declared goal not only to defend its security but likewise to promote its values to increase the degree of democratization and development worldwide, as the best protection for its own security is 'a world of well-governed democratic states'.[21] Hence, in this normative approach, the promotion of good governance, the support of social and political reform, rule of law and protecting human rights become central objectives of EU policy when engaging in international peacekeeping operations. This can also include 'rapid, and when necessary, robust intervention'[22] in states of concern.

Although these new developments in the international discourse on matters of security and sovereignty find resonance in China's academic circles and are incorporated in Chinese foreign policy elite discussions,[23] the Chinese leadership currently rejects this broad definition of security. In his speech at the 17th National People's Congress in October 2007, Hu Jintao instead endorsed his 'pet concept' – the scientific outlook on development. This 'people-centred approach' to development and prosperity includes the dimension of national security. However, it links the security of people inextricably to the unity and security of the state, which is the provider of this respective 'safety'. Instead of human security the term 'people's safety' is often referred to in a Chinese context, clearly distinguishing between a security (state) and a safety (individual) dimension. Not all threats falling in the category of human security following the general definition of the International Commission on Intervention and State Sovereignty (ICISS) are regarded as grave enough to threaten national security. Non-traditional threats, such as environmental degradation, terrorism or pandemics, are recognized as new challenges to international security by the Chinese administration and are also mentioned in the recently published Defence White Paper, giving them a clear security political dimension.[24] However, other challenges such as poverty, unsafe food or water supplies and natural disasters, albeit severely endangering people's lives, are not perceived as direct threats to security. According to Li Dongyan, in Chinese policy, the two concepts, human and national security, are not separated. Chinese human security scholars 'emphasize the interrelated and complementary relations between the two security concepts, especially the role of the state to protect people and safeguard human security'.[25] Despite this rhetoric adherence in the Chinese position with regard to the idea of sovereignty, the concept is undergoing significant adjustments on a case-by-case basis in the political practice. This momentum allows for flexibility in Chinese foreign policy making and international cooperation.

A valid example for these recent developments within the context of an overall discussion on aspects of human security is the debate surrounding the so-called Responsibility to Protect (R2P), which was also put forward by the ICISS and is linked to UN peacekeeping operations. The 2005 World Summit Outcome document, an agreement of 190 heads of states and governments, marking the 60th anniversary of the United Nations, sets the framework for the current debate as it picks up the idea of R2P. In this document R2P is defined as limited to specific sets of crimes, namely: genocide, ethnic cleansing, war crimes and crimes against humanity. It is argued that 'every state has the responsibility to use appropriate diplomatic, humanitarian and other peaceful means, in accordance with Chapters VI and VIII of the Charter, to help protect populations' from these crimes 'on a case-by-case basis and in cooperation with relevant regional organizations as appropriate, should peaceful means be inadequate and national authorities manifestly fail' in their duty to provide the necessary protection.[26]

Despite being generally opposed to all forms of interventionism and automatisms for international deployments, China's willingness to agree to this (albeit non-binding) resolution, underlines that it has become increasingly flexible in international peace and security affairs.[27] China's operative engagement in UN peacekeeping operations demonstrates these developments well and shall thus be subject to a more detailed analysis against the backdrop of the European approach.

Chinese engagement in UN peacekeeping operations

After regaining membership in the world body and reclaiming its seat in the Security Council in 1971, the People's Republic of China was generally opposed to international peacekeeping operations, regarding them as mere interventionism of Western powers. It refrained from voting on respective issues in the Council and refused to pay its assessed contributions to the peacekeeping budget. This policy became more nuanced with the opening up process in the late 1970s and early 1980s. Despite still not being actively involved, rhetorical support for peacekeeping missions strictly abiding by the principles of the UN Charter began in 1981.[28]

With accession to the UN Special Committee on Peacekeeping Operations, which is responsible for the review and assessment of all missions carried out under the authority of the DPKO since 1988, the gradual integration process into the UN peacekeeping architecture continued. It led to the first deployment of civilian election observers to Namibia and a small group of military observers to the Middle East at the turn of the decade.

China continuously increased its engagement in numbers and capacity of deployed personnel. China has also provided support for missions which – under considerations of ongoing rhetorical constraint concerning the intervention in the domestic affairs of other states – have gone far beyond the tasks of classic peacekeeping: for example, by financially contributing to the UN Transitional Authority in Cambodia (UNTAC) and simultaneously deploying 800 engineers in 1992/93,[29] or by sending police officers to the UN Mission in Bosnia-Herzegovina (UNMIBH) in 2001 and the UN Assistance Mission in Afghanistan (UNAMA) in 2004.[30] The policy of limited support on a case-by-case basis evolved, allowing for a pragmatic approach.

Currently China is involved in 10 operations worldwide providing a total of 2,143 military personnel and police officers thereby ranking 13th among the troop-contributing nations. The People's Republic is thus the largest troop contributor among the permanent members of the Security Council.[31] Marking a roughly twenty-fold increase in Chinese contributions compared to 2001, the rise in Chinese engagement can hardly be overstated. From being an opponent and later a sceptic of UN peacekeeping, China has evolved into a significant force in this realm of UN activity. Increasingly stressing the dimension of being a responsible player in international affairs, China is a significant supporter of the UN's ability to legitimize the use of force in international relations.

In a recent meeting of the Security Council considering the overall situation of UN peacekeeping, Chinese representative La Yifan stated that the demand for UN operations is continuously increasing. At the same time the missions were becoming larger, more complex and required a greater amount of human and management resources. Despite this trenchant analysis, he underlined the Chinese commitment to the three principles of host-nation consent, use of force merely for purposes of self-defence and the strict abidance to the principle of neutrality.[32] By declaring these principles the 'foundation' for success and the simultaneous acceptance of ever-changing realities in the theoretical as well as the practical realm, Beijing is left with enough leverage for political action despite rhetoric moderation. No concrete commitments are being made. The necessity of providing logistic support is mentioned and directed at 'countries with the means' to do so[33] – clearly distancing China from any direct responsibility in this field.

China has not yet deployed any combat forces to UN operations, although it has offered to do so in the case of UNIFIL (Lebanon) – an offer that was welcomed but later turned down, due to logistic considerations.[34] Its police and military officers as well as engineers and other non-combat forces deployed are praised by DPKO as well as by UN staff in the respective missions for their well-trained and highly qualified efforts.[35]

The recently published International Crisis Group Report (ICG Report) on Chinese peacekeeping activities identifies a major Chinese strength in its capacity to deploy so-called 'force enablers' (e.g. medical personnel, logistics experts and engineering troops) as well as a substantive number of police forces, both highly needed in peacekeeping scenarios.[36] These contributions are of dual value to the mission as they not only offer a substantive asset to the operation by themselves but also multiply the capacities of other troops on the ground by providing targeted assistance. Likewise, Chinese police forces are highly experienced in important tasks of crowd control and dispersion,[37] which can be valuable in post-conflict scenarios. Currently China does not possess sufficient military transport capacity for international operations and draws on civilian resources for transportation in international humanitarian deployments. According to Holslag,

> Beijing is still hoping to buy an additional batch of 34 Il-76 and four Il-78 refuelling tankers, which would substantially increase China's long-range airlift capacity. At the same time, China is investing massively in developing its own large long-range aircraft

– a project which is supposed to be completed by 2020.[38]

The Hu Administration has set out the goal of laying the foundation for China's military modernization up to 2010. Full modernization is supposed to be completed by 2050, while significant steps in the use of information technology will be undertaken up to 2020. These considerable efforts will have the effect that China, more than ever before, is able to back its global interests with military power. However, while the European arms embargo against China, which was established in the aftermath of the Tiananmen Square events in 1989, is still in effect, China remains cut off from important technological advancements, which slows down its development of military capacities in comparison with the Europeans especially in the high-technology realm.[39]

Recent developments in China's military sector indicate that a modernized People's Liberation Army (PLA) is putting greater emphasis on mobility and projection capabilities. Despite the self-evident deterrent capacity in terms of national security, which are the main reason for these developments, a more sophisticated PLA could also offer the UN a diversification of potential providers of military capacities, especially with regard to the constantly problematic realm of transport and airlift capabilities. Currently, however, China is not only unwilling but also mostly unable to conduct complex operations independently.

In June 2009 a new Peacekeeping Training Centre was opened in Huairou, near Beijing.[40] Up to then, the Langfang Training Centre for Civilian Police was the only centre dedicated to the preparation of Chinese personnel in UN Operations.[41] The new facility indicates the increased professionalization of the Chinese peacekeeping apparatus and allows for the assumption that the Chinese leadership is also preparing for combat forces in the realm of UN peacekeeping operations.

The People's Republic takes part in the UN Stand-by Arrangements System (UNSAS). UNSAS was developed in 1994 to improve the deployment time for peacekeeping operations. Member states can indicate resources, which are earmarked and can generally be provided to the UN upon request and with national (parliamentary) consent. The system has 4 levels, while the last level (4) of 'contingent owned equipment' has not yet been agreed to by any member state.[42] China upgraded its engagement in UNSAS in 2002. Ambassador Wang stated that China supports 'the Secretariat to adjust and improve UNSAS in accordance with the development of the situation and to enhance the rapid deployment capacity of peacekeeping operations'.[43] He signalled that

> [i]n addition to contributing engineering corps, military observers, civilian police and civilian personnel to relevant peacekeeping missions over the past years, the Chinese Government decided to upgrade its participation in UNSAS by designating non-combat formed units to take part in UNSAS ... includ[ing] one Engineering Unit, one Medical Unit and two Transport Units.[44]

Up to now China's engagement has not exceeded level 1 participation – merely necessitating the submission of a list of resources, which could potentially be provided to UN operations.[45]

Although European member states mostly cooperate on level 2, implicating the supply of detailed technical information on civilian and military capabilities, or level 3, which includes the additional signing of the Memoranda of Understanding (MoU) concerning international deployments, the UNSAS system itself has proven rather unreliable 'due to member states lack of definite commitment'.[46] In summary, despite an increasingly active posture on the ground, China has so far been reluctant to take a lead in the conduct of peacekeeping operations, often rhetorically retreating to its principle-driven stand on security, sovereignty and non-intervention.

Beijing, however, has begun to broaden its sphere of interest beyond the Chinese territory and has taken a pragmatic case-by-case approach to international crisis management and conflict resolution. This multifaceted approach can be seen in the international efforts in the Gulf of Aden, where China has deployed the largest maritime mission for the past 600 years of its history. With this UN-mandated[47] deployment to safeguard trade routes and commercial sea traffic from pirate activities the People's Republic has reached a new degree of engagement. With the deployment of two destroyers and a supply ship Beijing indicates that it is willing to protect economic interests and assume greater responsibility in international affairs,[48] cooperating with various international partners and a respective EU mission (Atalanta) in the region (see Chapter 11 for details). In its maritime mission China remains hesitant to cooperate more closely with European partners,[49] which might be because China is still inexperienced in conducting these kinds of operations. China has to get used to its new global role.

EU engagement in UN peacekeeping operations

Before 2003, EU member states contributed to the UN peacekeeping sector only on an individual basis, with nations such as France and Italy being more strongly involved than others. These individual contributions of European nations have – as indicated above – generally decreased since the 1990s.

Instead of deploying their troops within a UN context EU member states began to resort to alternative concepts of peacekeeping and a more regional approach, leading Tardy to the assessment that EU operations also became necessary because of the absence of EU member states in UN operations.[50] The year 2003 marked the initial deployment of a UN-mandated EU mission. That same year the European Security Strategy was adopted outlining the EU's understanding of its role in the international security architecture as being 'committed to reinforcing its cooperation with the UN to assist countries emerging from conflicts, and to enhancing its support for the UN in short-term crisis management situations'.[51] Its engagement as an actor in UN peacekeeping operations was initiated by the deployment of Operation Artemis in the Democratic Republic of Congo. Upon request for support by UN Secretary General Kofi Annan, France proved to be the driving force behind the process. In contrast to previous decades of going it alone on the African continent, Paris was striving for legitimacy and support of the EU.[52]

Artemis served as a test case for European capacities and the structures of a European Security and Defence Policy (ESDP) – it performed well within the very strict (geographical and operational) limitations of its mandate. Likewise it set a precedent for European engagement on the African continent with robust and sophisticated military capabilities.[53] Nevertheless, the selective and brief operation served as a mere crisis intervention and did not provide solutions for a sustainable peace.

EU–UN cooperation has since been institutionalized in a formal joint declaration on crisis management to enhance mutual coordination especially in the fields of planning, training, communication and in the identification of best practices.[54] In evaluating the EU's second military operation on the African continent, EUFOR Chad/Central African Republic (CAR), the authors of the *Annual Review of Global Peace Operations 2009* concluded that neither MINUCRAT (the respective UN support operation) nor EUFOR, which were simultaneously deployed, assisted significantly in improving the situation in the region. Both missions lacked a substantive mandate to encounter the *political* challenges of the underlying conflict. The EU mandate was limited to a one-year term and its duties were taken over by a larger UN force – equipped with a Chapter VII mandate – on 15 March 2009.[55]

Inter-organizational operations implicate additional problems of organizational egoisms and rivalries, which in the case of Chad/CAR led to diverging perceptions of the realities on the ground. While the EU regarded its military deployment as a separate and complementary operation, the UN viewed the military component as 'part of a larger UN-led intervention'.[56] EU Peacekeepers failed to live up to their highly resourced and well-trained potential. They were mandated to

> contribute to protecting civilians in danger, particularly refugees and displaced persons; facilitate the delivery of humanitarian aid and the free movement of humanitarian personnel by helping to improve security in the area of operations; contribute to protecting United Nations personnel, facilities, installations and equipment and to ensure the security and freedom of movement of its staff and United Nations and associated personnel.[57]

It became obvious, however, that the mission's mandate and the EU's capacities in a military operation were ill-fit for the actual internal conflict in Chad, as the EU's personnel was trained to address a military threat. The EU regards its activities in Chad as a successful mission. As it plans to stay involved in Chad as well as in the Central African Republic and neighbouring Sudan, a significant number of EUFOR soldiers have merely exchanged their badges and are now serving within the context of MINUCRAT.[58] See Table 10.1 for a list of UN-mandated EU military operations.

Currently[59] 23 of the 27 EU member states contribute to UN peacekeeping operations comprising a total of 9,022 troops and police, which amounts to less than 10 per cent of the total troops and police in UN peacekeeping operations.[60] Nine of the EU troop-contributing nations deploy less than 100 troops and police overall for the various UN operations worldwide. There is no European country among the Top 10 troop-contributing nations. Italy ranks 12th and deploys 2,287 staff, roughly 25 per cent of the overall European troops and police – significantly more than any other European nation. Among the top 20 troop-contributing nations only one

Table 10.1 UN-mandated EU Military Operations since 2003

Mission	Country	Time Frame	Size
Artemis	Democratic Republic of Congo	2003	1800 troops
EUFOR Althea*	Bosnia-Herzegovina	since 2004	2084 troops
EUFOR DR Congo	Democratic Republic of Congo	2006	2300 troops
EUFOR Chad/CAR	Chad/Central AfricanRepublic	2008–2009	3700 troops
EU NAVFOR Atalanta*	Maritime Mission at the Horn of Africa/Somalia	since 2008	1200 troops

*Ongoing missions as of April 2009.

Source: based on http://www.consilium.europa.eu/uedocs/cmsUpload/map-ENApril09.pdf.

further European nation can be found – France, ranking 16th with an overall contribution of 1,791.[61]

All states share the expenses for UN peacekeeping operations. Based on the scale of assessments for the peacekeeping budget the respective expenses are determined by the UN General Assembly. It takes into account the economic capacity and size of a country and requires the P5 to pay comparatively higher dues because of their special responsibility for the maintenance of international peace and security.[62] Additionally, countries can add voluntary contributions, which are generally non-reimbursable and include concrete operational assistance, such as transportation and supplies or financial contributions exceeding their required share.[63] When it comes to the financing of UN operations European nations remain a significant pillar of the UN system, which currently allows them to exert influence on the structuring and design of the missions. European nations provide significant support, assisting in keeping the UN peace and security sector financially operational despite its very limited options to fulfil the tasks conferred upon it.

The EU in its self-conception as normative power has a significant responsibility for maintaining peace and security on the global level. However, the tendency of EU member states to resort to deploying their troops in UN-mandated missions under regional (EU/NATO) command in so-called 'stand-alone missions' has severe implications for the overall crisis response capability of the United Nations. 'The fact that northern countries are involved in crisis management through other institutions, such as the EU or NATO, tends to accentuate the divide'[64] between the global North and South. In its selectivity, EU engagement can lead to a two-class system in UN peacekeeping, leaving various UN missions severely understaffed in qualified and well-trained personnel, as well as under-equipped for reconnaissance and logistics.[65]

Against the backdrop of an identified difference in understanding of security and sovereignty, the development towards a decreasing European engagement in overall troop contributions and a comparatively significant increase in Chinese activity in UN missions does not immediately reveal itself. What are the reasons leading to the divergence in the Chinese and the European approach to UN peacekeeping operations?

Rationale behind the respective approaches to peacekeeping operations

China's rationale of cooperating more closely in the international security system is motivated by a combination of domestic considerations and external determinants.

First and foremost, the Communist Party is highly interested in stabilizing its domestic position and deferring criticism of its authoritarian rule. Social and political stability in China are largely based on extensive economic growth and the improvement of living conditions for the majority of the population. The Party has increased its efforts to promote a multilateral agenda, intended to assist China in generating a more positive image internationally, rendering its gradual rise less hostile to the outside world. This behaviour has repercussions on the way in which the population appreciates its government for an internationally engaged responsible China, finally able to return to its desired place amongst the world's leading powers. Likewise, the deployment of military personnel also has a nationalist component, as Chinese peacekeepers are domestically praised for their service thereby increasing identification with the PLA engaged abroad. Each casualty is mourned by underlining the army's importance in safeguarding world peace.[66]

Beijing is also aware of the necessity of protecting its global economic interests. Instability and crises especially on the African continent, which serves as one of the People's Republic's most important suppliers of resources and is a significant site of Chinese investment, hold the potential to hamper its development. By adhering to the principle of host nation consent and Security Council mandate China is clearly positioning itself as opposed to unilateral interventions – an attitude highly regarded by authoritarian leaders of states in crisis regions. By engaging more strongly in peacekeeping operations, China has a greater potential to shape the international agenda in its interest.

A third important factor making the deployment of Chinese troops within the context of UN peacekeeping operations attractive to the Chinese leadership is the operational benefit, which can be gained from the experience of international exposure and cooperation. Despite the fact that the PRC is currently not deploying combat forces, military officers working as observers or commanders attain valuable knowledge and leadership capabilities. Police forces also become increasingly capable and exposed to innovative methods and modern techniques when working in cooperation with advanced and experienced international comrades.[67] As indicated above China's military capacities are being strengthened – a tendency regarded with scepticism by the outside world. China has therefore come to embrace military diplomacy as a tool for a more favourable international security environment.[68]

The EU on the other hand has much less to gain from deploying its highly trained and well-equipped forces under UN command. Although a UN mandate implicates an undeniable legitimizing power, it remains undesirable for the democratic nations of the EU to justify troop deployments to their domestic constituents in regions where a national or strategic interest cannot be clearly detected. The EU has not experienced a direct external state threat since the end of the Cold War. Nevertheless, it has found itself confronted with an increasing number of non-traditional risks and has therefore adopted a wider definition of security incorporating its aspirations to serve as a normative power in the international system.[69]

Distancing themselves to a certain degree from UN peacekeeping and providing stand-alone EU missions under UN-mandate is also to a significant degree an attempt by some European powers to emancipate themselves from transatlantic security structures in the realm of international security, thus serving organizational egoisms and interest driven national policies. Autonomous EU action is possible, however, only 'to the extent that a few key powers allow it to be',[70] and especially in the military realm the EU remains to a great degree dependent upon transatlantic capacities to guarantee the necessary support. European potential to set normative standards in the international peace and security sector, however, will stay limited as long as engagement remains selective.

Conclusion

UN peacekeeping operations offer an interesting field of analysis for emerging dynamics in the international system. China's and the EU's engagement in UN peacekeeping operations have been contrasted. The EU promotes 'the development of a stronger international society, well functioning international institutions and a rule-based international order'[71] while China stresses the merits of international cooperation and international relations based on equality and international law. Both actors follow different approaches to peacekeeping operations based on their respective national interest and understanding of security and sovereignty.

The EU is a valuable partner for the UN, as it not only has the technical and financial capabilities to staff robust operations but also because its normative approach to peacekeeping corresponds well with the broad understanding of security, human rights and development advocated by the world body.[72] It has, however, proven less reliable in providing the means necessary to reach common goals, due to specific national interests and domestic considerations.

An increasingly active 'peacekeeping dragon' poses challenges and offers opportunities to the UN peace and security system. Up to now China's engagement has been based on case-by-case decision making, which leaves the UN in uncertainty about the continuity of Chinese contributions. China has raised expectations by engaging in a more cooperative and responsible attitude especially in the developing world. The durability of this commitment remains to be seen and is largely dependent upon the domestic situation in the People's Republic.

The assessment of China's current capacities shows that thus far it remains unable to provide all necessary equipment, technical skills and training to conduct complex operations. Additionally, the principle-driven Chinese approach – albeit being re-evaluated on a case-by-case basis – hampers Chinese support for multidimensional operations.

China has not yet fully defined its future objectives in terms of a clear foreign policy strategy going beyond the current ad-hoc approach.

It therefore seems ever more important to pay close attention to the existing plurality of thought amongst Beijing's foreign policy elites. China has left the path of proclaiming its 'peaceful rise' as in the West this phrase was mainly perceived as a 'camouflage'[73] manoeuvre to hide its increased ambitions. The Chinese leadership has since preferred to translate its interests and strategic orientation into concrete political action – an enlarged involvement in UN peacekeeping operations being only one of many areas in which policy shifts can be detected.

In the current situation of severe overstretch of the UN peacekeeping sector, Chinese contributions can serve as a valuable alternative for the conduct of the respective missions. Peacekeeping operations, however, are more directly related to normative questions than bilateral engagement or military-to-military cooperation, as they call into question how China sees the world and what it regards as appropriate conduct on the international stage. This can be seen especially in changing positions on highly sensitive issues, such as questions of international intervention as well as newly emerging standards like the Responsibility to Protect. In the debate surrounding the moving of R2P from theory to practice, China remains a 'firm, but cautious'[74] supporter of the principle. Force can be a way of reacting to mass atrocities as a last resort, however, but only with a necessary Security Council mandate. China supports capacity building within states to prevent a situation from escalating and prefers UN measures in the humanitarian or diplomatic realm.[75] While Beijing remains rhetorically cautious, political actions show significant signs of adaptation, as China sees international peace and stability to be in its interests for domestic stability and prosperity.[76]

A closer Chinese integration into the international security architecture by means of participation in UN peacekeeping operations could strengthen Beijing's commitment to regional stability and security and deepen its acknowledgement of international norms while increasing the collective contribution to conflict resolution and post-conflict reconstruction.

China's current reluctance to lead and its tendency to 'keep a low profile', however, could put these developments into perspective. It will, for a variety of reasons, be considerably more difficult for China to keep up this approach as it finds itself more and more in the position of having to protect its interests on a global scale. If Western nations leave a vacuum in the staffing of UN peacekeeping operations, China has the potential to fill this void in the future – to accomplish this, however, it will have to overcome strategic considerations of the past.

Increased Chinese and European engagement within a UN context could greatly contribute to regional stability and international security especially in current conflict hotspots of common interest. It could likewise enlarge transparency amongst the two global actors and serve as a confidence-building measure, especially in the military realm, as cooperation between the EU and China is currently hesitant on the ground. To use the visible potential of complementary or even cooperative engagement, however, China has to prove its willingness to continuously support UN mechanisms and standards as well as its ability to act as a responsible power on the international scene. At the same time the EU has to recommit itself to UN peacekeeping operations and find a collective approach amongst its member states to avoid declining influence. As Tardy accurately summarizes for EU–UN relations '[c]ooperation is crucial and recognised as such on both sides, but comes second for institutions that are constantly struggling for their own comparative advantages, visibility and identity'.[77]

Notes

1 UN Charter, Preamble.
2 The term 'peacekeeping' has two dimensions. It not only refers to classic peace-keeping, consisting of truce supervision, and buffer functions between conflicting groups, but is also used as a generic term under which, e.g., conflict prevention and peacemaking, peacekeeping and peacebuilding can be subsumed. In this analysis, when referring to the term 'peacekeeping', peace operations in general will be alluded to; when talking about a specific peacekeeping mission with the relevant characteristics qualifying it as a traditional peacekeeping operation the term 'classic peacekeeping' will be employed.
3 Almost 45.8% of UN Military Personnel originate from the Asia-Pacific region, whereas Europe merely contributes 13.4%. Deployment, however takes place predominantly in Africa (71.4%) and not in Europe (1.3%) or Asia (0.2%): *Annual Review of Global Peace Operations 2009*, Center on International Cooperation, 2009 (GPO 2009), p. 148.
4 UN Doc. GA/PK/202 and UN Doc. A/AC/.121/2-009/L.3.
5 A full-text version of the report is available online on the DPKO's website: http://www.un.org/en/peacekeeping/documents/newhorizon.pdf; the New Horizons non-paper draws also on the conclusions of a recent report by the NYU Center on International Cooperation by Bruce Jones, Richard Gowan and Jake Sherman entitled 'Building on Brahimi: Peacekeeping in an era of strategic uncertainty' published in April 2009, available at: http://www.peacekeepingbestpractices.unlb.org/PBPS/Library/CIC%20New%20Horizon%20Think%20Piece.pdf. This independent advisory report equally identifies major obstacles on the way to improved strategies for the UN peacekeeping sector.
6 Together Pakistan, Bangladesh, India and Nigeria place more than 35,500 soldiers at the UN's disposal (as of October 2009) (UN DPKO).
7 UN Doc. GA/PK/202 and UN Doc. A/AC/.121/2-009/L.3.
8 William J. Durch and Madeline L. England, 'The Purposes of Peace Operations', in *Annual Review of Global Peace Operations 2009*, p. 15.
9 DefenceWeb, 'China Now a Major Peacekeeping Player', SIPRI, available at: http://www.defenceweb.co.za/index.php? option=com_content&task=view&id=1604&Itemid=380 (10 April 2009).
10 'China's Growing Role in UN Peacekeeping', International Crisis Group Asia Report, 166, 17 April 2009, (ICG Report), p. 32.
11 Volker Rittberger and Bernard Zangl, *International Organization: Polity, Politics and Policies*, Basingstoke: Palgrave Macmillan, 2006, p. 134.
12 UN Doc. A/55/305 - S/2000/809.
13 Capstone Doctrine: jointly published by the Department of Peacekeeping Operations and the newly established Department of Field Support, available at: http://pbpu.unlb.org/pbps/Library/Capstone_Doctrine_ENG.pdf.

14 See Michael W. Doyle and Nicholas Sambanis, 'Peacekeeping Operations', in Thomas G. Weiss and Sam Daws (eds), *The Oxford Handbook on the United Nations*, Oxford and New York: Oxford University Press, 2007, p. 324, and Capstone Doctrine, p. 19.

15 *Handbook on United Nations Multidimensional Peacekeeping Operations*, Peace-keeping Best Practices Unit, Department of Peacekeeping Operations (DPKO), United Nations, December 2003, p. 1, available at: pbpu.unlb.org/Pbps/library/Handbook%20on%20UN%20PKOs.pdf (11 March 2009).

16 See the so-called Brahimi-Report, UN Doc. A/55/305 - S/2000/809, Section E.48, as well as *Annual Review of Global Peace Operations 2009*.

17 Bates Gill and James Reilly, 'Sovereignty, Intervention and Peacekeeping: The View from Beijing', *Survival* 42(3), Autumn 2000, 42.

18 Whereas the ICISS (also known as the Canadian version) focuses on the human rights dimension, the Japanese definition, also prominent amongst the scholars engaging in the debate about the subject, emphasizes the development dimension of the broad conceptual framework of human security. For more on the topic of human security see: *Human Security Report 2005: War and Peace in the 21st Century*, New York and Oxford: Human Security Centre, 2005.

19 Andrea Ellner, 'Regional Security in a Global Context: A critical appraisal of European approaches to security', *European Security* 17(1), March 2008, 10.

20 'The Responsibility to Protect', Report of the International Commission on Intervention and State Sovereignty (ICISS), December 2001, p. 15.

21 'A Secure Europe in a Better World: The European security strategy', European Council, Brussels, 11–12 December 2003, (ESS) p. 10.

22 Ibid.

23 Li Dongyan, 'China's Approach to Non-Traditional Security (NTS)', Conference Report, Institute of East Asian Studies, Berkeley, 8 March 2007, available at: http://ieas.berkeley.edu/events/pdf/2007.03.08_Li_Dongyan.pdf.

24 'China's National Defense in 2008', White Paper issued by the Information Office of the State Council of the People's Republic of China on 20 January 2009, available at: http://www.gov.cn/english/official/2009-01/20/content_1210227.htm.

25 Li, 'China's Approach to Non-Traditional Security'.

26 UN Doc. A/60/L.1, p. 31 (paras 138/139).

27 Pang Zhonying, 'China's Non-Intervention Question', in *Global Responsibility to Protect* 1, 2009, Leiden, pp. 237–52.

28 ICG Report ('China's Growing Role in UN Peacekeeping'), p. 5.

29 Bonny Ling, 'China's Peacekeeping Diplomacy', *China Rights Forum*, 1, 2007, p. 47

30 ICG Report, p. 6.

31 For data see UN Department of Peacekeeping Operations as of November 2009.

32 See statement by La Yifan at Security Council Meeting 6075, 23 January 2009, UN Doc. S/PV.6075, p. 28.

33 Ibid.

34 ICG Report, p. 29.

35 Ling, 'China's Peacekeeping Diplomacy', p. 48.

36 ICG Report, pp. 9f.

37 Minxin Pei, 'Will the Chinese Communist Party Survive the Crisis?', *Foreign Affairs*, 12 March 2009, available at: http://www.foreignaffairs.com/articles/64862/minxin-pei/will-the-chinese-communist-party-survive-the-crisis?page=2 (10 April 2009).

38 Jonathan Holslag, 'Embracing Chinese Global Security Ambitions', *The Washington Quarterly*, July 2009, pp. 109f.

39 See Sophie Brune, Sascha Lange and Janka Oertel, 'China's Militärische Ent-wicklung: Modernisierung und Internationalisierung der Streitkräfte', SWP Study, 29 October 2009.
40 'China's Military Opens First Peacekeeping Training Center near Beijing', *Xinhua*, 26 June 2009, available at: http://english.people.com.cn/90001/90776/90785/6686691.html (10 July 09).
41 Bates Gill and Chin-hao Huang, 'China Spreads Its Peacekeepers', *Asia Times Online*, 4 February 2009, available at: http://www.atimes.com/atimes/China/KB04Ad01.html (08 June 2009).
42 Information supplied by the German Foreign Office.
43 Statement by HE Ambassador Wang Ying-Fan, Permanent Representative of China to the United Nations at the Special Committee on Peacekeeping Opera-tions, 12 February 2002, available at: http://www.fmprc.gov.cn/ce/ceun/eng/chinaandun/securitycouncil/thematicissues/peacekeeping/t29434.htm.
44 Ibid.
45 National Institute for Defense Studies (Ministry of Defense, Japan), *East Asian Security Review 2007*, pp. 118ff., available at: http://www.nids.go.jp/english/dissemination/east-asian/pdf/2007/east-asian_e2007_04.pdf.
46 Joachim Koops and Johannes Varwick, 'Ten Years of SHIRBRIG: Lessons learned, development prospects and strategic opportunities for Germany', GPPi Research Paper Series 11, 2008, p. 6.
47 Decision based on UN Resolutions S/RES/1816 (2008), S/RES/1838 (2008), S/RES/1846 (2008) and S/RES/1851 (2008).
48 'China Focus: Chinese fleet to escort ships off Somalia', *China Military Online*, 27 December 2008, available at: http://english.chinamil.com.cn/site2/special-reports/2008-12/27/content_1599921.htm (14 March 2009).
49 Personal interview.
50 Thierry Tardy, 'UN–EU Relations in Military Crisis Management: Institution-alisation and key constraints', in Joachim A. Koops (ed.), 'Military Crisis Management: The challenge of inter-organizationalism', *Studia Diplomatica: The Brussels Journal of International Relations*, 62/3, 2009, p. 50.
51 ESS, p. 11.
52 See Ståle Ulriksen, Catriona Gourlay and Catriona Mace, 'Operation Artemis: The shape of things to come?', *International Peacekeeping*, 11(3), Autumn 2004, 509.
53 Ibid. 521ff.
54 Joint Declaration on UN–EU Cooperation in Crisis Management, 24 September 2003 (New York), available at: http://www.eu-un.europa.eu/articles/en/article_2768_en.htm (12 April 2009).
55 'Global Peace Operations 2009', p. 32.
56 Ibid. p. 37.
57 UN Doc. S/RES/1778 (2007) and also Council Joint Action 2007/677/CFSP of 15 October 2007 on the European Union military operation in the Republic of Chad and in the Central African Republic.
58 EU Council conclusions on operation EUFOR Tchad/RCA, 16 March 2009, Brussels: Council of the European Union, 2932nd GENERAL AFFAIRS Council meeting, Conclusion on operation EUFOR Tchad/RCA, available at: http://www.europa-eu-un.org/articles/en/article_8570_en.htm.
59 Data as of November 2009.
60 According to UN DPKO, the total number of troops and police deployed in December 2009 was 98,114: http://www.un.org/en/peacekeeping/contributors/2009/nov09_1.pdf (12 December 2009).
61 'Global Peace Operations 2009', pp. 175 ff.

62 See UN Doc. A/61/139/Add. 1. The top-10 providers of assessed contributions to peace operations in 2008 were the United States, Japan, Germany, the United Kingdom, France, Italy, China, Canada, Spain and the Republic of Korea.

63 See http://www.un.org/Depts/dpko/dpko/contributors/financing.html; for the scale of assessment for the apportionment of the expenses of United Nations peacekeeping operations see UN Doc. A/61/139/Add.1, assessments for 1 January 2007 to 31 December 2009; EU member states accounted for 41.64% of the overall peacekeeping budget for 2008/2009, China accounts for 3.15 %, figures deducted from UN Doc. A/61/139/Add.1.

64 Tardy, 'UN–EU Relations', p. 48.

65 Sven B. Gareis and Johannes Varwick, 'Frieden erster und zweiter Klasse: Die Industriestaaten lassen die Vereinten Nationen bei Peacekeeping-Einsätzen im Stich', *Internationale Politik*, May 2007, pp. 71f.

66 Ling, 'China's Peacekeeping Diplomacy', p. 48.

67 For a detailed evaluation of Chinese motivations see also: ICG Report, par.III, pp. 11ff.

68 *East Asian Security Review 2007*, pp. 118ff.

69 Ellner, 'Regional Security in a Global Context', pp. 9–31.

70 Giovanna Bono, 'The EU's Military Doctrine: An assessment', *International Peacekeeping* 11(3), Autumn 2004, 453f.

71 ESS 2003, p. 9.

72 Bono, 'EU's Military Doctrine', p. 453 and Tardy, 'UN–EU Relations', p. 45.

73 Orville Schell, 'China Reluctant to Lead', *Yale Global*, 11 March 2009, p. 4, available at: http://yaleglobal.yale.edu.

74 Sarah Teitt, 'China and the Responsibility to Protect', 19 December 2008, available at: http://www.r2pasiapacific.org/images/stories/food/china_and_r2p.pdf.

75 Ibid.

76 Pang, 'China's Non-Intervention Question', pp. 237–52.

77 Tardy, 'UN–EU Relations', p. 52.

11 Europe sails East, China sails West

Somali piracy and shifting geopolitical relations in the Indian Ocean

Susanne Kamerling and
Frans-Paul van der Putten

Introduction[1]

The emergence of new maritime actors in the Indian Ocean is causing major changes in great power relations in the region. Somali piracy in the north-western Indian Ocean is accelerating this process, as a great number of countries have become involved in counter-piracy missions. In 2008 piracy attacks on international shipping in the Gulf of Aden and other parts of the western Indian Ocean reached such a level that they generated widespread attention in international media. For both Europe and China, their naval responses to Somali piracy represent a new stage in their involvement in international maritime security. On the European side, the EU is undertaking its first ever naval operation under its Common Security and Defence Policy (CSDP). Although individual member states have been active in the region through NATO missions and the US-led Combined Maritime Forces (CMF),[2] the EU as a joint actor was previously not active in waters beyond the Atlantic Ocean and the Mediterranean Sea. For China, the Somali mission is the first major naval operation outside the western Pacific Ocean.

This chapter explores how counter-piracy missions affect relations between China and Europe in international security. Three questions in particular will be addressed. First, what are the interests and activities of China and Europe with regard to counter-piracy activities off Somalia? Second, how do China's and the EU's counter-piracy missions relate to each other? And, third, how does the involvement of the EU and China in counter-piracy affect Indian Ocean geopolitics? Regarding the European side, this chapter focuses on the counter-piracy mission by the EU (in which Europe acts autonomously) rather than on those that take place through NATO or CMF.

The geopolitical context

The United States is the key element that connects the strategic outlook of both China and Europe in the Indian Ocean region. For Europe, the US is its primary security ally. For China, the US is the most important strategic rival. Direct security interaction between China and Europe is limited, but counter-piracy activities near Somalia have provided opportunities for establishing some preliminary contacts. Given the centrality of the US role, this chapter will analyse the shifting geopolitical relationship between Europe and China against the background of Europe–US and China–US relations.

At the global level, China is increasingly regarded by Washington as an indispensable partner to manage international security. Beijing's influence in issues and regions where the US has major interests is already too great to be ignored. While this influence continues to grow, the importance of Europe is diminishing. Due to the collapse of the Soviet Union and the economic rise of Asia, Europe itself no longer has the unique strategic value that it had for the US during the twentieth century. At the global level the trilateral relationship between the US, Europe and China is changing in the sense that the US–China relationship is becoming more important, while the US–Europe relationship is becoming less prominent. The Europe–China side of the relationship does not seem to be changing much and remains weakly developed.

In the Indian Ocean arena, the key relationship is between the US and China and reflects the situation at the global level. US naval power dominates in the region and its economic and diplomatic influence is well-established in many littoral states.[3] China is its most important potential challenger, both at sea and on land. The EU has so far not been a significant geopolitical player in the Indian Ocean, but its role in this part of the world is growing rather than declining. Europe in this region is not necessarily the most important ally for the United States as it is at the global level. Because of the crucial role that it plays in the US military strategy towards China, Japan potentially also has a key role in the US–China relationship in the Indian Ocean. India is another potential leading ally for Washington in this region. Although India is reluctant to enter into a formal alliance with the US, it is an indigenous great power in the Indian Ocean and a strategic rival of China. The expansion of Chinese influence in the Indian Ocean region is a cause of concern for the Indian government.[4] In the Indian Ocean, the relationship between China on the one hand and the US, India and Japan on the other is characterized by a lack of 'strategic trust'.[5] The role of Europe in this context is as yet unclear.

China sails west

Arguably, beyond the East and South China seas, the Indian Ocean is the most important maritime region in China's security strategy.[6] Access to energy[7] and other raw materials from the Middle East and Africa, and to the European market, depends on SLOCs in the Indian Ocean.[8] The key 'choke points' for Chinese shipping are the Malacca Strait in the east and the

Persian Gulf and the Red Sea in the west. In terms of great power relations, the Indian Ocean offers more opportunities for maritime newcomers such as China than do the Pacific or Atlantic Oceans. India excluded, the Indian Ocean littoral states are not regarded as major maritime powers.[9] At the same time, several international security issues, most notably piracy and terrorism, are linked to the Indian Ocean region. More so than the other two major oceans, the Indian Ocean is a region for the great powers to show responsibility for and leadership in international maritime security.

Increased cooperation between the US and India in maritime security is a potential source of concern for China. This could be a precursor of a closer strategic relationship between Delhi and Washington, and possibly also Tokyo. Each year the US and India hold the joint MALABAR naval exercise. In 2009, Japan participated in this exercise.[10] The 2005 joint statement by President Bush and Prime Minister Singh regarding the so-called Indo-US nuclear deal has been regarded as a sign of closer strategic relations between the two nations.

There is a fundamental gap between China's interests and influence in international maritime security. In the long run, the country's programme of military modernization is aimed at limiting this gap, with the maritime component aimed both at dealing with a Taiwan contingency and – in the longer term – at enabling missions to protect China's maritime and economic interests 'beyond Taiwan'.[11] But military means are only a part of Beijing's approach. Analysts of China's strategic thinking have pointed out that Chinese strategists strongly favour security solutions that preclude the need for military engagement.[12] It is likely therefore that even when Beijing's military reach spans the globe, it will still favour non-violent means to protect its maritime security interests.[13] At the same time, this should not be taken to mean that military assets are absent from China's strategy. Military means complement China's non-military means.

Beijing has close economic and diplomatic ties with many countries in the Indian Ocean region. Relations are particularly close with Myanmar, Sri Lanka, Pakistan, Iran, Saudi Arabia, Sudan and South Africa – all of which have great strategic importance for China. The Chinese defence industry supplies weapons to the governments of several of these countries. Moreover, in Pakistan, Myanmar and Sri Lanka the Chinese government is involved in the development of major port facilities. As pointed out by American observers, these facilities could in the future be used by Chinese commercial as well as naval ships.[14]

Beijing's permanent membership of the UN Security Council is of key importance regarding security issues in many of the littoral states in the Indian Ocean. To the extent that security issues relate to South-East Asia or Africa, China's importance for members of the Association of South-East Asian States (ASEAN) and the African Union (AU) makes it unlikely that these organizations would support policies that would hurt Beijing's strategic goals. All this makes it easier for the Chinese government to pursue its interests in the Indian Ocean region. But what China lacked was a naval presence in this part of the world.

This changed on 6 January 2009, when the Chinese People's Liberation Army's Navy (PLAN) counter-piracy mission, consisting of two destroyers and a supply ship, arrived in the Gulf of Aden.[15] The main task of the mission was to protect Chinese commercial shipping. Since the PRC regards Taiwan as a part of China, this also included Taiwanese ships. A number of Chinese- or Hong Kong-flagged ships had been attacked by pirates.[16] The resupplying of the supply ship itself has been done through local ports. China's naval presence in the Gulf of Aden has been continuous, with successive task forces each consisting of two warships and one supply ship. The ships are equipped with helicopters and carry about 70 special forces able to engage in on-board counter-piracy operations.[17] The Chinese warships have been escorting commercial vessels without participating in the International Recommended Transit Corridor (IRTC), a corridor through the Gulf of Aden patrolled by the US, NATO and the Combined Task Force 151 (CTF-151) of the CMF.

The Chinese government has several objectives in sending warships to Somalia. Although the PLAN presence in the Gulf of Aden is small, it has made China highly visible as one of the great powers in Indian Ocean security.[18] That Beijing takes the counter-piracy effort seriously is signalled by the fact that the PLAN as been sending some of its most modern warships.[19] This deployment has allowed Beijing to join the various multilateral counter-piracy initiatives that are being undertaken. This includes membership of the Contact Group on Piracy off the Coast of Somalia (CGPCS) and its various working groups, and the monthly Shared Awareness and Deconfliction (SHADE) meetings in Bahrain. SHADE, co-chaired by the EU and the Combined Maritime Force (CMF), is an inclusive structure that brings together representatives from countries and organizations that have deployed military assets in the region, as well as from the shipping industry and Interpol.[20] It was solely designed to work at the tactical and operational level to coordinate military activity off Somalia, recognizing that there will be strategic differences between all key actors. The Chinese are now starting to coordinate their activities in the Gulf of Aden smoothly with the other navies present.[21] Through being visible and involved, Beijing increases its ability to direct new developments in maritime security in a direction that suits its needs.[22] This allows the Chinese government to contribute to effective measures against Somali piracy. At a more general level it also strengthens China's image as a responsible power.[23] Moreover, it can boost multilateralism in maritime security. Increased multilateralism, including a greater role for the UN Security Council wherever possible, is in China's interest because it limits the hegemony of the US Navy on the high seas.[24] This can be illustrated by an early attempt by the Chinese to have all military forces conducting counter-piracy missions off Somalia working under direct UN Command. This was raised through both SHADE and the CGPCS, but was not politically acceptable to any other significant actor.[25]

A second interest served by the mission is the increased protection of Chinese economic activities. It remains unclear how much damage Somali piracy causes to international shipping.[26] On the one hand, insurance costs have risen and slow-moving ships have had difficulty in obtaining naval protection. On the other hand, piracy attacks affect only a very small portion of total shipping in the western Indian Ocean directly. Another question is to what extent it is really necessary for Chinese ships to make use of Chinese naval protection, as alternative sources of protection are available. But, at a more general level, the Chinese counter-piracy mission can be seen in the same light as China's participation in UN peacekeeping missions in Africa. These troop deployments are a legitimate means for Beijing to achieve 'a level of tactical and operational familiarity' with a region where it has crucial economic interests.[27] According to some sources, there is a growing interest among Chinese strategy experts for the idea of establishing permanent facilities to support overseas (non-war) military operations.[28]

Thirdly, China's government has an interest in showing its own population that it is capable of protecting Chinese nationals and Chinese-flagged ships abroad.[29] Rather than merely relying on protection by foreign navies, the PRC should show that it can do no less than the other great powers. Historically, the Chinese Communist Party derives its legitimacy from its ability to make China strong enough to be able to withstand foreign powers. The escort mission is a good opportunity for the Chinese government to show that at least in this regard it is in the same league as the other maritime powers.[30] At the same time, hijackings of Chinese vessels represent a major threat to the legitimacy of the Chinese government. The hijacking in October 2009 of the Chinese bulk carrier *Dexinhai*, with 25 crewmembers, by Somali pirates highlighted the fact that the presence of Chinese warships in the waters off Somalia is insufficient to prevent attacks on Chinese vessels.[31] The incident seems to have increased pressure on the Chinese government to show that it is capable of protecting Chinese shipping, and may be the explanation for Chinese representatives at a SHADE meeting in Bahrain in November 2009 to express their country's willingness to play a leading role – alongside the EU and the US-led CMF – in chairing future SHADE meetings.[32] In late January 2010, following a meeting of the SHADE grouping, China, the US, the EU and NATO reached an agreement that China would join the rotating task of coordinating the international counter-piracy effort.[33] It is not immediately clear what this role of coordinator entails. It probably relates to the SHADE meetings in Bahrain, but it may also mean that China is to become involved in the International Recommended Transit Corridor.

A fourth interest is strengthening China's claim on Taiwan. The Chinese government has stated that it regards Taiwanese-flagged vessels as Chinese. Consequently the PLAN also escorts Taiwanese ships.[34] Any involvement by Taiwan in maritime security in the Indian Ocean would run counter to

China's efforts to isolate the island militarily and diplomatically. Diplomatic isolation – combined with economic incentives – is the PRC's main tool to push Taiwan towards reunification with the mainland. Any display of Taiwan's de facto independence by joining international maritime security initiatives would be highly unwelcome for the Chinese government.

Because the Taiwanese navy has no presence in the Gulf of Aden,[35] this further emphasizes the political isolation of Taiwan, while at the same time showing China's resolve and ability to act on behalf of Taiwan in international security.

Finally, the process of military modernization that China is going through also benefits from the mission. The Chinese navy is still underdeveloped in terms of operating far from its own shores and operating in an international setting. The counter-piracy mission provides the PLAN with valuable experience in this regard.[36] Also, for the Chinese navy it is very beneficial to be able to operate in close contact with highly advanced navies, such as those of the United States and various European countries.[37]

Europe sails east

For Europe, the main security issue in the maritime sphere – at the global level – is safeguarding the critical sea lines of communication (SLOC) and with that the vital flows of resources, trade and commodities from Asia and the Middle East to Europe. Disruption of the SLOC would have a disastrous effect on the stability of the European economy as a whole. However, another concern that has more recently stepped in the limelight is that maritime security is now becoming one of Europe's first lines of defence against contemporary regional threats (drug smuggling, human trafficking and illegal immigration) as well as global security threats (maritime terrorism, piracy and proliferation of conventional and unconventional weapons). The worst case scenario is a maritime 9/11, in which both the economic and security environment would be strongly affected.[38]

Given that the EU has so far been primarily focused on the Atlantic Ocean and the Mediterranean, strategic thinking about the role and ambitions of the EU outside its own waters remains relatively limited.[39] The EU's Green Paper of 2006 and Blue Book and accompanying Action Plan of 2007 have most recently enunciated Europe's policy on sea. However, they mainly focus on the economic perspective of an integrated European maritime policy.[40] Although these policies recognize the cross-border character of maritime challenges and the potential of a maritime Europe, they neglect to reflect on other parts of the maritime domain than Europe's direct neighbouring waters. Although agencies such as the European Maritime Safety Agency (EMSA) and initiatives focused on the Baltic Sea (HELCOM, Northern dimension), the North Sea, the Black Sea and the Mediterranean Sea (FRONTEX, MPTF) are crucial for Europe when dealing with regional challenges, global security threats that can possibly affect Europe and in which the EU can play a role are not yet considered in the policies currently in place.[41] The EU still needs to find a way to approach maritime security in a broader and more global sense, and it lacks a comprehensive maritime security policy that takes into account (security) challenges of other regions than just its own spatial domain. Yet, maritime security is becoming more and more a matter of global governance.[42] It is clear that Europe has important maritime security interests outside its own region, particularly in the Indian Ocean. The proposal to set up an EU Rapid Response Force could be a step forward in this regard.[43] The three most critical maritime security interests for Europe relate to: its sea lines of communication (SLOC); global security threats that manifest themselves at sea; and positioning itself in the shift in great power relations that is taking place in the Indian Ocean.

Europe's economic security depends heavily on the imports and exports of energy and trade from and to Asia and the Middle East, that go through the Indian Ocean. Europe is a maritime power with 90 per cent of its external trade and 40 per cent of its internal trade carried by sea. European maritime regions account for 40 per cent of the EU's total GDP and Europeans own or control 40 per cent of the world merchant fleet.[44] The EU's cargo trade with Asia accounts for 26 per cent of the global container shipping traffic, one of the most important trade routes on earth.[45] Moreover, along this route through the Indian Ocean seven of the EU's fifteen largest trading partners including China can be found, with imports of 437.1 billion euros and exports of 223.6 billion euros in 2007.[46] And, while the maritime infrastructure of world trade is robust enough to withstand attacks on its structure, the system's interconnectedness may mean that any attack or any conflict will affect Europe's prosperity and security as such.[47] In this light, Eurasian SLOC are of growing geopolitical importance and the Indian Ocean is the strategic gateway for Europe.

Secondly, regional as well as global security threats are increasingly manifesting themselves at sea, in particular in strategic chokepoints such as the Gulf of Aden, as Somali piracy has clearly shown. The Suez Canal, Bab-el-Mandeb, the Strait of Hormuz and the Strait of Malacca are strategically just as important as the Gulf of Aden,[48] and before 2005 the Strait of Malacca was the hotspot for piracy. Drugs smuggling, human trafficking and illegal migration are among the everyday security challenges southern Europe is faced with on a large scale. FRONTEX is the EU agency that is specialized in the border control of this region.[49] But the risk that global security threats such as the proliferation of WMD, the scenario of a terrorist attack or a combination of these two originate and manifest themselves in the Indian Ocean is ever more likely. The attacks in Mumbai in 2008 were carried out by Pakistani terrorists who travelled to India by sea. And piracy raises its head not only in the Gulf of Aden but also in other parts of the Indian Ocean. The Indian Ocean region is therefore also from the security perspective an important region for Europe to take into account, and not only for defence reasons.

The third interest for Europe in the Indian Ocean is its positioning in the shift in great power relations in this region. The EU has a more extensive counter-piracy presence in the western Indian Ocean than other actors, and this should be seen as an opportunity to establish contacts with other great powers in the Indian Ocean region.[50] The EU has so far grabbed this opportunity by cooperating with China in SHADE and by temporarily exchanging liaison officers between the operational commanding frigate of Atalanta and with China's PLAN *Zhoushan* warship.[51] The EU could possibly even play a role in mediating, and thereby avoiding a naval arms race, and by facilitating and actively supporting regional and global maritime partnerships.

Like China, the EU has a fundamental gap between its interests, its influence and its strategy with regard to international maritime security. Europe's security strategy, as outlined in the 2003 document 'A secure Europe in a better world',[52] recognizes primary objectives of the EU as being:

- to bring about a ring of well-governed countries around its borders;
- to establish strategic partnerships with emerging powers such as China and India; and
- to strive for effective multilateralism.

However, the Indian Ocean region is not taken into account sufficiently in the EU's strategy and policies. If the EU wants to play a role, and be 'more effective and visible around the world', as the 2008 'Report on the Implementation of the European Security Strategy' suggests, it has to work – with others – towards a maritime security strategy that takes its interests in the Indian Ocean region into account. Besides, Europe's influence in this region has been rather limited, for the United States has been in de facto control of the world seas and has acted as guardian of the SLOC since the Second World War. However, the vast increase in maritime traffic, coupled with an increased non-military threat to shipping, has driven the US to seek assistance in 'policing' the world's waters.[53] The growing interests of other great powers such as China, but also India and Japan, in maritime security in the Indian Ocean, could be a prime opportunity for Europe to establish the contacts as enunciated in its security strategy and to position itself in this region and in the shift in great power relations. As a military power, the EU has great potential. Naval capabilities of EU member states together account for 8 carriers, 24 assault ships, 58 submarines, 26 destroyers and 108 frigates. Compared with China, which has no carriers, 1 assault ship, 62 submarines, 28 destroyers and 50 frigates, the EU is still in the lead.[54] The EU, as China, will probably favour non-military means of involvement in international maritime security, if only because it has no comprehensive security strategy as a basis of military (maritime) power and capabilities. But as the CSDP advances, missions such as Atalanta to combat piracy, can complement the EU's non-military means, and thereby form a combined response of civilian and military components to counter such threats.[55]

The basis for Europe's security strategy, including its strategy for maritime security, is its economic and diplomatic influence. To protect its SLOC and maritime interests, the EU benefits from its status as a major economic player. Although the EU is less of a dominant power in a political or military sense, its economic power is the basis for its diplomatic influence in the Indian Ocean region. The EU maintains economic ties with all the important countries in the region, including bilateral relations and (strategic) partnerships with Saudi Arabia, India, Japan and China. The EU also invests in development cooperation relations with among others Djibouti, Ethiopia, Somalia, Madagascar and the Seychelles. Besides EU's economic power and external relations, the EU's diplomatic and military reach is also strengthened by the permanent membership of France and the United Kingdom in the UN Security Council, and the membership of 21 EU member states of NATO and other multilateral organizations. The result is that the EU is an influential member in organizations that are of importance to maritime security such as the UN and NATO. EU member states individually also have a military presence in the Indian Ocean region. The UK has a naval base in Diego Garcia (which it leases to the United States) and in Brunei. France has a base in Djibouti and recently opened a military base in the United Arab Emirates. France has moreover conducted joint military exercises in the Mediterranean Sea with China for search and rescue operations to improve their ability to cope with unconventional security threats.[56]

In 2008 the EU and individual EU member states have actively participated in the many counter-piracy missions that have promptly been set up after the explosion in piracy attacks in the Gulf of Aden and Somali basin. Countries such as France, Denmark and the Netherlands have – by UN request – individually contributed to protecting food supply ships from the World Food Programme to Somalia since 2007. In December 2008 the EU decided, under French presidency, that it would initiate its first ever naval operation, Atalanta. Belgium, Germany, France, Greece, Italy, the Netherlands, Norway, Portugal, Spain, Sweden, Turkey and the UK were the countries that are or have been involved in this. Candidate members Croatia and Montenegro have also announced their assistance.[57] The EU Naval Force (EUNAVFOR) moreover runs the Maritime Security Centre (Horn of Africa) (MSC(HOA)) tasked with safeguarding merchant shipping and improving information sharing and coordination between the maritime actors and the shipping industry. This is made possible by a website accessible by members of the shipping industry as well as participating countries such as NATO members, China, Russia, India and many others.[58] In November 2009 the EU decided to prolong the Atalanta mission until at least 13 December 2010. Some of the European countries (Denmark, France, Germany, the Netherlands, Spain and UK) were also involved in the

Combined Maritime Force. Besides all these efforts, EU member states have also participated in NATO missions Allied Provider and Allied Protector in 2008 and Ocean Shield in 2009 of NATO Standing Maritime Groups (SNMG) 1 and 2. All these international maritime missions and forces are sharing information and 'deconflicting' their efforts under the umbrella of the SHADE meetings in Bahrain. The EU has been one of the main drivers behind SHADE and the International Recommended Transit Corridor. Thus the EU has actively participated in fighting the security threat of piracy in a region where it was less visible beforehand. This has greatly contributed to the EU's common operational and tactical experiences in large and longer-term out of area operations with international alliances and cooperation with maritime forces they had not worked with before.

The EU has several objectives in deploying warships and setting up missions to the Indian Ocean region. Although EU presence in the western Indian Ocean might be temporary, an operational period of at least two years for the EU's first naval mission (2008–2010) provides a massive source of experience for the countries and navies involved in working together to combat the unconventional but, until recently, reasonably manageable security threat of piracy. Working together with other parties including the shipping industry, coast guards and port authorities, intelligence agencies such as Interpol and local groups such as fishermen can provide a major source of information and operational knowledge. Improving international maritime cooperation on a technical level (communication, data and intelligence sharing, surveillance, maritime domain awareness, synchronizing systems), operational level (doctrines and rules of engagement) and judicial level (prosecution, detention, safeguarding evidence) could help improve the effectiveness of possible future operations in maritime security.[59]

The second objective is related to this. So far, all CSDP missions have been land based. The counter-piracy mission Atalanta is its first maritime mission ever, and offers the opportunity to EU member states[60] to cooperate and deal with this unexplored area.[61] It has created a momentum in forging the CSDP itself, as well as the role and experience of Europe's navies.[62] It also creates an opportunity in pushing forward strategic thinking about Europe's role in maritime security and its own naval power now and in the future.[63]

Thirdly, the EU has become highly visible as one of the players in maritime security in the Indian Ocean region. This is of importance because, although it has no collective experience in the region of that kind, this could be of help when other maritime security threats occur in the future. But, perhaps more importantly, in combating piracy, the EU has shown itself to be a reliable partner to all great powers with a presence in the Indian Ocean region. The EU is seen by many as a neutral partner, while its military presence in the Gulf of Aden provides the EU with 'a seat at the table'. This could be a prime opportunity for the EU to position itself in the shift in great power relations that is taking place, either as a partner or possibly as a mediator or facilitator of international maritime partnerships and cooperation.

Fourthly, and for the national governments of EU member states probably the most important reason: the EU has displayed the willingness and ability to step up when the SLOC and its shipping industry are under threat. The EU has moreover shown its decisiveness and its capability to act quickly when such a security threat is disturbing its energy and trade flows. This reaffirms at least part of its relevance at a time when Euroscepticism across its member states is rampant.

Finally, the recent developments are good news for EU navies that have been sidelined in post-Cold War warfare: they can again claim their raison d'être at a time when defence budgets are shrinking.[64] The recent decade is marked by a certain 'sea-blindness' in which navies were present in supporting land operations in Iraq and Afghanistan but their merits were less visible.[65] Piracy operations have refocused the attention on one of the basic naval objectives: providing maritime security. Moreover, maritime diplomacy has been shown to be quite effective. The cooperation between the EU and Asian maritime actors such as China has revealed this quite clearly.

China and Europe

China's escort mission reveals several new insights into where it is heading in international security. Beijing is willing to deploy military assets in order to protect Chinese citizens and Chinese economic interests abroad. Whereas China has already been very active in deploying troops as part of UN peace-keeping missions, this is new in the sense that the counter-piracy mission is linked more directly to Chinese interests and that it comprises combat troops and major warships. In addition, Beijing seemingly aims for an active role in maritime security far outside its own region and it is willing to do so in cooperation with other countries.[66] In fact, the Chinese government even showed signs of wanting to play a leading role by becoming one of the organizers of the SHADE meetings. Thus the PLAN mission indicates that China is expanding its military role as well as its diplomatic influence, but without directly challenging the position of the United States.[67]

The EU's involvement in counter-piracy also shows important new elements. The European military presence in the Indian Ocean is expanding. Whereas navies of individual member states had previously been active in and around the Persian Gulf, the EU as an exclusively European actor for the first time has a significant presence off the Horn of Africa. Europe can show itself more clearly and it has wider policy options in the Indian Ocean region when it operates through the EU rather than within NATO or the US-led Combined Maritime Force. The EU has the most extensive mission compared with others (including NATO), co-chairs SHADE and runs the online coordination centre MSC(HOA) that is open to all the other actors. Furthermore, European countries are represented through three parallel missions: by the EU, by the CMF and by NATO. It is noteworthy that the EU took a rapid and significant step by sending a naval taskforce. But it is even more striking that the EU together with the United States and potentially China is playing a leading role in the international coordination of the maritime efforts in the Gulf of Aden and the western Indian Ocean. The EU seized this opportunity by cooperating with the other countries and alliances present and it has – together with NATO and the CMF – established a workable operational situation.[68]

Conclusion: geopolitical implications

The Chinese and European counter-piracy roles affect geopolitics in a number of ways. For the first time the naval forces of these two actors are in contact with each other at the operational level. The exchange of liaison officers with China as an initiative of EU mission Atalanta is an example of this explorative but promising cooperation. Europe and China had already appeared on each other's military horizons through NATO's mission in Afghanistan and both sides' peacekeeping missions in various parts of the world. The counter-piracy missions are a further development in this regard. Both sides will now find it easier to regard the other side as a potential partner but also as a potential rival. In this regard it is important to keep in mind that so far there is little structured coordination, while there is much mutual uncertainty.

Furthermore, US leadership in maritime security in the Indian Ocean – although still well-established – is becoming somewhat less obvious than it has long been. The prominent role of the EU and the increasingly prominent role of China in counter-piracy point in the direction of greater maritime multilateralism. However, neither actor is directly challenging the United States. Their counter-piracy efforts in the western Indian Ocean are so far welcomed by the US government. There is a growing conviction in the US that it needs not only its traditional allies but also China's help to tackle many international issues – piracy being one of them.[69] The United States, as the dominant power on the high seas, needs to address the piracy issue in order not to lose its legitimacy as the leading maritime power. So far the US has not been able to eradicate Somali piracy single-handedly. The best alternative then is to work together with other major powers. A key question for American strategists is how to strike a balance between cooperating with China and avoiding a decline of US influence.[70] The Somali piracy issue helps Washington and Beijing to experiment with approaches to manage their changing relationship.[71]

In the third place, the EU's role in maritime security in the Indian Ocean is a new potential avenue for Europe to play a role in US–China security relations. Given that the American and Chinese need to work with each other while also being strategic rivals, new possibilities for Europe to make itself useful seem to be emerging. For instance, the EU might take the initiative to expand coordinating mechanisms such as SHADE that bring together Europe, the US and China as the three leading actors. China did not previously respond positively to the American proposal to establish a global partnership for maritime security.[72] This Global Maritime Partnership Initiative, or '1000 Ship Navy', has been seen by the Chinese government as undermining the authority of the Security Council and as a way for the United States to expand its control of maritime affairs.[73] Through European participation it might become easier for Beijing and Washington to work together in maritime security at a coordinating level.

Fourthly, the counter-piracy operations can also have implications for Europe's security relations with Japan and India. As the US–China relationship becomes more important in international affairs, there is a growing rationale for other major powers to establish closer relations. Europe's security relations with India and Japan are still underdeveloped, and – as in the case of EU–China – the Gulf of Aden is a setting for operational interaction. At the same time, from Beijing's perspective, the threat of more naval cooperation between the US, Europe, Japan and India is growing. Avoiding a naval arms race and increasing stability in great power relations should therefore be one of the goals in international maritime cooperation that is currently taking place in the Indian Ocean. For Somali piracy has turned out to be a window of opportunity for promising and as of yet unprecedented possibilities for (operational) cooperation, amongst others between the EU and China.

Notes

1 The authors are very grateful for and have benefited much from advice given by Jonathan Holslag, Jerry Liang, Snowy Lintern and May-Britt Stumbaum.
2 The Combined Maritime Forces are a multinational force patrolling the western Indian Ocean to counter terrorism and improve maritime security. There are three main task forces ('Combined Task Forces'): CTF-150 (counterterrorism activities in the Red Sea, Gulf of Aden, Arabian Sea), CTF-151 (established January 2009 for counterpiracy activities in the Gulf of Aden), and CTF-152 (counterterrorism activities in the Persian Gulf): http://www.cusnc.navy.mil/cmf/cmf_command.html.
3 On the relationship between Somali piracy and the US geopolitical role in the Indian Ocean, see James R. Holmes, 'The Interplay between Counterpiracy and Indian Ocean Geopolitics', in Bibi van Ginkel and Frans-Paul van der Putten (eds), *The International Response to Somali Piracy: Challenges and Opportunities*, Leiden: Martinus Nijhoff, forthcoming.
4 Swaran Singh, 'China's Expanding Energy Deficit: Security implications for the Indian Ocean Region', in Dennis Rumley and Sanjay Chaturvedi (eds), *Energy Security and the Indian Ocean*, New Delhi: South Asian Publishers, 2005, p. 167; Vijay Sakhuja, 'Maritime Multilateralism: China's strategy for the Indian Ocean', *China Brief* 9(22), 4 November 2009, p. 14.
5 Li Mingjiang, 'China's Gulf of Aden Expedition: Stepping stone to East Asia?', *RSIS Commentaries*, Singapore, 9 January 2009, available at: https://www.rsis.edu.sg.

6 James R. Holmes and Toshi Yoshihara, *Chinese Naval Strategy in the 21st Century: The turn to Mahan*, London and New York: Routledge, 2008, p. 123.
7 Singh, 'China's Expanding Energy Deficit', p. 177.
8 Alison A. Kaufman 'China's Participation in Counterpiracy Operations off the Horn of Africa: Drivers and implications', conference report, Alexandria VA: CNA China Studies, July 2009, p. 8.
9 Singh, 'China's Expanding Energy Deficit', pp. 176–7.
10 http://www.marinebuzz.com/2009/04/24/exercise-malabar-09-usjapanindia-to-participate-off-the-coast-of-okinawajapan/.
11 Andrew S. Erickson, 'Can China Become a Maritime Power?', in Toshi Yoshihara and James R. Holmes (eds), *Asia Looks Seaward: Power and maritime strategy*, Westport CT and London: Praeger Security International, 2008, p. 107; James R. Holmes and Toshi Yoshihara, 'The Influence of Mahan upon China's Maritime Strategy', *Comparative Strategy* 24, 2005, p. 43. On the relationship between China's overseas economic interests and military means see Jonathan Holslag, 'Khaki and Commerce: The military implications of China's trade ambitions', *Issues & Studies* 45(3), September 2009, pp. 37–67.
12 Jacqueline Newmyer, 'Oil, Arms, and Influence: The indirect strategy behind China's military modernization', *Orbis*, Spring 2009, pp. 205–19.
13 Geoffrey Till, *Seapower: A guide for the twenty-first century*. London and New York: Routledge, 2009, p. 332.
14 Christopher J. Pehrson, 'String of Pearls: Meeting the challenge of China's rising power across the Asian littoral', Carlisle Papers in Security Strategy, Carlisle PA: Strategic Studies Institute of the United States Army War College, 2006. However, it is not clear if Beijing really sees these facilities as having a major military purpose: Jason J. Blazevic, 'Defensive Realism in the Indian Ocean: Oil, sea lanes and the security dilemma', *China Security* 5(3), 2009, p. 63.
15 Philip C. Saunders, 'Uncharted Waters: The Chinese navy sails to Somalia', *Pacnet Newsletter* 3, 15 January 2009, distributed by pacnet@hawaiibiz.rr.com. By late 2009, there had been four rotations, the first deployment comprising the two guided missile destroyers *Haikou* and *Wuhan* and the supply ship *Weishanhu*. The second deployment began in April 2009, when the two destroyers were replaced with two other destroyers: *Shenzhen* and *Huangshan*. The supply ship remained until the start of the third deployment, on 1 August 2009. This deployment consisted of the missile frigates *Zhoushan* and *Xuzhou* and the supply ship *Qiandaohu*: US–China Economic and Security Review Commission, '2009 Report to Congress', Washington DC: US Government Printing Office, 2009, p. 119. The fourth deployment began late November 2009, when the missile frigates *Ma'anshan* and *Wenzhou* relieved *Zhoushan* and *Xuzhou*. In December 2009 they were joined by a fourth ship, the guided-missile frigate *Chaohu*: http://eng.chinamil.com.cn/special-reports/2008hjdjhd/indexg.htm (1 December 2009); http://eng.mod.gov.cn/DefenseNews/2009-12/22/content_4113304.htm (21 January 2010).
16 'Piracy and Armed Robbery against Ships: Annual report 1 January – 31 December 2008', London: International Maritime Bureau of the International Chamber of Commerce, January 2009.
17 Saunders, 'Uncharted Waters'.
18 With many other major powers present it would have been 'conspicuous' if the PLAN were to remain absent: J. Peter Pham, 'The Chinese Navy's Somali Cruise', *World Defense Review*, 12 March 2009, available at: http://worlddefensereview.com.
19 Richard Weitz, 'Operation Somalia: China's first expeditionary force?', *China Security* 5(1), Winter 2009, pp. 27–42; Pham, 'Somali Cruise'.
20 http://www.marad.dot.gov/documents/Third_Plenary_Meeting_of_CGPCS.pdf (10 August 2009).

21 James R. Holmes and Toshi Yoshihara, 'Is China a "Soft" Naval Power?', *China Brief*, 9(17), 20 August 2009, p. 4.
22 Weitz, 'Operation Somalia', p. 32. As Sakhuja, 'Maritime Multilateralism', p. 13, points out, during the 2004 Tsunami disaster relief operations China was not a member of the core group of nations, which comprised the US, Australia and India. This experience may have been an extra stimulus for the PLAN to join multinational initiatives to maritime security. Indeed, China had already stepped up its maritime cooperation with other Asian countries prior to the counter-piracy mission: Li, 'Stepping stone'. On the relationship between disaster relief and geopolitics in Asia see D. Suba Chandran, N. Manoharan, Vibhanshu Shekhar, Jabin T. Jacob, Raghav Sharma and Sandeep Bhardwaj, 'India's Disaster Relief Diplomacy', *Indian Foreign Affairs Journal* 4(2), April–June 2009, pp. 63–80.
23 S. Rajasimman, 'China's Naval Projection off Somalia', Institute for Defence Studies and Analyses, 2 March 2009, available at: http://www.idsa.in; Saunders, 'Uncharted Waters'; Li, 'Stepping stone'; Kaufman, 'China's Participation', p. 9.
24 International counterpiracy missions are supported by the Security Council; operations in Somali territorial waters are allowed by the Somali transitional government and through Security Council Resolutions. The Chinese mission therefore operates in line with Beijing's principles of working under a Security Council mandate and not intervening in another country without its consent.
25 The United Nations also stated that they did not have the manpower or skill sets required to command a large multinational maritime group.
26 Kaufman, 'China's Participation', p. 2.
27 Pham, 'Somali Cruise'.
28 Michael S. Chase and Andrew S. Erickson, 'Change in Beijing's Approach to Overseas Basing?', *China Brief*, 9(19), 24 September 2009, p. 10.
29 Kaufman, 'China's Participation', p. 7. However, according to some analysts, only one Chinese and one Hong Kong flagged ship had been seized by pirates by late 2008, and this was unlikely to be a sufficient reason for Beijing to dispatch warships: Rajasimman, 'China's Naval Projection'.
30 And there has been widespread media attention in China for the counter-piracy mission: Robert S. Ross, 'China's Naval Nationalism', *International Security* 34(2), Fall 2009, p. 64.
31 http://english.sina.com/china/p/2009/1020/279108.html (22 November 2009).
32 Richard Weitz, 'Priorities and Challenges in China's Naval Deployments in the Horn of Africa', *China Brief* 9(24), 3 December 2009, p. 10.
33 Lauren Gelfand, 'China Enhances Anti-Piracy Effort off Somali Coast', *Jane's Defence Weekly*, 10 February 2010, p. 5.
34 Pham, 'Somali Cruise'.
35 In January 2009, the Taiwanese government appears to have considered the idea of sending warships to Somalia to protect Taiwanese vessels: 'Government Still Mulling Use of Anti-Piracy Frigates', *Taipei Times*, 10 January 2009, available at: http://www.taipeitimes.com/News/taiwan/archives/2009/01/10/2003433360.
36 Rajasimman, 'China's Naval Projection'; Li, 'Stepping stone'; Weitz, 'Operation Somalia', p. 34.
37 Sakhuja 'Maritime Multilateralism', p. 13; Pham, 'Somali Cruise'.
38 Teodoro E. López-Calderón, 'An Approach to EU–NATO Cooperation in "Maritime Security"', in John Chapman (ed.), 'The Question Marks over Europe's Maritime Security', SDA Discussion paper, Brussels 2008, p. 9, available at: http://www.securitydefenceagenda.org/Portals/7/Reports/2007/Final_Discussion_Paper.pdf.
39 J. Rogers, 'From Suez to Shanghai: The European Union and Eurasian maritime security', European Union Institute for Security Studies (EUISS), Occasional Paper 77, March 2009, pp. 8, 31–3.

40 'Re-Thinking Europe's Naval Power', report of roundtable meeting of 16 March 2009, Security and Defense Agenda (SDA), Brussels, p. 9.
41 Rogers, 'From Suez to Shanghai', and Chapman, 'Question Marks'.
42 M. Mueller-Hennig, 'Maritime Security Requires Regional and Global Governance', in Chapman, 'Question Marks', p. 11.
43 'Re-Thinking Europe's Naval Power', p. 9.
44 'Commissioner Joe Borg in Hamburg: Let's Design a European Maritime Strategy for Greater Prosperity and Wellbeing', Press release, European Commission, Maritime Affairs, 4 December 2006.
45 Rogers, 'From Suez to Shanghai', pp. 21–2.
46 The others are Japan, South Korea, India, Taiwan, Singapore and Saudi Arabia: Rogers, 'From Suez to Shanghai', pp. 21–2.
47 Lee Willett, 'Maritime Security: A choice or obligation – and the implications for the European Union?', in Chapman, 'Question Marks', p. 19.
48 Per Gullestrup and May-Britt J. Stumbaum, 'Coping with Piracy, The European Union and the shipping industry', in Bibi van Ginkel and Frans-Paul van der Putten (eds), *The International Response to Somali Piracy: Challenges and Opportunities*, Leiden: Martinus Nijhoff, forthcoming.
49 'Re-Thinking Europe's Naval Power' p. 5.
50 Gullestrup and Stumbaum, 'Coping with Piracy'.
51 'Chinese and Dutch Naval Officers in On-Board Study and Exchange Activity', *PLA Daily*, 26 November. 2009.
52 'A Secure Europe in a Better World', European Union, Brussels, 12 December 2003.
53 The US Navy Global Maritime Partnership initiative of 2006, seeking maritime partners to assist in providing stability, was endorsed in late 2007 by 'A Cooperative Strategy for 21st Century Seapower', the current US maritime doctrine: see http://www.navy.mil/maritime/MaritimeStrategy.pdf.
54 Rogers, 'From Suez to Shanghai', annex 2, p. 42; International Institute of Strategic Studies, *The Military Balance 2009*, London: Routledge, 2009.
55 Gullestrup and Stumbaum, 'Coping with Piracy'.
56 'China, France Hold Joint Naval Exercise in Mediterranean', *China Daily,* 26 September 2007, available at: http://www.chinadaily.com.cn/china/2007-09/26/content_6145193.htm.
57 European countries are for the purpose of this article not defined as EU member states but in a broader (geographical) sense.
58 Gullestrup and Stumbaum, 'Coping with Piracy'. See also http://www.mschoa.eu. The online centre is run from Atalanta's headquarter in Northwood, United Kingdom.
59 'Re-Thinking Europe's Naval Power', p. 6.
60 Also non EU member states such as Norway and candidate members such as Croatia and Macedonia have participated or announced their assistance in EU mission Atalanta.
61 Gullestrup and Stumbaum, 'Coping with Piracy'.
62 Ibid.
63 'Re-Thinking Europe's Naval Power'.
64 Gullestrup and Stumbaum, 'Coping with Piracy'.
65 Geoffrey Till, 'Making waves; naval power evolves for the 21st century', in *Jane's Intelligence Review,* December 2009, p. 29.
66 Kaufman, 'China's Participation', p. 4.
67 Ibid., p. 9.
68 Gullestrup and Stumbaum, 'Coping with Piracy'.
69 Kaufman, 'China's Participation', p. 12.
70 On this challenge see also Ross, 'China's Naval Nationalism'.

71 On this theme see also Eric McVadon, 'China and the United States on the High Seas', *China Security*, 3(4), Autumn 2007, pp. 3–28; Weitz, 'Operation Somalia', p. 39.
72 Mike Mullen, 'We Can't Do It Alone', *Honolulu Advertiser*, 29 October 2006.
73 McVadon, 'High Seas'.

Conclusion

*Frans-Paul van der Putten
and Chu Shulong*

This chapter summarises the views of the contributors to this book. It does so by addressing the three questions raised in the introduction:

- How do Europe and China view each other's security roles?
- In which direction is the bilateral security relationship developing?
- How are China's and Europe's changing roles affecting international security?

Perception of the other's security role

From a Chinese perspective, Europe is a leading security actor and will become even more important as the European integration process continues. While it is recognised that there are major obstacles to this process of integration, Chinese experts and policymakers believe that the capacity of the EU will continue to grow, and the EU is generally regarded as a rising power in international security.[1] However, the EU is seen as a collective entity, and so as clearly distinct from a single nation. China itself is seen by Europe as an inevitable factor in addressing global challenges. As leading European countries and the EU have ambitions to play a role in global security governance and crisis management, there is growing awareness that China needs to be engaged.[2]

For the Chinese, Europe is among the three main security actors of the coming decades, the other two being the US and China itself. Whereas it is not expected to achieve the military capabilities that the US has, Europe – especially the EU – is seen in China as, compared with the US, a relatively constructive and peaceful actor in international security. In this context, the elements that are especially important are the EU's emphasis on multilateralism and institution building.[3] On the European side, China is widely seen as rapidly becoming a major great power and potentially the most significant actor apart from the US and Europe itself. In the long run, Russia and other major countries – India, Japan, Brazil – appear to be regarded as having less potential than either the EU or China when it comes to leadership in security affairs.

China does not see Europe as a potential security threat since there seems no likelihood of Europe damaging China's sovereignty or its territorial integrity. The Taiwan, Tibet, and Xinjiang issues are the areas in which European actions are thought to be most potentially dangerous to China's core security interests.[4] Likewise, China is not seen as a security threat to Europe. However, there is a concern in Europe that China's rise could threaten the current, Western-shaped international system.[5] Europe thus has two main motives in engaging China on global security issues. One is to cooperate with China in order to increase stability in international affairs. The other is to make sure that China grows into a leading security actor within the existing institutional framework of global security governance. China does not seem to reject these strategic goals.

The bilateral security relationship

Until now, bilateral security relations have remained a weakly developed element in the overall relationship between Europe and China. There are two levels of bilateral relations: apart from the bilateral EU–China relationship there are also bilateral relations between China and individual European countries.[6] In spite of the EU's efforts at strengthening its capacity to manage external relations – most recently by appointing a high representative for foreign affairs and security policy – it seems likely that the dual-level aspect of EU–China relations will continue to exist for some time to come.

Until recently, Sino–European relations in the traditional security sphere were to a large extent shaped by the fact that each side's defence-related activities did not overlap geographically. In this context, exchanges in the field of defence technology were potentially one of the main ways to achieve closer security ties. This was indeed attempted from autumn 2003 onwards.[7] The EU moved towards ending the arms embargo against China that has been in existence since 1989. It also agreed with China that it could contribute to the Galileo project, Europe's global navigation satellite system. However, the challenges involved in both processes proved too great for the EU. For a variety of reasons, neither initiative was successful. One of the relevant factors was pressure exerted by the US on the EU. The United States continues to have a dominant influence on Sino–European relations. Also today there are no signs that European countries want to diminish the role of their security alliance with the US. Another insight that emerged from the failed attempt at closer technological cooperation is that this was not a top priority for either the EU or China.

The embargo remains an important obstacle to a deepening of security ties, as it stands in the way of closer technological cooperation. Although there are military exchanges, the arms embargo limits the possibility of European countries providing significant levels of training to Chinese military personnel.[8] The scope for joint exercises is also limited, although there have been a number of joint maritime exercises.[9] It may also be noted that, in spite of the embargo, there have been sales from various EU member states to China of arms-related materials.[10] Apart from defence technology, another important security area in which bilateral cooperation is possible is non-proliferation of weapons of mass destruction. In this regard, Europe and China have worked well together.[11] One notable exception is the Iranian nuclear issue, which will be discussed below.

In the field of non-traditional security issues, there has been much progress with regard to addressing climate change, while there have also been differences. There have been various joint dialogues and workshops on these issues, and there are significant technology exchanges.[12] With regard to energy security, there is concern on the European side that China's attempts at gaining access to foreign energy sources involves backing regimes that violate human rights. Another worry in Europe is that China's state-controlled energy companies might interfere with free market principles. And a third potential or actual cause for concern in Europe is that in the future China might compete with Europe for access to Russian energy resources.[13]

The rise of new centres of power – such as China – signifies a relative decline by the United States. This fundamental power shift creates new security challenges. Europe and China share an interest in stabilising the changing world order.[14] Both strive to strengthen the multilateral system of global security governance. Apart from the US itself they are the most influential and therefore best positioned actors to contribute to international stability. However, so far bilateral cooperation between Europe and China on global security management is fragmentary and hardly institutionalised. Through NATO, the security role of Europe is expanding. The geographic reach of the Chinese military is likewise increasing. The People's Liberation Army is engaged in numerous peacekeeping missions in Africa and other areas in the world, as well as in a counter-piracy mission in the Gulf of Aden.[15] Still, the number of geographic regions where both China and Europe are directly active in security issues remains limited.

Europe, in spite of being a former centre of colonial power and a leading international actor in the post-Cold War world, is largely absent from security management in East Asia. This is notable because Europe has a major interest in stability in this region, where two major hotspots are located: the Taiwan Strait and the Korean Peninsula. Were the EU or any other European actor actively involved in East Asian security, then this would have a major impact on Europe–China security relations. It is not likely that a European security presence in East Asia will materialise in the foreseeable future. On the one hand, none of the leading actors in the region – including the United States – seem eager to see a more substantial European involvement. On the other, the EU does not have clear priorities, a roadmap or a monitoring mechanism for its policy on East Asian security.[16] Regardless of a possible European role in East Asian security, the EU does not even seem to have decided how to respond to a potential military conflict related to either Taiwan or the Korean Peninsula.[17]

In the coming years and decades, both the EU and China may join the United States as the leading actors in global security. However, the position of the EU vis-à-vis the other two powers is still relatively little defined. Although Europe and the US have a long-standing security alliance, the EU as such is not a part of NATO, and it is not clear how the transatlantic alliance relates to the US–China relationship.[18] The EU has not yet made up its mind on where it stands in US–China security relations. This is the case with regard to a potential military conflict between the two Pacific powers, such as could result from a crisis in the Taiwan issue. But it is likewise true with regard to the possibility of bilateral US–China cooperation on international security affairs – the G-2 scenario.

The impact of Sino–European relations on international security

From 2003 to 2005, the intended cooperation between the EU and China in the spheres of defence and space technology was a potential challenge to US supremacy in these fields.[19] But this cooperation proved to be short-lived, partly due to pressure from Washington on the relevant European actors. Although the US, China and Europe regard one another as primary actors in international security, they communicate either bilaterally or in the context of broader multilateral forums. As yet there is no platform or mechanism for trilateral interaction on security issues.

Various obstacles exist on the way to a system of trilateral engagement. Europe does not have a unified external security policy, NATO is still in the process of defining the direction and scope of its overall mission, the US and Europe have different approaches to global security governance, and there is a fundamental distrust between China on the one side and Europe and the US on the other.[20] Besides the United States, Russia is another important security actor whose position is potentially affected by Sino–European security interaction. However, so far this proves not to be the case. Here, too, there is no trilateral security interaction. The relationship between Europe and China is less active and developed than the bilateral relations each of them maintains with Russia.[21]

Both China and Europe support the United Nations system, including the Security Council, as the main mechanism to manage global security. Although Europe is not collectively represented in the Security Council, the UK and France are permanent members. Due to their military and political weight, these are the two most influential security actors within Europe, including in the security domain of the EU and the European component of NATO. So, although the European security interests are only partially represented in the Security Council, the Council is the most important multilateral security platform where Europe and China interact with each other.

For the further development of the capacities of the Security Council it is relevant that Europe and China have differing views on its functioning.[22]

China maintains that host nation consent, neutrality and using force exclusively for self-defence are the preconditions for any UN peace operation. Most European nations favour a less restrictive approach, based on norms and focused on the civilian population, human rights and conflict prevention. Important developments are currently taking place with regard to the Chinese position. On the one hand, as China becomes more influential in international affairs it is in a better position to defend its views and interests in multilateral organisations. On the other, Beijing is becoming more flexible in its stance on state sovereignty. While adhering to the same basic principles, the Chinese government seems increasingly prepared to decide on its implementation on a case-by-case basis.

The Europe–China relationship is also important at the level of UN peace operations.[23] While European countries have become reluctant to commit troops to UN operations, China has become one of the leading troop suppliers. However, for the time being, Europe is better positioned in terms of equipment, technical skills and training to conduct complex operations. This means that the two actors could significantly boost UN capabilities if they could coordinate and expand their complementary roles. However, for now it remains to be seen to which extent Europe is committed in the longer term to UN peace operations and China is able to balance its domestic insecurities with its expanding global interests.

Closely related to this is Sino–European cooperation in the field of counter-piracy.[24] With the support of the UN Security Council and Somalia's provisional government, both sides have deployed warships in the Gulf of Aden and the western Indian Ocean. They are now increasingly cooperating in a multinational setting that involves also the United States and other actors. The actual scope of this cooperation is limited: it does not involve major concessions from either side, nor do the naval missions by themselves seem able to end the piracy threat to international shipping. But still this instance of cooperating is a highly symbolic process that opens the door to further joint initiatives in maritime security. Unlike UN peace operations, this model of cooperation involves direct contacts between military units that do not operate on behalf of the United Nations.

There is thus at least the potential of China and Europe increasingly working together to address security threats in Africa and the western Indian Ocean. Afghanistan is another place where both sides have a direct and major interest in increasing stability. However, although China complements Europe's military and development activities in Afghanistan through its involvement in the Afghan economy, there are no signs of a joint approach – either bilaterally or in a multilateral setting – to stabilising the country and neighbouring Pakistan. Even less promising are the prospects for a joint approach on Iran's nuclear program.

In the Iranian nuclear issue, the primary security interest at stake for the Chinese side is energy security. Europe, however, is more concerned about the danger of proliferation of nuclear weapons and regional destabilisation.

Partly related to this, the two sides have taken different approaches to dealing with this crisis.[25] The European actors involved – the three leading European nations and the EU – have shown an increasing tendency to side with the United States in calling for sanctions. Beijing favours a less confrontational approach and emphasises the principle of national sovereignty. The Iranian crisis has brought China and Europe together in an ad hoc multilateral forum (consisting of the five permanent members of the UN Security Council plus Germany) to deal with this major security issue. However, this particular instance of joint security management has shown important limitations to the ability of Europe and China to work together. Although the main protagonists are Iran and the US, and both China and Europe have an interest in preventing a military conflict, they have so far failed to come up with a common approach.

All these developments suggest that, although the rise of China and the integration of Europe are processes with far-reaching implications, the relationship between China and Europe is not yet having a significant effect on international security. The bilateral relationship has not seriously affected the position of either the US or Russia. Nor has it had a significant impact on a major security hotspot. And yet the potential for bilateral Sino–European relations to play a major security role is clearly great. If Europe and China continue to believe that the world is becoming multipolar and that multilateralism is the way to deal with global issues, then it is likely that the two actors will play corresponding and increasing global roles. It is up to the leaders and peoples on both sides to decide what the level of mutual cooperation on international issues should be, including those in the security sphere.

Notes

 1 Chapter 2.
 2 Chapter 1.
 3 Chapter 2.
 4 Chapter 2.
 5 Chapter 2.
 6 Chapter 2.
 7 Chapter 4.
 8 Chapter 3.
 9 Chapter 8.
10 Chapter 8.
11 Chapter 3.
12 Chapter 3.
13 Chapter 3.
14 Chapter 5.
15 Chapter 11.
16 Chapter 8.
17 Chapter 8.
18 Chapter 6.
19 Chapter 4.

20 Chapter 6.
21 Chapter 7.
22 Chapter 10.
23 Chapter 10.
24 Chapter 11.
25 Chapter 9.

Index